Cassandra High Performance Cookbook

Over 150 recipes to design and optimize large-scale
Apache Cassandra deployments

Edward Capriolo

BIRMINGHAM - MUMBAI

Cassandra High Performance Cookbook

First published: July 2011

Production Reference: 2070711

Published by Packt Publishing Ltd.
32 Lincoln Road
Olton
Birmingham, B27 6PA, UK.

ISBN 978-1-849515-12-2

www.packtpub.com

Cover Image by Rakesh Shejwal (shejwal.rakesh@gmail.com)

Credits

Author

Edward Capriolo

Reviewers

Vineet Daniel

Matthew Tovbin

Seth Long

Jing Song

Acquisition Editor

Dilip Venkatesh

Development Editor

Roger D'souza

Technical Editors

Prashant Macha

Gauri Iyer

Manasi Poonthottam

Pooja Pande

Project Coordinator

Michelle Quadros

Proofreader

Jonathan Todd

Indexers

Hemangini Bari

Tejal Daruwale

Graphics

Nilesh Mohite

Production Coordinators

Aparna Bhagat

Arvindkumar Gupta

Cover Work

Aparna Bhagat

Arvindkumar Gupta

About the Author

Edward Capriolo is a member of the Apache Software Foundation and a committer for the Hadoop-Hive project. He has experience as a developer as well Linux and network administrator and enjoys the rich world of Open Source software.

Edward Capriolo is currently working as a System Administrator at Media6degrees where he designs and maintains distributed data storage systems for the Internet advertising industry.

To Stacey, my wife and best friend. To my parents, grandparents, and family. To friends who have supported me through many endeavors. To my educators and employers who gave me the tools.

To those who have contributed to Cassandra, including (but not limited to) Jonathon Ellis, Brandon Williams, Jake Luciani, and others who have developed an amazing project to learn and write about. Also deserving of recognition is the amazing community, including (but not limited to) Robert Coli (my Cassandra sensei) and Jeremy Hanna. Special thanks to Matt Landolf, Mubarak Seyed, Tyler Hobbs, and Eric Tamme who contributed the knowledge and free time to add to the content of the book.

To the team at Packt Publishing. They did an excellent job by beautifully redrafting my crude drawings, fixing my grammatical errors, and reviewing and suggesting content. The book got better with every new person who became involved.

About the Reviewers

Vineet Daniel is a Systems Architect and has worked at various startups and managed high traffic web applications. He has over eight years of experience in Software development, managing servers/cloud, and team. The experience has made him a learned individual in technologies like optimization, high-availability, and scalability. He loves to use Linux commands and has a never ending appetite for penetration testing. Find him on `www.vineetdaniel.me`, `@vineetdaniel`.

This is for my Parents, brother, Annie, and two wonderful kids in my life Ana and Aman for encouraging me to go ahead with the task. I would like to thank the team at Packt publishing especially Michelle for guiding me and providing me with this wonderful opportunity to work with Packt Publishing.

Matthew Tovbin received a BSc degree in computer science from the Hadassah Academic College, Jerusalem, Israel in 2005. He has been a software engineer in Intelligence Corps, **Israel Defense Force** (**IDF**), 2005-2008, working on a variety of military IT systems, and later a software engineer and a team leader in web-based startup named AnyClip, making a dream of "Find any moment from any film, instantly" to come true.

Currently Matthew is an MSc student in the Department of Computer Science, Hadassah Academic College and a software engineer of data infrastructure at Conduit.

His experience covers aspects of the architecture, design, and development of high performance distributed web and data analysis systems. His background includes a wide range of programming languages (including Java and C#), search engines (including Lucene), databases, and NoSQL distributed data stores.

Matthew's research interests include search engines, distributed computing, image processing, computer vision, and machine learning.

I would like to thank my beloved girlfriend, Luba, for her thoughtful feedback and support, during the review process of this book.

Jing Song has been working in the IT industry as an engineer for more than 12 years after she graduated school. She enjoys solving problems and learning about new technologies in computer science space. Her interests and experiences lie across multiple tiers, from web frontend GUI to middleware, from middleware to backend SQL RDBMS and NoSQL data storage. In the last five years, she has mainly focused on the enterprise application performance and cloud computing areas.

Jing currently works for Apple as a tech lead with the Enterprise Technology Service group, leading various Java applications from design, to implementation, to performance tuning. She was one of the contributors to the internal private cloud application last year. Her team has POC on most of the NoSQL candidates, for example, Cassandra, CouchDB, MongoDB, Redis, Voldeomort, MemCache, as well as EC2, EMC atmos, and so on.

www.PacktPub.com

Support files, eBooks, discount offers and more

You might want to visit www.PacktPub.com for support files and downloads related to your book.

Did you know that Packt offers eBook versions of every book published, with PDF and ePub files available? You can upgrade to the eBook version at www.PacktPub.com and as a print book customer, you are entitled to a discount on the eBook copy. Get in touch with us at service@packtpub.com for more details.

At www.PacktPub.com, you can also read a collection of free technical articles, sign up for a range of free newsletters and receive exclusive discounts and offers on Packt books and eBooks.

http://PacktLib.PacktPub.com

Do you need instant solutions to your IT questions? PacktLib is Packt's online digital book library. Here, you can access, read and search across Packt's entire library of books.

Why Subscribe?

- ▶ Fully searchable across every book published by Packt
- ▶ Copy & paste, print and bookmark content
- ▶ On demand and accessible via web browser

Free Access for Packt account holders

If you have an account with Packt at www.PacktPub.com, you can use this to access PacktLib today and view nine entirely free books. Simply use your login credentials for immediate access.

Table of Contents

Preface   **1**

Chapter 1: Getting Started   **7**

   Introduction   7

   A simple single node Cassandra installation   8

   Reading and writing test data using the command-line interface   10

   Running multiple instances on a single machine   11

   Scripting a multiple instance installation   13

   Setting up a build and test environment for tasks in this book   15

   Running in the foreground with full debugging   19

   Calculating ideal Initial Tokens for use with Random Partitioner   20

   Choosing Initial Tokens for use with Partitioners that preserve ordering   22

   Insight into Cassandra with JConsole   23

   Connecting with JConsole over a SOCKS proxy   26

   Connecting to Cassandra with Java and Thrift   27

Chapter 2: The Command-line Interface   **29**

   Connecting to Cassandra with the CLI   30

   Creating a keyspace from the CLI   30

   Creating a column family with the CLI   31

   Describing a keyspace   32

   Writing data with the CLI   33

   Reading data with the CLI   34

   Deleting rows and columns from the CLI   35

   Listing and paginating all rows in a column family   36

   Dropping a keyspace or a column family   37

   CLI operations with super columns   38

   Using the assume keyword to decode column names or column values   39

   Supplying time to live information when inserting columns   40

Using built-in CLI functions	41
Using column metadata and comparators for type enforcement	42
Changing the consistency level of the CLI	43
Getting help from the CLI	44
Loading CLI statements from a file	45
Chapter 3: Application Programmer Interface	**47**
Introduction	47
Connecting to a Cassandra server	48
Creating a keyspace and column family from the client	49
Using MultiGet to limit round trips and overhead	51
Writing unit tests with an embedded Cassandra server	53
Cleaning up data directories before unit tests	56
Generating Thrift bindings for other languages (C++, PHP, and others)	58
Using the Cassandra Storage Proxy "Fat Client"	59
Using range scans to find and remove old data	62
Iterating all the columns of a large key	66
Slicing columns in reverse	68
Batch mutations to improve insert performance and code robustness	69
Using TTL to create columns with self-deletion times	72
Working with secondary indexes	74
Chapter 4: Performance Tuning	**77**
Introduction	78
Choosing an operating system and distribution	78
Choosing a Java Virtual Machine	79
Using a dedicated Commit Log disk	80
Choosing a high performing RAID level	81
File system optimization for hard disk performance	83
Boosting read performance with the Key Cache	84
Boosting read performance with the Row Cache	86
Disabling Swap Memory for predictable performance	88
Stopping Cassandra from using swap without disabling it system-wide	89
Enabling Memory Mapped Disk modes	89
Tuning Memtables for write-heavy workloads	90
Saving memory on 64 bit architectures with compressed pointers	92
Tuning concurrent readers and writers for throughput	92
Setting compaction thresholds	94
Garbage collection tuning to avoid JVM pauses	95
Raising the open file limit to deal with many clients	97
Increasing performance by scaling up	98

Chapter 5: Consistency, Availability, and Partition Tolerance with Cassandra   101

Introduction   102
Working with the formula for strong consistency   102
Supplying the timestamp value with write requests   105
Disabling the hinted handoff mechanism   106
Adjusting read repair chance for less intensive data reads   107
Confirming schema agreement across the cluster   109
Adjusting replication factor to work with quorum   111
Using write consistency ONE, read consistency ONE for low latency operations   114
Using write consistency QUORUM, read consistency QUORUM for strong consistency   118
Mixing levels write consistency QUORUM, read consistency ONE   119
Choosing consistency over availability consistency ALL   120
Choosing availability over consistency with write consistency ANY   121
Demonstrating how consistency is not a lock or a transaction   122

Chapter 6: Schema Design   127

Introduction   127
Saving disk space by using small column names   128
Serializing data into large columns for smaller index sizes   130
Storing time series data effectively   131
Using Super Columns for nested maps   134
Using a lower Replication Factor for disk space saving and performance enhancements   137
Hybrid Random Partitioner using Order Preserving Partitioner   138
Storing large objects   142
Using Cassandra for distributed caching   145
Storing large or infrequently accessed data in a separate column family   145
Storing and searching edge graph data in Cassandra   147
Developing secondary data orderings or indexes   150

Chapter 7: Administration   155

Defining seed nodes for Gossip Communication   156
Nodetool Move: Moving a node to a specific ring location   157
Nodetool Remove: Removing a downed node   159
Nodetool Decommission: Removing a live node   160
Joining nodes quickly with auto_bootstrap set to false   161
Generating SSH keys for password-less interaction   162
Copying the data directory to new hardware   164
A node join using external data copy methods   165

Nodetool Repair: When to use anti-entropy repair 167
Nodetool Drain: Stable files on upgrade 168
Lowering gc_grace for faster tombstone cleanup 169
Scheduling Major Compaction 170
Using nodetool snapshot for backups 171
Clearing snapshots with nodetool clearsnapshot 173
Restoring from a snapshot 174
Exporting data to JSON with sstable2json 175
Nodetool cleanup: Removing excess data 176
Nodetool Compact: Defragment data and remove deleted data from disk 177

Chapter 8: Multiple Datacenter Deployments 179
Changing debugging to determine where read operations are being routed 180
Using IPTables to simulate complex network scenarios in a local
environment 181
Choosing IP addresses to work with RackInferringSnitch 182
Scripting a multiple datacenter installation 183
Determining natural endpoints, datacenter, and rack for a given key 185
Manually specifying Rack and Datacenter configuration with a property
file snitch 187
Troubleshooting dynamic snitch using JConsole 188
Quorum operations in multi-datacenter environments 189
Using traceroute to troubleshoot latency between network devices 190
Ensuring bandwidth between switches in multiple rack environments 191
Increasing rpc_timeout for dealing with latency across datacenters 192
Changing consistency level from the CLI to test various consistency
levels with multiple datacenter deployments 193
Using the consistency levels TWO and THREE 194
Calculating Ideal Initial Tokens for use with Network Topology Strategy
and Random Partitioner 196

Chapter 9: Coding and Internals 199
Introduction 199
Installing common development tools 200
Building Cassandra from source 200
Creating your own type by sub classing abstract type 201
Using the validation to check data on insertion 204
Communicating with the Cassandra developers and users through IRC
and e-mail 206
Generating a diff using subversion's diff feature 207
Applying a diff using the patch command 208

Using strings and od to quickly search through data files   209
Customizing the sstable2json export utility   210
Configure index interval ratio for lower memory usage   212
Increasing phi_convict_threshold for less reliable networks   213
Using the Cassandra maven plugin   214

Chapter 10: Libraries and Applications   **217**
Introduction   217
Building the contrib stress tool for benchmarking   218
Inserting and reading data with the stress tool   218
Running the Yahoo! Cloud Serving Benchmark   219
Hector, a high-level client for Cassandra   221
Doing batch mutations with Hector   223
Cassandra with Java Persistence Architecture (JPA)   224
Setting up Solandra for full text indexing with a Cassandra backend   226
Setting up Zookeeper to support Cages for transactional locking   227
Using Cages to implement an atomic read and set   229
Using Groovandra as a CLI alternative   231
Searchable log storage with Logsandra   232

Chapter 11: Hadoop and Cassandra   **237**
Introduction   237
A pseudo-distributed Hadoop setup   238
A Map-only program that reads from Cassandra using the
ColumnFamilyInputFormat   242
A Map-only program that writes to Cassandra using the
CassandraOutputFormat   246
Using MapReduce to do grouping and
counting with Cassandra input and output   248
Setting up Hive with Cassandra Storage Handler support   250
Defining a Hive table over a Cassandra Column Family   251
Joining two Column Families with Hive   253
Grouping and counting column values with Hive   254
Co-locating Hadoop Task Trackers on Cassandra nodes   255
Setting up a "Shadow" data center for running only MapReduce jobs   257
Setting up DataStax Brisk the combined stack of Cassandra, Hadoop,
and Hive   258

Chapter 12: Collecting and Analyzing Performance Statistics   **261**
Finding bottlenecks with nodetool tpstats   262
Using nodetool cfstats to retrieve column family statistics   263
Monitoring CPU utilization   264
Adding read/write graphs to find active column families   266

Using Memtable graphs to profile when and why they flush   267
Graphing SSTable count   268
Monitoring disk utilization and having a performance baseline   269
Monitoring compaction by graphing its activity   271
Using nodetool compaction stats to check the progress of compaction 272
Graphing column family statistics to track average/max row sizes 273
Using latency graphs to profile time to seek keys   274
Tracking the physical disk size of each column family over time   275
Using nodetool cfhistograms to see the distribution of query latencies 276
Tracking open networking connections   277

Chapter 13: Monitoring Cassandra Servers   **279**
Introduction   279
Forwarding Log4j logs to a central sever   280
Using top to understand overall performance   282
Using iostat to monitor current disk performance   284
Using sar to review performance over time   285
Using JMXTerm to access Cassandra JMX   286
Monitoring the garbage collection events   288
Using tpstats to find bottlenecks   289
Creating a Nagios Check Script for Cassandra   290
Keep an eye out for large rows with compaction limits   292
Reviewing network traffic with IPTraf   293
Keep on the lookout for dropped messages   294
Inspecting column families for dangerous conditions   295

Index   **297**

Preface

Apache Cassandra is a fault-tolerant, distributed data store which offers linear scalability allowing it to be a storage platform for large high volume websites.

This book provides detailed recipes that describe how to use the features of Cassandra and improve its performance. Recipes cover topics ranging from setting up Cassandra for the first time to complex multiple data center installations. The recipe format presents the information in a concise actionable form.

The book describes in detail how features of Cassandra can be tuned and what the possible effects of tuning can be. Recipes include how to access data stored in Cassandra and use third party tools to help you out. The book also describes how to monitor and do capacity planning to ensure it is performing at a high level. Towards the end, it takes you through the use of libraries and third-party applications with Cassandra and Cassandra integration with Hadoop.

What this book covers

Chapter 1, Getting Started: The recipes in this chapter provide a whirlwind tour of Cassandra. Setup recipes demonstrate how to download and install Cassandra as a single instance or simulating multiple instance clusters. Trouble-shooting recipes show how to run Cassandra with more debugging information and how to use management tools. Also included are recipes for end users which connect with the command like interface and setup an environment to build code to access Cassandra.

Chapter 2, Command-line Interface: This chapter provides recipes on using Cassandra's command line interface. Recipes cover how the CLI is used to make changes to the metadata such as key spaces, column families, and cache settings. Additionally recipes show how to use the CLI to set, get and scan data.

Chapter 3, Application Programmer Interface: Cassandra provides an application programmer interface for programs to insert and access data. The chapter has recipes for doing common operations like inserting fetching, deleting, and range scanning data. Also covered in this chapter are recipes for batch mutate and multi-get which are useful in batch programs.

Chapter 4, Performance Tuning: Many configuration knobs and tunable settings exist for Cassandra. Additionally hardware choices and operating system level tuning effect performance. The recipes in this chapter show configuration options and how changing them optimizes performance.

Chapter 5, Consistency, Availability, and Partition Tolerance with Cassandra: Cassandra is designed from the ground up to store and replicate data across multiple nodes. This chapter has recipes that utilize tunable consistency levels and configure features like read repair. These recipes demonstrate how to use features of Cassandra that make available even in the case of failures or network partitions.

Chapter 6, Schema Design: The Cassandra data model is designed for storing large amounts of data across many nodes. This chapter has recipes showing how common storage challenges can be satisfied using Cassandra. Recipes include techniques for serializing data, storing large objects, time series, normalized, and de-normalized data.

Chapter 7, Administration and Cluster Management: Cassandra allows nodes to be added and remove from the cluster without downtime. This chapter contains recipes for adding, moving, and removing nodes as well as administrative techniques for backing up and restoring data. Also covered administrative techniques such as backing up or restoring data.

Chapter 8, Multiple Datacenter Deployments: Cassandra is designed to work both when nodes are deployed in a local area network and when nodes are separated by larger geographical distances such as a wide area network. The recipes in this chapter show how to configure and use features that control and optimize how Cassandra works in multiple datacenter environments.

Chapter 9, Coding and Internals: This chapter covers programming recipes that go beyond the typical application programmer interface, including building Cassandra from source, creating custom types for use with Cassandra, and modifying tools like the JSON export tools.

Chapter 10, Third-party Libraries and Applications: A variety of libraries and applications exist for Cassandra. This chapter introduces tools that make coding easier such as the high-level client Hector, ot the object mapping tool Kundera. Recipes also show how to setup and use applications built on top of Cassandra such as the full text search engine solandra.

Chapter 11, Hadoop and Cassanda: Hadoop is a distributed file system, HDFS that provides high throughput and redundant storage and MapReduce, a software framework for distributed processing of large data sets on compute clusters. This chapter provides recipes with tips on setting up Hadoop and Cassandra both individually and on shared hardware. Recipes show how to use Cassandra as the input or output of map reduce jobs, as well as common tasks like counting or joining data that can be done with Cassandra data inside Hadoop.

Chapter 12, Collecting and Analyzing Statistics: This chapter covers techniques for collecting performance data from the Cassandra and the operating system. Recipes collect and display performance data and how to interpret that data and use the information tune Cassandra servers.

Chapter 13, Monitoring: The monitoring chapter has recipes which show how to install and use tools to help understand the performance of Cassandra. Recipes include how to forward log events to a central server for aggregation. Othere recipes show how to monitor logs for dangerous conditions.

What you need for this book

To run the examples in this book the following software will be required:

- ▸ Java SE Development Kit 1.6.0+, 6u24 recommended
- ▸ Apache Cassandra 0.7.0+, 7.5 recommended
- ▸ Apache Ant 1.6.8+
- ▸ Subversion Client 1.6+
- ▸ Maven 3.0.3+

Additionally the following tools are helpful, but are not strictly required:

- ▸ Apache Thrift, latest stable release recommended
- ▸ Apache Hadoop 0.20.0+,0.20.2 recommended (needed for Hadoop Chapter)
- ▸ Apache Hive 0.7.0+, 0.7.0 recommended (needed for Hadoop Chapter)
- ▸ Apache Zookeeper 3.3.0+, 3.3.3 recommended (needed 1 for locking recipe)

Who this book is for

This book is designed for administrators, developers, and data architects who are interested in Apache Cassandra for redundant, highly performing, and scalable data storage. Typically these users should have experience working with a database technology, multiple node computer clusters, and high availability solutions.

Conventions

In this book, you will find a number of styles of text that distinguish between different kinds of information. Here are some examples of these styles, and an explanation of their meaning.

Code words in text are shown as follows: "Edit the configuration file `conf/cassandra.yaml` to set where commit logs will be stored."

A block of code is set as follows:

```
package hpcas.c03;
import hpcas.c03.*;
import java.util.List;
import org.apache.cassandra.thrift.*;
```

When we wish to draw your attention to a particular part of a code block, the relevant lines or items are set in bold:

```
<path id="hpcas.test.classpath">
    <pathelement location="${test.build}"/>
    <pathelement location="${test.conf}" />
    <path refid="hpcas.classpath"/>
</path>
```

Any command-line input or output is written as follows:

```
$ ant test
test:
    [junit] Running Test
    [junit] Tests run: 1, Failures: 0, Errors: 0, Time elapsed: 0.42 sec
    [junit] Running hpcas.c05.EmbeddedCassandraTest
    [junit] All tests complete
    [junit] Tests run: 1, Failures: 0, Errors: 0, Time elapsed: 3.26 sec
```

New terms and **important words** are shown in bold. Words that you see on the screen, in menus or dialog boxes for example, appear in the text like this: "Click on the **attributes** and the **Scores** information will appear in the right panel."

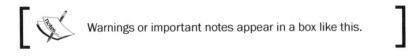

Warnings or important notes appear in a box like this.

Tips and tricks appear like this.

Reader feedback

Feedback from our readers is always welcome. Let us know what you think about this book—what you liked or may have disliked. Reader feedback is important for us to develop titles that you really get the most out of.

To send us general feedback, simply send an e-mail to feedback@packtpub.com, and mention the book title via the subject of your message.

If there is a book that you need and would like to see us publish, please send us a note in the **SUGGEST A TITLE** form on www.packtpub.com or e-mail suggest@packtpub.com.

If there is a topic that you have expertise in and you are interested in either writing or contributing to a book, see our author guide on www.packtpub.com/authors.

Customer support

Now that you are the proud owner of a Packt book, we have a number of things to help you to get the most from your purchase.

Downloading the example code for this book

You can download the example code files for all Packt books you have purchased from your account at http://www.PacktPub.com. If you purchased this book elsewhere, you can visit http://www.PacktPub.com/support and register to have the files e-mailed directly to you.

Errata

Although we have taken every care to ensure the accuracy of our content, mistakes do happen. If you find a mistake in one of our books—maybe a mistake in the text or the code—we would be grateful if you would report this to us. By doing so, you can save other readers from frustration and help us improve subsequent versions of this book. If you find any errata, please report them by visiting http://www.packtpub.com/support, selecting your book, clicking on the **errata submission form** link, and entering the details of your errata. Once your errata are verified, your submission will be accepted and the errata will be uploaded on our website, or added to any list of existing errata, under the Errata section of that title. Any existing errata can be viewed by selecting your title from http://www.packtpub.com/support.

Piracy

Piracy of copyright material on the Internet is an ongoing problem across all media. At Packt, we take the protection of our copyright and licenses very seriously. If you come across any illegal copies of our works, in any form, on the Internet, please provide us with the location address or website name immediately so that we can pursue a remedy.

Please contact us at copyright@packtpub.com with a link to the suspected pirated material.

We appreciate your help in protecting our authors, and our ability to bring you valuable content.

Questions

You can contact us at questions@packtpub.com if you are having a problem with any aspect of the book, and we will do our best to address it.

1

Getting Started

In this chapter, you will learn the following recipes:

- ▶ A simple single node Cassandra installation
- ▶ Reading and writing test data using the command-line interface
- ▶ Running multiple instances on a single machine
- ▶ Scripting a multiple instance installation
- ▶ Setting up a build and test environment for tasks in this book
- ▶ Running the server in the foreground with full debugging
- ▶ Calculating ideal Initial Tokens for use with Random Partitioner
- ▶ Choosing Initial Tokens for use with Order Preserving Partitioners
- ▶ Connecting to Cassandra with JConsole
- ▶ Using JConsole to connect over a SOCKS proxy
- ▶ Connecting to Cassandra with Java and Thrift

Introduction

The Apache Cassandra Project develops a highly scalable second-generation distributed database, bringing together a fully distributed design and a ColumnFamily-based data model. The chapter contains recipes that allow users to hit the ground running with Cassandra. We show several recipes to set up Cassandra. These include cursory explanations of the key configuration files. It also contains recipes for connecting to Cassandra and executing commands both from the application programmer interface and the command-line interface. Also described are the Java profiling tools such as JConsole. The recipes in this chapter should help the user understand the basics of running and working with Cassandra.

A simple single node Cassandra installation

Cassandra is a highly scalable distributed database. While it is designed to run on multiple production class servers, it can be installed on desktop computers for functional testing and experimentation. This recipe shows how to set up a single instance of Cassandra.

Getting ready

Visit `http://cassandra.apache.org` in your web browser and find a link to the latest binary release. New releases happen often. For reference, this recipe will assume `apache-cassandra-0.7.2-bin.tar.gz` was the name of the downloaded file.

How to do it...

1. Download a binary version of Cassandra:

   ```
   $ mkdir $home/downloads
   $ cd $home/downloads
   $ wget <url_from_getting_ready>/apache-cassandra-0.7.2-bin.tar.gz
   ```

2. Choose a base directory that the user will run as he has read and write access to:

   > **Default Cassandra storage locations**
   >
   > Cassandra defaults to wanting to save data in `/var/lib/cassandra` and logs in `/var/log/cassandra`. These locations will likely not exist and will require root-level privileges to create. To avoid permission issues, carry out the installation in user-writable directories.

3. Create a `cassandra` directory in your **home directory**. Inside the `cassandra` directory, create `commitlog`, `log`, `saved_caches`, and `data` subdirectories:

   ```
   $ mkdir $HOME/cassandra/
   $ mkdir $HOME/cassandra/{commitlog,log,data,saved_caches}
   $ cd $HOME/cassandra/
   $ cp $HOME/downloads/apache-cassandra-0.7.2-bin.tar.gz .
   $ tar -xf apache-cassandra-0.7.2-bin.tar.gz
   ```

4. Use the `echo` command to display the path to your home directory. You will need this when editing the configuration file:

   ```
   $ echo $HOME
   /home/edward
   ```

This tar file extracts to `apache-cassandra-0.7.2` directory. Open up the `conf/cassandra.yaml` file inside in your text editor and make changes to the following sections:

```
data_file_directories:
- /home/edward/cassandra/data
commitlog_directory: /home/edward/cassandra/commit
saved_caches_directory: /home/edward/cassandra/saved_caches
```

5. Edit the `$HOME/apache-cassandra-0.7.2/conf/log4j-server.properties` file to change the directory where logs are written:

    ```
    log4j.appender.R.File=/home/edward/cassandra/log/system.log
    ```

6. Start the Cassandra instance and confirm it is running by connecting with `nodetool`:

    ```
    $ $HOME/apache-cassandra-0.7.2/bin/cassandra

     INFO 17:59:26,699 Binding thrift service to /127.0.0.1:9160
     INFO 17:59:26,702 Using TFramedTransport with a max frame size of
    15728640 bytes.

    $ $HOME/apache-cassandra-0.7.2/bin/nodetool --host 127.0.0.1 ring

    Address        Status   State   Load          Token
    127.0.0.1        Up      Normal  385 bytes        398856952452...
    ```

How it works...

Cassandra comes as a compiled Java application in a tar file. By default, it is configured to store data inside `/var`. By changing options in the `cassandra.yaml` configuration file, Cassandra uses specific directories created.

> **YAML**: YAML Ain't Markup Language
>
> YAML™ (rhymes with "camel") is a human-friendly, cross-language, Unicode-based data serialization language designed around the common native data types of agile programming languages. It is broadly useful for programming needs ranging from configuration files and Internet messaging to object persistence and data auditing.
>
> See `http://www.yaml.org` for more information.

After startup, Cassandra detaches from the console and runs as a daemon. It opens several ports, including the **Thrift** port 9160 and **JMX** port on 8080. For versions of Cassandra higher than 0.8.X, the default port is 7199. The `nodetool` program communicates with the JMX port to confirm that the server is alive.

There's more...

Due to the distributed design, many of the features require multiple instances of Cassandra running to utilize. For example, you cannot experiment with **Replication Factor**, the setting that controls how many nodes data is stored on, larger than one. Replication Factor dictates what **Consistency Level** settings can be used for. With one node the highest Consistency Level is ONE.

See also...

The next recipe, *Reading and writing test data using the command-line interface.*

Reading and writing test data using the command-line interface

The **command-line interface** (**CLI**) presents users with an interactive tool to communicate with the Cassandra server and execute the same operations that can be done from client server code. This recipe takes you through all the steps required to insert and read data.

How to do it...

1. Start the Cassandra CLI and connect to an instance:
   ```
   $ <cassandra_home>/bin/cassandra-cli
   [default@unknown] connect 127.0.0.1/9160;
   Connected to: "Test Cluster" on 127.0.0.1/9160
   ```

2. New clusters do not have any preexisting keyspaces or column families. These need to be created so data can be stored in them:
   ```
   [default@unknown] create keyspace testkeyspace
   [default@testkeyspace] use testkeyspace;
   Authenticated to keyspace: testkeyspace
   [default@testkeyspace] create column family testcolumnfamily;
   ```

3. Insert and read back data using the set and get commands:
   ```
   [default@testk..] set testcolumnfamily['thekey']
   ['thecolumn']='avalue';
   Value inserted.
   [default@testkeyspace] assume testcolumnfamily validator as ascii;
   [default@testkeyspace] assume testcolumnfamily comparator as ascii;
   [default@testkeyspace] get testcolumnfamily['thekey'];
   => (column=thecolumn, value=avalue, timestamp=1298580528208000)
   ```

How it works...

The CLI is a helpful interactive facade on top of the Cassandra API. After connecting, users can carry out administrative or troubleshooting tasks.

See also...

Chapter 2, Command-line Interface is dedicated to CLI recipes defined in the preceding statements in greater detail.

Running multiple instances on a single machine

Cassandra is typically deployed on clusters of multiple servers. While it can be run on a single node, simulating a production cluster of multiple nodes is best done by running multiple instances of Cassandra. This recipe is similar to *A simple single node Cassandra installation* earlier in this chapter. However in order to run multiple instances on a single machine, we create different sets of directories and modified configuration files for each node.

How to do it...

1. Ensure your system has proper loopback address support. Each system should have the entire range of 127.0.0.1-127.255.255.255 configured as localhost for loopback. Confirm this by pinging `127.0.0.1` and `127.0.0.2`:

```
$ ping -c 1 127.0.0.1
PING 127.0.0.1 (127.0.0.1) 56(84) bytes of data.
64 bytes from 127.0.0.1: icmp_req=1 ttl=64 time=0.051 ms
$ ping -c 1 127.0.0.2
PING 127.0.0.2 (127.0.0.2) 56(84) bytes of data.
64 bytes from 127.0.0.2: icmp_req=1 ttl=64 time=0.083 ms
```

2. Use the `echo` command to display the path to your home directory. You will need this when editing the configuration file:

```
$ echo $HOME
/home/edward
```

3. Create a `hpcas` directory in your **home directory**. Inside the `cassandra` directory, create `commitlog`, `log`, `saved_caches`, and `data` subdirectories:

```
$ mkdir $HOME/hpcas/
$ mkdir $HOME/hpcas/{commitlog,log,data,saved_caches}
$ cd $HOME/hpcas/
$ cp $HOME/downloads/apache-cassandra-0.7.2-bin.tar.gz .

$ tar -xf apache-cassandra-0.7.2-bin.tar.gz
```

4. Download and extract a binary distribution of Cassandra. After extracting the binary, move/rename the directory by appending '1' to the end of the filename.$ mv apache-cassandra-0.7.2 apache-cassandra-0.7.2-1 Open the `apache-cassandra-0.7.2-1/conf/cassandra.yaml` in a text editor. Change the default storage locations and IP addresses to accommodate our multiple instances on the same machine without clashing with each other:

```
data_file_directories:
    - /home/edward/hpcas/data/1
commitlog_directory: /home/edward/hpcas/commitlog/1
    saved_caches_directory: /home/edward/hpcas/saved_caches/1
listen_address: 127.0.0.1
rpc_address: 127.0.0.1
```

Each instance will have a separate logfile. This will aid in troubleshooting. Edit `conf/log4j-server.properties`:

```
log4j.appender.R.File=/home/edward/hpcas/log/system1.log
```

Cassandra uses **JMX (Java Management Extensions)**, which allows you to configure an explicit port but always binds to all interfaces on the system. As a result, each instance will require its own management port. Edit `cassandra-env.sh`:

```
JMX_PORT=8001
```

5. Start this instance:

```
$ ~/hpcas/apache-cassandra-0.7.2-1/bin/cassandra

 INFO 17:59:26,699 Binding thrift service to /127.0.0.101:9160
 INFO 17:59:26,702 Using TFramedTransport with a max frame size of
15728640 bytes.
```

```
$ bin/nodetool --host 127.0.0.1 --port 8001 ring
```

```
Address        Status State    Load        Token
127.0.0.1      Up     Normal   385 bytes   398856952452...
```

At this point your cluster is comprised of single node. To join other nodes to the cluster, carry out the preceding steps replacing '1' with '2', '3', '4', and so on:

```
$ mv apache-cassandra-0.7.2 apache-cassandra-0.7.2-2
```

6. Open ~/hpcas/apache-cassandra-0.7.2-2/conf/cassandra.yaml in a text editor:

```
data_file_directories:
    - /home/edward/hpcas/data/2
commitlog_directory: /home/edward/hpcas/commitlog/2
    saved_caches_directory: /home/edward/hpcas/saved_caches/2
listen_address: 127.0.0.2
rpc_address: 127.0.0.2
```

7. Edit ~/hpcas/apache-cassandra-0.7.2-2/conf/log4j-server. properties:

```
log4j.appender.R.File=/home/edward/hpcas/log/system2.log
```

8. Edit ~/hpcas/apache-cassandra-0.7.2-2/conf/cassandra-env.sh:

```
JMX_PORT=8002
```

9. Start this instance:

```
$ ~/hpcas/apache-cassandra-0.7.2-2/bin/cassandra
```

How it works...

The **Thrift** port has to be the same for all instances in a cluster. Thus, it is impossible to run multiple nodes in the same cluster on one IP address. However, computers have multiple **loopback** addresses: 127.0.0.1, 127.0.0.2, and so on. These addresses do not usually need to be configured explicitly. Each instance also needs its own storage directories. Following this recipe you can run as many instances on your computer as you wish, or even multiple distinct clusters. You are only limited by resources such as memory, CPU time, and hard disk space.

See also...

The next recipe, *Scripting a multiple instance installation* does this process with a single script.

Scripting a multiple instance installation

Cassandra is an active open source project. Setting up a multiple-node test environment is not complex, but has several steps and smaller errors happen. Each time you wish to try a new release, the installation process will have to be repeated. This recipe achieves the same result of the *Running multiple instances on a single machine* recipe, but only involves running a single script.

How to do it...

1. Create a shell script `hpcbuild/scripts/ch1/multiple_instances.sh` with this content:

    ```sh
    #!/bin/sh
    CASSANDRA_TAR=apache-cassandra-0.7.3-bin.tar.gz
    TAR_EXTRACTS_TO=apache-cassandra-0.7.3
    HIGH_PERF_CAS=${HOME}/hpcas
    mkdir ${HIGH_PERF_CAS}
    mkdir ${HIGH_PERF_CAS}/commit/
    mkdir ${HIGH_PERF_CAS}/data/
    mkdir ${HIGH_PERF_CAS}/saved_caches/
    ```

2. Copy the tar to the base directory and then use `pushd` to change to that directory. The body of this script runs five times:

    ```sh
    cp  ${CASSANDRA_TAR} ${HIGH_PERF_CAS}
    pushd ${HIGH_PERF_CAS}
    for i in 1 2 3 4 5 ; do
      tar -xf ${CASSANDRA_TAR}
      mv ${TAR_EXTRACTS_TO} ${TAR_EXTRACTS_TO}-${i}
    ```

    Cassandra attempts to auto detect your memory settings based on your system memory. When running multiple instances on a single machine, the memory settings need to be lower:

    ```sh
      sed -i '1 i MAX_HEAP_SIZE="256M"' ${TAR_EXTRACTS_TO}-${i}/conf/
    cassandra-env.sh
      sed -i '1 i HEAP_NEWSIZE="100M"' ${TAR_EXTRACTS_TO}-${i}/conf/
    cassandra-env.sh
    ```

3. Replace `listen_address` and `rpc_address` with a specific IP, but do not change the seed from `127.0.0.1`:

    ```sh
      sed -i "/listen_address\|rpc_address/s/localhost/127.0.0.${i}/g"
    ${TAR_EXTRACTS_TO}-${i}/conf/cassandra.yaml
    ```

4. Set the `data`, `commit log`, and `saved_caches` directory for this instance:

    ```sh
      sed -i "s|/var/lib/cassandra/data|${HIGH_PERF_CAS}/data/${i}|g"
    ${TAR_EXTRACTS_TO}-${i}/conf/cassandra.yaml
      sed -i "s|/var/lib/cassandra/commitlog|${HIGH_PERF_CAS}/
    commit/${i}|g" ${TAR_EXTRACTS_TO}-${i}/conf/cassandra.yaml
      sed -i "s|/var/lib/cassandra/saved_caches|${HIGH_PERF_CAS}/
    saved_caches/${i}|g" ${TAR_EXTRACTS_TO}-${i}/conf/cassandra.yaml
    ```

5. Change the JMX port for each instance:

```
 sed -i "s|8080|800${i}|g" ${TAR_EXTRACTS_TO}-${i}/conf/
cassandra-env.sh
done
popd
```

6. Change the mode of the script to executable and run it:

```
$ chmod a+x multiple_instances.sh
```

```
$ ./multiple_instances.sh
```

How it works...

This script accomplishes the same tasks as the recipe. This script uses borne shell scripting to handle tasks such as creating directories and extracting tars, and uses the `sed` utility to locate sections of the file that need to be modified to correspond to the directories created.

Setting up a build and test environment for tasks in this book

Cassandra does not have a standardized data access language such as **SQL** or **XPATH**. Access to Cassandra is done through the **Application Programmer Interface** (**API**). Cassandra has support for **Thrift**, which generates bindings for a variety of languages. Since Cassandra is written in Java, these bindings are well established, part of the Cassandra distribution, and stable. Thus, it makes sense to have a build environment capable of compiling and running Java applications to access Cassandra. This recipe shows you how to set up this environment. Other recipes in the book that involve coding will assume you have this environment setup.

Getting ready

You will need:

▶ The apache-ant build tool (`http://ant.apache.org`)

▶ Java SDK (`http://www.oracle.com/technetwork/java/index.html`)

▶ JUnit jar (`http://www.junit.org/`)

How to do it...

1. Create a top-level folder and several sub folders for this project:

```
$ mkdir ~/hpcbuild
$ cd ~/hpcbuild
$ mkdir src/{java,test}
$ mkdir lib
```

2. Copy JAR files from your Cassandra distribution into the `lib` directory:

```
$ cp <cassandra-home>/lib/*.jar ~/hpcbuild/lib
```

From the JUnit installation, copy the `junit.jar` into your library path. Java applications can use JUnit tests for better code coverage:

```
$ cp <junit-home>/junit*.jar ~/hpcbuild/lib
```

3. Create a `build.xml` file for use with Ant. A `build.xml` file is similar to a **Makefile**. By convention, properties that represent critical paths to the build are typically specified at the top of the file:

```
<project name="hpcas" default="dist" basedir=".">
  <property name="src" location="src/java"/>
  <property name="test.src" location="src/test"/>
  <property name="build" location="build"/>
  <property name="build.classes" location="build/classes"/>
  <property name="test.build" location="build/test"/>
  <property name="dist"  location="dist"/>
  <property name="lib" location="lib"/>
```

Ant has tags that help build paths. This is useful for a project that requires multiple JAR files in its `classpath` to run:

```
<path id="hpcas.classpath">
  <pathelement location="${build.classes}"/>
  <fileset dir="${lib}" includes="*.jar"/>
</path>
```

We want to exclude test cases classes from the final JAR we produce. Create a separate source and build path for the test cases:

```
<path id="hpcas.test.classpath">
  <pathelement location="${test.build}"/>
  <path refid="hpcas.classpath"/>
</path>
```

An Ant target does a unit of work such as `compile` or `run`. The init target creates directories that are used in other parts of the build:

```
<target name="init">
  <mkdir dir="${build}"/>
  <mkdir dir="${build.classes}"/>
  <mkdir dir="${test.build}"/>
</target>
```

The `compile` target builds your code using the `javac` compiler. If you have any syntax errors, they will be reported at this stage:

```
<target name="compile" depends="init">
  <javac srcdir="${src}" destdir="${build.classes}">
    <classpath refid="hpcas.classpath"/>
  </javac>
</target>
<target name="compile-test" depends="init">
  <javac srcdir="${test.src}" destdir="${test.build}">
    <classpath refid="hpcas.test.classpath"/>
  </javac>
</target>
```

The `test` target looks for filenames that match certain naming conventions and executes them as a batch of JUnit tests. In this case, the convention is any file that starts with `Test` and ends in `.class`:

```
<target name="test" depends="compile-test,compile" >
  <junit printsummary="yes" showoutput="true" >
    <classpath refid="hpcas.test.classpath" />
    <batchtest>
      <fileset dir="${test.build}" includes="**/Test*.class" />
    </batchtest>
  </junit>
</target>
```

If the build step succeeds, the `dist` target creates a final JAR `hpcas.jar`:

```
<target name="dist" depends="compile" >
  <mkdir dir="${dist}/lib"/>
  <jar jarfile="${dist}/lib/hpcas.jar" basedir="${build.classes}"/>
</target>
```

The `run` target will allow us to execute classes we build:

```
<target name="run" depends="dist">
  <java classname="${classToRun}" >
    <classpath refid="hpcas.classpath"/>
  </java>
</target>
```

The `clean` target is used to remove files left behind from older builds:

```
<target name="clean" >
  <delete dir="${build}"/>
  <delete dir="${dist}"/>
</target>
</project>
```

Now that the `build.xml` file is constructed, we must verify it works as expected. Create small Java applications in both the build and test source paths. The first is a JUnit test in `src/test/Test.java`:

```
import junit.framework.*;
public class Test extends TestCase {
    public void test() {
        assertEquals( "Equality Test", 0, 0 );
    }
}
```

4. Next, write a simple "yo cassandra" program `hpcbuild/src/java/A.java`:

```
public class A {
  public static void main(String [] args){
    System.out.println("yo cassandra");
  }
}
```

5. Call the `test` target:

    $ ant test

```
    Buildfile: /home/edward/hpcbuild/build.xml
    . . .
        [junit] Running Test
        [junit] Tests run: 1, Failures: 0, Errors: 0,
    Time elapsed: 0.012 sec
    BUILD SUCCESSFUL
    Total time: 5 seconds
```

6. Call the `dist` target. This will compile source code and build a JAR file:

    $ ant dist

```
compile:
    dist:
            [jar] Building jar: /home/edward/hpcbuild/dist/lib/hpcas.
    jar
    BUILD SUCCESSFUL
    Total time: 3 seconds
```

The `jar` command will build empty JAR files with no indication that you had specified the wrong path. You can use the `-tf` arguments to verify that the JAR file holds the content you believe it should:

$ jar -tf /home/edward/hpcbuild/dist/lib/hpcas.jar

```
    META-INF/
    META-INF/MANIFEST.MF
    A.class
```

7. Use the `run` target to run the A class:

```
$ ant -DclassToRun=A run

run:
     [java] yo cassandra
BUILD SUCCESSFUL
Total time: 2 seconds
```

How it works...

Ant is a build system popular with Java projects. An Ant script has one or more **targets**. A target can be a task such as compiling code, testing code, or producing a final JAR. Targets can depend on other targets. As a result, you do not have to run a list of targets sequentially; the `dist` target will run its dependents such as `compile` and `init` and their dependencies in proper order.

There's more...

If you want to work with an **IDE**, the NetBeans IDE has a type of project called **Free-Form project**. You can use the preceding `build.xml` with the Free-Form project type.

Running in the foreground with full debugging

When working with new software or troubleshooting an issue, every piece of information can be valuable. Cassandra has the capability to both run in the foreground and to run with specific debugging levels. This recipe will show you how to run in the foreground with the highest possible debugging level.

How to do it...

1. Edit `conf/log4j-server.properties`:

   `log4j.rootLogger=DEBUG,stdout,R`

2. Start the instance in the foreground using `-f`:

   `$ bin/cassandra -f`

How it works...

Without the -f option, Cassandra disassociates itself from the starting console and runs like a system daemon. With the -f option, Cassandra runs as a standard Java application.

Log4J has a concept of log levels DEBUG, INFO, WARN, ERROR, and FATAL. Cassandra normally runs at the INFO level.

There's more...

Setting a global DEBUG level is only appropriate for testing and troubleshooting because of the overhead incurred by writing many events to a single file. If you have to enable debug in production, try to do it for the smallest set of classes possible, not all org.apache.cassandra classes.

Calculating ideal Initial Tokens for use with Random Partitioner

Cassandra uses a **Consistent Hashing** to divide data across the ring. Each node has an **Initial Token** which represents the node's logical position in the ring. Initial Tokens should divide the **Keyspace** evenly. Using the row key of data, the partitioner calculates a token. The node whose Initial Token is closest without being larger than the data's token is where the data is stored along with the other replicas.

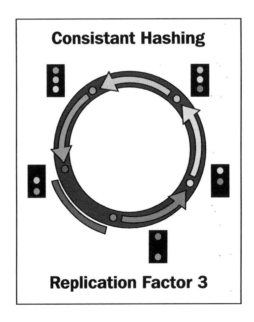

Consistant Hashing

Replication Factor 3

Initial Tokens decide who is "responsible for" data.

The formula to calculate the ideal Initial Tokens is:

```
Initial_Token= Zero_Indexed_Node_Number  * ((2^127) / Number_Of_Nodes)
```

For a five node cluster, the initial token for the 3rd node would be:

```
initial token=2 * ((2^127) / 5)
initial token=68056473384187692692674921486353642290
```

Initial Tokens can be very large numbers. For larger clusters of 20 or more nodes, determining the ideal Initial Token for each node in a cluster is a time consuming process. The following Java program calculates the Initial Tokens for each node in the cluster.

Getting ready

You can easily build and run this example following *Setting up a build and test environment* earlier in this chapter.

How to do it...

1. Create a file `src/hpcas/c01/InitialTokes.java`:

```java
package hpcas.c01;
import java.math.*;
public class InitialTokens {
  public static void main (String [] args){
    if (System.getenv("tokens")==null){
      System.err.println("Usage: tokens=5 ant
-DclassToRun=InitialTokens run");
      System.exit(0);
    }
    int nodes = Integer.parseInt(System.getenv("tokens"));
    for (int i = 0 ;i <nodes;i++){
      BigInteger hs = new BigInteger("2");
      BigInteger res = hs.pow( 127 );
      BigInteger div = res.divide( new BigInteger( nodes+"") );
      BigInteger fin = div.multiply( new BigInteger(i+"") );
      System.out.println(fin);
    }
  }
}
```

2. Set the environment variable `tokens` to the number of nodes in the cluster. Then, call the `run` target, passing the full class name `hpcas.c01.InitialTokens` as a Java property:

```
$ tokens=5 ant -DclassToRun=hpcas.c01.InitialTokens run

run:
    [java] 0
    [java] 34028236692093846346337460743176821145
    [java] 68056473384187692692674921486353642290
    [java] 102084710076281539039012382229530463435
    [java] 136112946768375385385349842972707284580
```

How it works

Generating numbers equidistant from each other helps keep the amount of data on each node in the cluster balanced. This also keeps the requests per nodes balanced. When initializing systems running the server for the first time, use these numbers in the `initial_tokens` field of the `conf/cassandra.yaml` file.

There's more...

This technique for calculating Initial Tokens is ideal for the **Random Partitioner**, which is the default partitioner. When using the **Order Preserving Partitioner**, imbalances in key distribution may require adjustments to the Initial Tokens to balance out the load.

See also...

If a Cassandra node has already joined the cluster, see in *Chapter 7, Administration*, the recipe *Nodetool Move: Move a node to a specific ring location* to see how to move a node to an initial token.

Choosing Initial Tokens for use with Partitioners that preserve ordering

Some partitioners in Cassandra preserve the ordering of keys. Examples of these partitioners include `ByteOrderedPartitioner` and `OrderPreservingPartitioner`. If the distribution of keys is uneven, some nodes will have more data than others. This recipe shows how to choose `initial_tokens` for a phonebook dataset while using `OrderPreservingPartitioner`.

How to do it...

In the `conf/cassandra.yaml` file, set the `partitioner` attribute.

```
org.apache.cassandra.dht.OrderPreservingPartitioner
```

Determine the approximate distribution of your keys. For names from a phonebook, some letters may be more common than others. Names such as Smith are very common while names such as Capriolo are very rare. For a cluster of eight nodes, choose initial tokens that will divide the list roughly evenly.

```
A, Ek, J, Mf, Nh, Sf, Su, Tf
```

Calculating Distributions

Information on calculating distributions using spreadsheets can be found online: `http://www.wisc-online.com/objects/ViewObject.aspx?ID=TMH4604`.

How it works...

Partitioners that preserve order can range scan across keys and return data in a natural order. The trade off is that users and administrators have to plan for and track the distribution of data.

There's more...

If a Cassandra node has already joined the cluster, see the recipe in *Chapter 7*, Administration, the recipe *Nodetool Move: Move a node to a specific ring location* to see how to move a node to an initial token.

Insight into Cassandra with JConsole

The Java Virtual Machine has an integrated system to do interactive monitoring of JVM internals called **JVM (Java Management Extensions)**. In addition to JVM internals, applications can maintain their own counters and provide operations that the user can trigger remotely. Cassandra has numerous counters and the ability to trigger operations such as clearing the Key Cache or disabling compaction over JMX. This recipe shows how to connect to Cassandra instances using **JConsole**.

Getting ready

JConsole comes with the Java Runtime Environment. It requires a windowing system such as **X11** to run on the system you start JConsole from, not on the server it will connect to.

How to do it...

1. Start JConsole:

    ```
    $ /usr/java/latest/bin/jconsole
    ```

2. In the **Remote Process** box, enter the host and port of your instance:

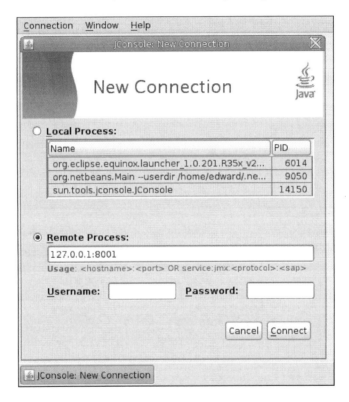

3. Click on the **Memory** tab to view information about the virtual memory being used by the JVM:

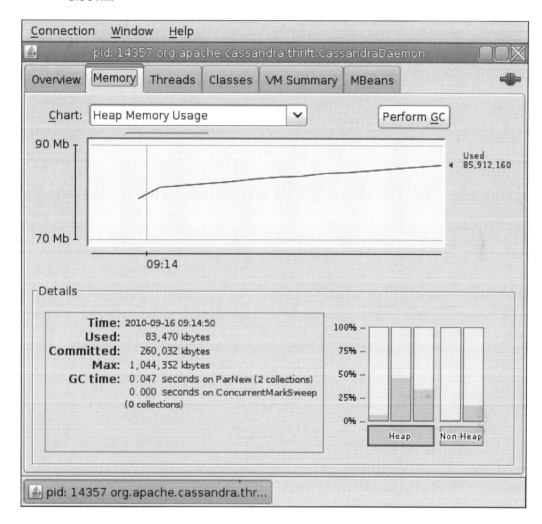

How it works...

JConsole can connect to local processes running as your user without host and port information by selecting the process in the **Local Process** list. Connecting to processes on other machines requires you to enter host and port information in the **Remote Process**.

See also...

The recipe *Connecting with JConsole over a SOCKS Proxy* shows how to use JConsole with a host only reachable by SSH.

Chapter 12, Collecting and Analyzing Performance Statistics covers Java and Cassandra counters in great detail.

Connecting with JConsole over a SOCKS proxy

Often, you would like to run **JConsole** on your desktop and connect to a server on a remote network. JMX uses **Remote Method Invocation** (**RMI**) to communicate between systems. RMI has an initial connection port. However, the server allocates dynamic ports for further communication. Applications that use RMI typically have trouble running on more secure networks. This recipe shows how to create a **dynamic proxy** over SSH and how to have JConsole use the proxy instead of direct connections.

Getting ready

On your management system you will need an SSH client from **OpenSSH**. This comes standard with almost any Unix/Linux system. Windows users can try **Cygwin** to get an OpenSSH client.

How to do it...

1. Start an SSH tunnel to your login server, for example `login.domain.com`. The -D option allocates the SOCKS proxy:

    ```
    $ ssh -f -D9998 edward@login.domain.com 'while true; do sleep 1;
    done'
    ```

2. Start up JConsole by passing it command-line instructions to use the proxy you created in the last step:

    ```
    $ jconsole -J-DsocksProxyHost=localhost -J-DsocksProxyPort=9998 \
    service:jmx:rmi:///jndi/rmi://cas1.domain.com:8080/jmxrmi
    ```

How it works...

A dynamic SOCKS proxy is opened up on the target server and tunneled to a local port on your workstation. JConsole is started up and configured to use this proxy. When JConsole attempts to open connections, they will happen through the proxy. Destination hosts will see the source of the traffic as your proxy system and not as your local desktop.

Connecting to Cassandra with Java and Thrift

Cassandra clients communicate with servers through API classes generated by Thrift. The API allows clients to perform data manipulation operations as well as gain information about the cluster. This recipe shows how to connect from client to server and call methods that return cluster information.

Getting ready

This recipe is designed to work with the build environment from the recipe *Setting up a build and test environment*. You also need to have a system running Cassandra, as in the *Simulating multiple node clusters* recipe.

How to do it...

1. Create a file `src/hpcas/c01/ShowKeyspaces.java`:

```
package hpcas.c01;
import org.apache.cassandra.thrift.*;
import org.apache.thrift.protocol.*;
import org.apache.thrift.transport.*;
public class ShowKeyspaces {
   public static void main(String[] args) throws Exception {
      String host = System.getenv("host");
      int port = Integer.parseInt(System.getenv("port"));
```

The objective is to create a `Cassandra.Client` instance that can communicate with Cassandra. The Thrift framework requires several steps to instantiate:

```
TSocket socket = new TSocket(host, port);
TTransport transport = new TFramedTransport(socket);
TProtocol proto = new TBinaryProtocol(transport);
transport.open();
Cassandra.Client client = new Cassandra.Client(proto);
```

We call methods from the `Cassandra.Client` that allow the user to inspect the server, such as describing the cluster name and the version:

```
System.out.println("version "+client.describe_version());
System.out.println("partitioner"
+client.describe_partitioner());
System.out.println("cluster name "
```

```
        +client.describe_cluster_name());
        for ( String keyspace: client.describe_keyspaces() ){
            System.out.println("keyspace " +keyspace);
        }
        transport.close();
    }
}
```

2. Run this application by providing host and port environment variables:

    **# host=127.0.0.1 port=9160 ant -DclassToRun=hpcas.c01.
    ShowKeyspaces run**

    ```
    run:
            [java] version 10.0.0
            [java] partitioner org.apache.cassandra.dht.
            RandomPartitioner
            [java] cluster name Test Cluster
            [java] keyspace Keyspace1
            [java] keyspace system
    ```

How it works...

Cassandra clusters are symmetric in that you can connect to any node in the cluster and perform operations. Thrift has a multi-step connection process. After choosing the correct transports and other connection settings, users can instantiate a `Cassandra.Client` instance. With an instance of the `Cassandra.Client`, users can call multiple methods without having to reconnect. We called some methods such as `describe_cluster_name()` that show some information about the cluster and then disconnect.

See also...

In *Chapter 5, Consistency, Availability, and Partition Tolerance with Cassandra, the recipe Working with the formula for strong consistency* shows how to create a simple wrapper that reduces the repeated code when connecting to Cassandra.

2

The Command-line Interface

In this chapter, you will learn:

- ▶ Connecting to Cassandra with the CLI
- ▶ Creating a keyspace from the CLI
- ▶ Creating a column family with the CLI
- ▶ Describing keyspaces
- ▶ Writing data with the CLI
- ▶ Reading data with the CLI
- ▶ Deleting rows and columns from the CLI
- ▶ Listing and paginating all rows in a column family
- ▶ Dropping a keyspace or a column family
- ▶ Using assume to decode column names or column values
- ▶ Supplying time to live information when inserting columns
- ▶ Changing the consistency level of the CLI
- ▶ Getting help from the CLI
- ▶ Loading CLI statements from a file

Connecting to Cassandra with the CLI

Users can connect to any node in the cluster and issue requests. This recipe shows how to connect to a node in the cluster.

How to do it...

1. Execute the `cassandra-cli` script to start an interactive session:

   ```
   $ <cassandra_home>/bin/cassandra-cli
   ```

2. Use the `connect` statement and specify a host and port to connect to. Connect to the Thrift port, which defaults to 9160, not the JMX or Storage Port:

   ```
   [default@unknown] connect 127.0.0.2/9160;
   Connected to: "Test Cluster" on 127.0.0.2/9160
   ```

3. Once connected, client/server commands can be issued:

   ```
   [default@testks] show api version;
   19.4.0
   [default@testks] describe cluster;
   Cluster Information:
       Snitch: org.apache.cassandra.locator.SimpleSnitch
       Partitioner: org.apache.cassandra.dht.RandomPartitioner
       Schema versions:
           b2046e4c-8cc7-11e0-ae9c-e700f669bcfc: [127.0.0.1]
   ```

How it works...

The CLI presents an interactive interface to execute operations with Cassandra. The underlying communication between the CLI and Cassandra uses the same Thrift interface that client applications use.

Creating a keyspace from the CLI

A **keyspace** is a top-level organizational unit that can hold one or more **column families**. An important setting for creating a keyspace is **replication factor**, which controls how many replicas of data will be in the cluster.

Replication factor can not exceed the number of nodes in the cluster.

How to do it...

Create a keyspace named `testkeyspace` with a replication factor of `3`.

```
[default@unknown] create keyspace testkeyspace with replication_factor=3;
```

How it works...

A keyspace does not store data directly. However, all the column families inside it inherit configuration from it. This is important because two column families inside the same keyspace must use the same replication factor and replication strategy. It is suggested to create a keyspace for each column family since there are no benefits in sharing one.

There's more...

The syntax in Cassandra 0.8.0 and higher will move the replication factor to a property of the `strategy_options`.

```
[default@unknown] CREATE KEYSPACE testkeyspace WITH strategy_class =
SimpleStrategy AND strategy_options:replication_factor = 1;
```

See also...

Other options that can be supplied when creating a keyspace are `placement_strategy` and `strategy_options`. These options are described in the multiple data center chapter.

Creating a column family with the CLI

A **column family** is a container for columns. To insert and read data, you first need to create a column family.

Getting ready

Columns families need to be created inside a keyspace. See the previous recipe, *Creating a keyspace from the CLI*.

How to do it...

1. Authenticate to an existing keyspace with the `use` command:

   ```
   [default@testkeyspace] use testkeyspace;
   Authenticated to keyspace: testkeyspace
   ```

2. Create a column family named `testcolumnfamily`:

```
[default@testkeyspace] create column family testcolumnfamily;
5ec1d928-3ee5-11e0-b34a-e700f669bcfc
Waiting for schema agreement...
... schemas agree across the cluster
```

3. Column families have several configurable parameters that are specified in a `with` clause and separated by `and`:

```
[default@testkeyspace] create column family testcolumnfamily with
rows_cached=200000 and read_repair_chance=0.4;
```

See also...

There are many parameters for a column family that significantly change how it operates.

Chapter 4, Performance Tuning discusses *Tuning Memtables for write-heavy workloads, Boosting read performance with the Key Cache, and Boosting read performance with the Row Cache.*

Chapter 7, Administration the recipe Lowering gc_grace for faster deletes.

Describing a keyspace

The `describe keyspace` command shows all the properties of a **keyspace**, including the information of each **column family** inside it.

How to do it...

1. Use the `describe keyspace` command and specify the name of a keyspace:

```
[default@unknown] describe keyspace testkeyspace;
Keyspace: testkeyspace:
  Replication Strategy: org.apache.cassandra.locator.
SimpleStrategy
    Replication Factor: 1
  Column Families:
    ColumnFamily: testcolumnfamily
      Columns sorted by: org.apache.cassandra.db.marshal.BytesType
      Row cache size / save period: 0.0/0
      Key cache size / save period: 200000.0/3600
      Memtable thresholds: 0.0703125/15/60
      GC grace seconds: 864000
      Compaction min/max thresholds: 4/32
      Read repair chance: 1.0
```

How it works...

The information about keyspaces and column families is meta-information that is stored and replicated across all nodes in the cluster. The `describe keyspace` command displays this information.

Writing data with the CLI

The command-line interface has a `set` command that is used for inserting data.

Getting ready

To insert data, a target keyspace and column family must already exist. An insert also requires a row key, a column name, and a column value information.

How to do it...

1. Authenticate to a keyspace:

    ```
    [default@unknown] use testkeyspace;
    Authenticated to keyspace: testkeyspace
    ```

2. For the row identified by 'server01', set the 'os' (operating system) to 'linux' using the `set` command:

    ```
    [default@testkeyspace] set testcolumnfamily['server01']
    ['os']='linux';
    Value inserted.
    ```

3. For the row identified by 'server01', set the 'distribution' to 'CentOS_5' using the `set` command:

    ```
    [default@testkeyspace] set testcolumnfamily['server01']
    ['distribution']='CentOS_5';
    Value inserted.
    ```

How it works...

`Set` command will create the column if it does not already exist. If the column does exist, the old value will be overwritten with the new value. Cassandra automatically writes the key to the proper node regardless of which node the CLI connects to.

There's more...

The CLI uses microseconds since epoch time as the value of timestamp when setting columns. This is a Cassandra convention.

Reading data with the CLI

The `get` operation allows users to retrieve data through the CLI.

Getting ready

To retrieve data using the `get` operation, a row key is required and a column name is optional.

How to do it...

1. Connect to an existing keyspace:

   ```
   [default@unknown] use testkeyspace;
   Authenticated to keyspace: testkeyspace
   ```

2. Issue the `get` command for a specific row key and column:

   ```
   [default@testkeyspace] get testcf['server01']['distribution'];
   => (column=6469737479269627574696f6e, value=43656e744f535f35,
   timestamp=1298461364486000)
   ```

3. Remove the column hash to fetch all the columns for a row key:

   ```
   [default@testkeyspace] get testcf['server01'];
   => (column=6469737479269627574696f6e, value=43656e744f535f35,
   timestamp=1298461364486000)
   => (column=6f73, value=6c696e7578, timestamp=1298461314264000)
   Returned 2 results.
   ```

4. Fetch some data that does not exist:

   ```
   [default@testks] get testcf['doesnotexist'];
   Returned 0 results.
   [default@testks] get testcf['doesnotexist']['nope'];
   Value was not found
   ```

How it works...

Cassandra uses the row key to locate and fetch the requested data from the proper node. The client does not need to specifically connect to the node with the data.

See also...

In this chapter, the recipe *Using the assume keyword to decode column names or column values* demonstrates how to force the CLI to display column names and values in more human-readable formats.

In this chapter, the recipe *Using column metadata and comparators for schema enforcement* stores meta-information inside the schema so it displays properly.

Deleting rows and columns from the CLI

Known rows and columns can be deleted by specifying the **row key** and/or the **column name** with the **del** (delete) command.

How to do it...

1. Connect to a Cassandra keyspace:

    ```
    [default@unknown] use testkeyspace;
    Authenticated to keyspace: testkeyspace
    ```

2. Issue a delete for the row key `server01` and the column `distribution`:

    ```
    [default@testkeyspace] del testcf['server01']['distribution'];
    column removed.
    ```

Caution

Supplying only a row key with no column will result in all the columns for that row being deleted.

3. Issue a delete for all the columns of the row key `server01`:

    ```
    [default@testkeyspace] del testcolumnfamily['server01'];
    row removed.
    ```

How it works...

Deletes in Cassandra are implemented as special writes known as **tombstones**. The data is not removed from disk until a time in the future, but reads done after the delete will not find this data.

See also...

Chapter 7, *Administration*, recipe, *Lowering GCGraceSeconds for faster deletes.*

Chapter 4, *Performance Tuning*, *Setting compaction thresholds* recipe.

Listing and paginating all rows in a column family

The `list` command pages through data.

Getting ready

Insert some sample data into a column family.

```
[default@testks] set testcf['a']['thing']='5';
[default@testks] set testcf['g']['thing']='5';
[default@testks] set testcf['h']['thing']='5';
```

How to do it...

1. Use the list keyword to show the first entries in the column family:

```
[default@testks] list testcf;
Using default limit of 100
RowKey: a
=> (column=7468696e67, value=35, timestamp=1306981...)
RowKey: h
=> (column=7468696e67, value=35, timestamp=1306981...)
RowKey: g
=> (column=7468696e67, value=35, timestamp=1306981...)
```

2. List using a specific start key 'h' and a limit of 2:

```
[default@testks] list testcf['h':] limit 2;
RowKey: h
=> (column=7468696e67, value=35, timestamp=1306981...)
RowKey: g
=> (column=7468696e67, value=35, timestamp=1306981...)
```

3. Run list using a start key of 'a' and an end key of 'h':

```
[default@testks] list testcf['a':'h'] limit 5;
RowKey: a
=> (column=7468696e67, value=35, timestamp=1306981...)
RowKey: h
=> (column=7468696e67, value=35, timestamp=1306981...)
```

How it works...

List uses range scanning to display data in a column family. If using `RandomParitioner`, the data will not be in a lexicographical order, but it will be in a constant order. The list moves through the data and provides commands to limit results, start at a specific key, and stop scanning at a specific key.

Dropping a keyspace or a column family

The `drop` statement can be used to drop a column family or a keyspace.

Warning

Dropping a column family or a keyspace will remove all data in it for all nodes in the cluster. It cannot be undone.

How to do it...

Use `drop column family` to remove the column family:

```
[default@testkeyspace] use testkeyspace;
Authenticated to keyspace: testkeyspace
[default@testkeyspace] drop column family testcolumnfamily;
Use the drop keyspace statement on 'testkeyspace',
[default@testkeyspace] drop keyspace testkeyspace;
```

How it works...

The `drop` command removes a keyspace or a column family across the cluster. After executing this statement, writes and reads to the entity will not be possible.

See also...

- ▶ In *Chapter 7, Administration*, the recipe *Using nodetool snapshot for backups*
- ▶ In *Chapter 7, Administration*, the recipe *Exporting data to JSON with sstable2json*

CLI operations with super columns

Super columns add another level of nesting over standard columns. The CLI allows inserts to super columns much like inserts of normal columns. They can be read with `get`, written with `set`, and deleted with `del`. The super column version of these commands uses an extra `['xxx']` to represent the extra level of the map called the **sub-column**.

How to do it...

1. Create a column family named `supertest` using the clause 'with column_type=super':

    ```
    [default@testkeyspace] create column family supertest with column_
    type='Super';
    ```

2. Now, insert data. Notice super columns have an extra level of the map ['XXX']:

    ```
    [default@test..] set supertest['mynewcar']['parts']
    ['engine']='v8';
    [default@test..] set supertest['mynewcar']['parts']
    ['wheelsize']='20"';
    [default@test..] set supertest['mynewcar']['options']['cruise
    control']='yes';
    [default@test..] set supertest['mynewcar']['options']['heated
    seats']='yes';
    ```

3. Use `assume` so CLI formats the columns as ASCII text, and then fetch all the columns of the 'mynewcar' row:

    ```
    [default@testkeyspace] assume supertest comparator as ascii;
    [default@testkeyspace] assume supertest sub_comparator as ascii;
    [default@testkeyspace] assume supertest validator as ascii;
    [default@testkeyspace] get supertest['mynewcar'];
    => (super_column=options,
    ```

```
        (column=cruise control, value=yes,
    timestamp=1298581426267000)
        (column=heated seats, value=yes, timestamp=1298581436937000))
    => (super_column=parts,
        (column=engine, value=v8, timestamp=1298581276849000)
        (column=wheelsize, value=20", timestamp=1298581365393000))
```

How it works...

Super columns bring an extra level of nesting to the data model. When working with super columns from the CLI, an extra '[]' specifies the sub-index level.

There's more...

Internally, super columns must be completely serialized and de-serialized to be accessed. This makes them inefficient for super columns with a large number of columns. While super columns look like an attractive option, it is almost always better to append the column and the super column together with a deliminator between them. The extra serialization involved in using super columns and extra space used makes them less efficient.

Using the assume keyword to decode column names or column values

The `assume` keyword does not modify data or column family metadata. Instead, it decodes and helps display results of `get` and `list` requests inside the command-line interface.

How to do it...

1. Use the `assume` statement to set the comparator, validator, and keys to ASCII type a subcomparator also exists for super columns:

   ```
   [default@testkeyspace] assume testcf comparator as ascii;
   Assumption for column family 'testcf' added successfully.
   [default@testkeyspace] assume testcf validator as ascii;
   Assumption for column family 'testcf' added successfully.
   [default@testkeyspace] assume testcf keys as ascii;
   Assumption for column family 'testcf' added successfully.
   ```

2. Read a row key. The column and value will be displayed rather than the hex code:

   ```
   [default@testkeyspace] get testcf ['server01'];
   => (column=distribution, value=CentOS_5,
   timestamp=1298496656140000)
   Returned 1 results.
   ```

How it works...

By default, columns with no metadata are displayed in a hex format. This is done because row keys, column names, and column values are byte arrays. These could have non-printable characters inside them such as a tab or newline that would affect the CLI output. `assume` converts and displays these values in specific formats.

There's more...

Cassandra has built-in types that can be used with `assume`. These are bytes, integer, long, lexicaluuid, timeuuid, utf8, and ASCII.

Supplying time to live information when inserting columns

Time To Live (**TTL**) is a setting that makes a column self-delete a specified number of seconds after the insertion time.

How to do it...

1. Append `with ttl` clause to a set statement that will expire a row after ten seconds:

   ```
   [default@testkeyspace] set testcf['3']['acolumn']='avalue' with
   ttl = 10;
   Value inserted.
   [default@testkeyspace] get testcf['3'];
   => (column=61636f6c756d6e, value=6176616c7565,
   timestamp=1298507877951000, ttl=10)
   Returned 1 results.
   ```

2. Wait ten seconds or longer before reading again and the column will be deleted:

   ```
   [default@testkeyspace] get testcf['3'];
   Returned 0 results.
   ```

See also...

In *Chapter 3, The Application Programmer Interface*, the recipe *Using TTL to create columns with self-deletion times*.

Using built-in CLI functions

By default, Cassandra treats data as **byte arrays**. However, support is offered for types such as **Long**, which is a serialized 64 bit integer. The CLI provides built-in functions that convert the user-supplied data from the CLI into other types such as a conversion from a string to a long. Other functions create values of `timeuuid()`, which are normally generated by a program.

How to do it...

1. Use the help command to determine which functions are available:

```
[default@unknown] help set;
set <cf>['<key>']['<col>'] = <value>;
set <cf>['<key>']['<super>']['<col>'] = <value>;
set <cf>['<key>']['<col>'] = <function>(<argument>);
set <cf>['<key>']['<super>']['<col>'] = <function>(<argument>);
set <cf>[<key>][<function>(<col>)] = <value> || <function>;
set <cf>[<key>][<function>(<col>) || <col>] = <value> ||
<function> with ttl = <secs>;
Available functions: bytes, integer, long, lexicaluuid, timeuuid,
utf8, ascii.
examples:
set bar['testkey']['my super']['test col']='this is a test';
set baz['testkey']['test col']='this is also a test';
set diz[testkey][testcol] = utf8('this is utf8 string.');
set bar[testkey][timeuuid()] = utf('hello world');
set bar[testkey][timeuuid()] = utf('hello world') with ttl = 30;
set diz[testkey][testcol] = 'this is utf8 string.' with ttl = 150;
```

2. Insert a column that uses the `timeuuid()` method as a column name and uses the `long()` method to turn the literal string `'7'` into an encoded long:

```
[default@testkeyspace] set testcf['atest'][timeuuid()] = long(7);
Value inserted.
```

How it works...

Functions are useful for converting strings into the other types from the CLI.

Using column metadata and comparators for type enforcement

Cassandra is designed to store and retrieve simple byte arrays. It is normally up to the user to encode and decode their data. Cassandra does have support for built-in types such as timeuuid, ASCII, long, and a few others. When creating or updating a column family, the user can supply **column metadata** that instructs the CLI on how to display data and help the server enforce types during insertion operations.

How to do it...

1. Create a column family named `cars` specifying the comparator as `LongType`:

   ```
   [default@testkeyspace] create column family cars with comparator=L
   ongType;
   46e82939-400c-11e0-b34a-e700f669bcfc
   ```

2. Try to insert a row with a column name that is not a number:

   ```
   [default@testkeyspace] set cars ['3']['343zzz42']='this should
   fail';
   '343zzz42' could not be translated into a LongType.
   ```

3. Supply an integer and use the built-in `long ()` method to encode it:

   ```
   [default@testkeyspace] set cars ['3'][long('3442')]='this should
   pass';
   Value inserted.
   ```

4. Cassandra can enforce that the values of columns with specific names are of specific types. Create a column family `cars2` and fill out the **column metadata** as shown:

   ```
   create column family cars2 with column_metadata=[{column_
   name:'weight', validation_class:IntegerType},{column_name:'make',
   validation_class:AsciiType}];
   ```

5. Attempt to write to the `'weight'` column. This should fail if the value is not an integer:

   ```
   [default@testkeyspace] set cars2['mynewcar']['weight']='200fd0';
   '200fd0' could not be translated into an IntegerType.
   ```

6. Write two entries with values of proper types:

   ```
   [default@testkeyspace] set cars2['mynewcar']
   ['weight']=Integer('2000');
   Value inserted.
   [default@testkeyspace] set cars2['mynewcar']['make']='ford';
   Value inserted.
   ```

7. Fetch the results:

```
[default@testkeyspace] assume cars2 comparator as ascii;
Assumption for column family 'cars2' added successfully.
[default@testkeyspace] get cars2['mynewcar'];
=> (column=make, value=ford, timestamp=1298580528208000)
=> (column=weight, value=2000, timestamp=1298580306095000)
Returned 2 results.
```

How it works...

Cassandra defaults to not enforcing types and accepts arbitrary byte data. Column metadata as well as comparators allow users to ensure the integrity of data during write operations. It also serves as meta information for users reading the data so it can be decoded properly.

See also...

in *Chapter 9, Coding and Internals*, the recipe *Creating your own type by sub classing abstract type*.

Changing the consistency level of the CLI

The Cassandra data mode stores data across many nodes and data centers. When operating on data, users choose the **consistency level** of the operation per requests. The default consistency level used by the CLI is ONE. This recipe shows how to use the consistencylevel keyword to change consistency level.

How to do it...

1. Use the consistencylevel statement to change the consistency level:

```
[default@ks33] consistencylevel as QUORUM;
Consistency level is set to 'QUORUM'.
```

2. After changing the level, do set, get, and list operations as normal:

```
[default@testkeyspace] get cars2['mynewcar'];
=> (column=make, value=ford, timestamp=1298580528208000)
=> (column=weight, value=2000, timestamp=1298580306095000)
Returned 2 results.
```

How it works...

Changing the consistency level only affects the current CLI session. Doing this is helpful when trying to troubleshoot errors that users may be reporting. Consistency level ONE is forgiving in that write or read operations will succeed with multiple node failures, while other levels such as ALL are less forgiving. This feature is also useful when working in multiple data center environments with levels such as LOCAL_QUORUM.

See also...

In *Chapter 5, Consistency, Availability, and Partition Tolerance with Cassandra*, the recipe *The formula for strong consistency*.

In *Chapter 8, Multiple Data Center Deployments*, the recipe *Changing consistency level from the CLI to test various consistency levels with multiple data center deployments*.

Getting help from the CLI

The CLI has built-in documentation that is accessed using the `help` statement. This recipe shows how to get help from the CLI.

How to do it...

1. Issue the help statement:

```
[default@testks] help;
List of all CLI commands:
help;
Display this help.
help <command>; Display detailed, command-specific help.

connect <hostname>/<port> (<username> '<password>')?; Connect to
thrift service.

use <keyspace> [<username> 'password'];                    Switch
to a keyspace.

...
del <cf>['<key>'];
Delete record.
```

```
del <cf>['<key>']['<col>'];
Delete column.

del <cf>['<key>']['<super>']['<col>'];
Delete sub column
...
```

2. Run the command 'help del' for help on the delete command:

```
[default@testks] help del;
del <cf>['<key>'];
del <cf>['<key>']['<col>'];
del <cf>['<key>']['<super>']['<col>'];

Deletes a record, a column, or a subcolumn.

example:
del bar['testkey']['my super']['test col'];
del baz['testkey']['test col'];
del baz['testkey'];
```

How it works...

The default help statement displays information about all the other statements available. When following help with the name of another statement such as del or list, the statement issues more details on that specific command.

Loading CLI statements from a file

The Cassandra CLI has a batch utility that processes commands from a file.

How to do it...

1. Create a file with a list of commands for the Cassandra CLI:

```
$ echo  "create keyspace abc;" >> bfile
$ echo  "use abc;" >> bfile
$ echo "create column family def;" >> bfile
$ echo "describe keyspace abc;" >> bfile
```

2. Start the Cassandra CLI using the `-b` argument to specify the batch file:

```
$ <cassandra_home>/bin/cassandra-cli --host localhost -p 9160 -f
bfile;
Connected to: "Test Cluster" on localhost/9160
Authenticated to keyspace: abc
Keyspace: abc:
   Replication Strategy: org.apache.cassandra.locator.
SimpleStrategy
      Replication Factor: 1

...
```

How it works...

The batch mode has access to the same commands as the CLI. This mode can be used for light scripting tasks. However, it is good practice to create a batch file for all meta operations done to the cluster for change management.

There's more...

The `-B, --batch` switch enables batch mode, which suppresses output and stops processing on any error.

3

Application Programmer Interface

In this chapter, you will learn the following recipes:

- ▶ Connecting to a Cassandra server
- ▶ Creating a keyspace and column family from the client
- ▶ Using `MultiGet` to limit round trips and overhead
- ▶ Writing unit tests with an embedded Cassandra server
- ▶ Cleaning up data directories before unit tests
- ▶ Generating Thrift bindings for other languages (C++, PHP, and others)
- ▶ Using the Cassandra Store Proxy "Fat Client"
- ▶ Using range scans to find and remove old data
- ▶ Iterating all the columns of a (large) key
- ▶ Slicing columns in reverse
- ▶ Batch mutations to improve insert performance and code robustness
- ▶ Using TTL to create columns with self-deletion times
- ▶ Working with secondary indexes

Introduction

Programmatic access to a cluster of Cassandra servers is done though the Application Programmer Interface. This client API is built using Apache Thrift. With Thrift, structures, exception, services, and methods are specified in a language-neutral file called an interface file. Thrift's code generation takes the interface file as input and generates network RPC clients in many languages. The multiple language code generation allows programs written in C++ or Perl to call the same methods as a Java client. The Java client is generated and comes packaged with Cassandra.

The Application Programmer Interface provided by Cassandra provides methods for users to create, modify, and remove the meta structures for storing data, **keyspaces**, and **column families**, as well as methods for inserting, removing, and fetching data from column families.

The clients' Thrift generates are more generic because they have to work with many languages. High-level clients usually exist for a given language. For example, Java has Hector and Pelops and Python has Pycassa. These high-level clients are typically suggested because they insulate users from the details of the generated Thrift code. This chapter uses the Thrift API as this is the most language-neutral way to present the material.

Connecting to a Cassandra server

The first step is connecting to a node in the Cassandra cluster. The process of opening and closing connections involves a few lines of code that are repeated often. This recipe demonstrates the connection opening and closing code and abstracts that code into a class for reuse.

How to do it...

Create text file `<hpc_build>/src/java/hpcas/c03/FramedConnWrapper.java`:

```java
package hpcas.c03;

import org.apache.cassandra.thrift.Cassandra;
import org.apache.thrift.protocol.*;
import org.apache.thrift.transport.*;
public class FramedConnWrapper {

  /* Declare the private properties used for client server
communication. */
  private TTransport transport;

  private TProtocol proto;

  private TSocket socket;

  /* Create a constructor that takes a host and port supplied by the
user. */
  public FramedConnWrapper(String host, int port) {
    socket = new TSocket(host, port);
    transport = new TFramedTransport(socket);
    proto = new TBinaryProtocol(transport);
  }
```

```
public void open() throws Exception {
   transport.open();
}

public void close() throws Exception {
   transport.close();
   socket.close();
}

public Cassandra.Client getClient() {
   Cassandra.Client client = new Cassandra.Client(proto);
   return client;
}
}
```

How it works...

Thrift-generated classes have a slightly complex connection process. This is due to different options and transports available to Thrift. The final product of the connection steps are an instance of type `TProtocol`. The `TProtocol` instance is used in the constructor of the `Cassandra.Client` class. Cassandra. Client has the methods users interact to Cassandra with.

There's more

Initializing connections in this manner does not account for server fail-over or retries. This is one of the reasons higher level clients are preferred. Betweeen Cassandra 0.7.X and 0.8.X, the replication factor was moved from a property of a KsDef object to a name value pair in the StrategyOptions.

Creating a keyspace and column family from the client

The top level element in the storage element is a keyspace; the column family is the structure that holds data. It is common to have an application detect if the proper metadata is created and, if they are not, to create them. This recipe adds a method to `hpcas.c03.Util.java`, which creates a keyspace and column family from three arguments.

How to do it...

Create the file `<hpcbuild>/src/hpcas/c03/Util.java`:

```java
package hpcas.c03;
import java.io.UnsupportedEncodingException;
import java.util.*;
import org.apache.cassandra.thrift.*;
public class Util {

  /* Returns a list of keyspaces, useful for quickly detecting if a
keyspace exists */
  public static List<String> listKeyspaces(Cassandra.Client c) throws
Exception{
    List<String> results = new ArrayList<String>();
    for (KsDef k : c.describe_keyspaces()) {
      results.add(k.getName());
    }
    return results;
  }
  /* creates a KsDef CfDef ready for use with system_add_keyspaces()
*/

  public static KsDef createSimpleKSandCF(String ksname, String
cfname,
int replication) {

    KsDef newKs = new KsDef();

    newKs.setStrategy_class("org.apache.cassandra.locator.
SimpleStrategy");

    newKs.setName(ksname);

    newKs.setReplication_factor(replication);

    CfDef cfdef = new CfDef();

    cfdef.setKeyspace(ksname);

    cfdef.setName(cfname);

    newKs.addToCf_defs(cfdef);

    return newKs;
  }

  /*Method that is used retrieve environment or -D options passed from
the user */

  public static String envOrProp(String name) {
    if (System.getenv(name) != null) {
      return System.getenv(name);
    } else if (System.getProperty(name) != null) {
```

```
        return System.getProperty(name);
    } else {
      return null;
    }
  }

}
```

How it works...

The `createSimpleKSandCF` method takes three arguments: a keyspace name, a column family name, and a replication factor. It produces a `KsDef` instance with an initialized `CfDef` instance inside it. The result can be used by methods such as `system_add_keyspace` or `system_add_column_family` to create a keyspace or column family across the cluster.

See also...

> ▶ *Chapter 2, Command-line Interface, Creating a Keyspace from the CLI*
>
> ▶ *Chapter 2, Command-line Interface, Creating a Column Family with the CLI*

Using MultiGet to limit round trips and overhead

`MultiGet` should be used as an alternative to multiple `get` operations when each `get` operation uses the same `SlicePredicate`. By using `MultiGet`, the number of requests and network round trips are reduced versus doing one get operation per row key.

How to do it...

1. Create a program `<hpc_build>/src/java/hpcas/c03/GetVMultiGet.java`:

```java
package hpcas.c05;
import hpcas.c03.*;
import java.util.*;
import org.apache.cassandra.thrift.*;

public class GetVMultiGet {
  public static void main (String [] args) throws Exception {
  /* The user will specify host,port,keyspace,columnfamily, and
insert count */
    int inserts = Integer.parseInt(Util.envOrProp("inserts"));
    String ks = Util.envOrProp("ks");
    String cf = Util.envOrProp("cf");
```

```
FramedConnWrapper fcw = new FramedConnWrapper
            (Util.envOrProp("host"), Integer.parseInt(Util.
envOrProp("port"))); 
    fcw.open();
    /* a ColumnParent is used to insert data */
    ColumnParent parent = new ColumnParent();
    parent.setColumn_family(cf);
    /* A ColumnPath is used to get data */
    ColumnPath path = new ColumnPath();
    path.setColumn_family(cf);
    path.setColumn("acol".getBytes("UTF-8"));
```

The number of keys written are user specified. A counter is created and the value of the counter is used as the row key and the value.

```
    Column c = new Column();
    fcw.getClient().set_keyspace(ks);
    c.setName("acol".getBytes());
    for (int j = 0; j < inserts; j++) {
      byte [] key = (j+"").getBytes();
      c.setValue(key);
      fcw.getClient().insert(key, parent, c, ConsistencyLevel.
ALL);
      fcw.getClient().get(key, path, ConsistencyLevel.ALL);
    }
```

2. Create a timer and then read the data one key at a time using the get method:

```
    long getNanos = System.nanoTime();
    for (int j = 0; j < inserts; j++) {
      byte [] key = (j+"").getBytes();
      c.setValue(key);
      fcw.getClient().get(key, path, ConsistencyLevel.ONE);
    }
    long endGetNanos = System.nanoTime()-getNanos;
```

3. The `MultiGet` operation requires a `SlicePredicate`. This can either be a list of columns or a slice range:

```
    SlicePredicate pred = new SlicePredicate();
    pred.addToColumn_names("acol".getBytes());
    long startMgetNanos = System.nanoTime();
```

4. Use looping to batch requests into groups of five. Then, call the `MultiGet` method, which fetches the group:

```
    for (int j = 0; j < inserts; j=j+5) {
      List<byte[]> wantedKeys = new ArrayList<byte[]>();
      for (int k=j;k<j+5;k++){
```

```
            wantedKeys.add((j+"").getBytes());
        }
        fcw.getClient().multiget_slice(wantedKeys, parent, pred,
        ConsistencyLevel.ONE);
    }
    long endMGetNanos = System.nanoTime()-startMgetNanos;
    System.out.println("get time "+endGetNanos);
    System.out.println("mget time "+endMGetNanos);
    }
}
```

5. Run the application supplying host, port, number of inserts, keyspace, and column family name:

```
$ host=127.0.0.1 port=9160  inserts=4000 ks=ks33 cf=cf33 ant
-DclassToRun=hpcas.c05.GetVMultiGet run

run:
        [java] get time 2632434394
        [java] mget time 1754092111
```

How it works...

The time savings from `MultiGet` is mostly attributed to saving network round trip time between the application and the server. This is significant when reading small rows in a linear manner. It is important to note that using `MultiGet` does not change how the data is located in caches or a disk; that time is the same when using both methods.

Writing unit tests with an embedded Cassandra server

The ability to bring up a fully functioning instance inside user code is a clear advantage to having to manage the code base and Cassandra service separately. This approach is ideal when a large number of developers are sharing a project, or with **continuous integration** tools such as Hudson that build and test code in a completely automated and unattended manner. This recipe shows how to use the `EmbeddedCassandraService` with JUnit test classes.

How to do it...

1. Ensure that `hpcbuild/build.xml` contains a property for the location of `test.conf`:

```
<property name="dist"  location="dist"/>
<property name="lib" location="lib"/>
<property name="test.conf" location="test_conf"/>
```

Also, ensure that the `test.classpath` is included in the test target.

```
<path id="hpcas.test.classpath">
    <pathelement location="${test.build}"/>
    <pathelement location="${test.conf}" />
    <path refid="hpcas.classpath"/>
</path>
```

2. Inside the `hpcbuild` directory, create a directory for test configuration files and copy a stock configuration directory to it:

```
$ mkdir hpcbuild/test_conf
$ cp <cassandra_home>/conf/ <home>/hpcbuild/test_conf/
```

3. Modify the `cassandra.yaml` so the test configuration does not overlap with other Cassandra instances:

```
data_file_directories:
    - /tmp/test_data
commitlog_directory: /tmp/test_commit
storage_port: 7009
rpc_port: 9169
```

4. Create a file `<hpcbuild>/src/test/hpcas/c05/ EmbeddedCassandraTest.java`:

```
package hpcas.c05;

/* Import org.junit.*.  For the assertEquals method using a static
import. */
import org.junit.*;
import static org.junit.Assert.assertEquals;
import org.apache.cassandra.service.*;
import org.apache.cassandra.thrift.*;
import hpcas.c03.FramedConnWrapper;

public class EmbeddedCassandraTest {
```

5. Declare an `EmbeddedCassandraService` instance as static. Many Cassandra internals not re-entrant and can only be used with the static modifier (one per JVM). It is currently not possible to start more than a single instance inside a JVM:

```
private static EmbeddedCassandraService cassandra;   .
```

6. `@BeforeClass` is a JUnit annotation that instructs JUnit to call this method before test cases inside this class. Inside `setup()` method, the Cassandra instance is initialized:

```
@BeforeClass
public static void setup() throws Exception {
    cassandra = new EmbeddedCassandraService();
    cassandra.init();
    Thread t = new Thread(cassandra);
    t.setDaemon(true);
    t.start();
}
```

7. The `@Test` annotation instructs JUnit to run a method as a **test case**. Ensure that the Cassandra instance is up and running by connecting to it and asserting the cluster name is what it is expected to be:

```
@Test
public void testInProcessCassandraServer()
        throws Exception {
    FramedConnWrapper fcw = new FramedConnWrapper
    ("127.0.0.1", 9169);
    fcw.open();
    Cassandra.Client client = fcw.getClient();
    assertEquals("Test Cluster", client.describe_cluster_name());
    fcw.close();
    System.out.println("All tests complete");
}
}
```

8. Run the unit test using the `ant test` target:

```
$ ant test

test:
    [junit] Running Test
    [junit] Tests run: 1, Failures: 0, Errors: 0, Time elapsed:
0.42 sec
    [junit] Running hpcas.c05.EmbeddedCassandraTest
    [junit] All tests complete
    [junit] Tests run: 1, Failures: 0, Errors: 0, Time elapsed:
3.26 sec
```

How it works...

The Cassandra threads have their daemon status set to true. When only daemon threads are running, the JVM will close. Running Cassandra in an embedded manner makes it fast and easy to develop applications that store their data inside Cassandra such as a custom middle-ware layer.

See also...

▶ The next recipe, *Cleaning up data directories before unit tests*

▶ *Chapter 9, Coding and Internals*, the recipe *Using the Cassandra maven plugin*

Cleaning up data directories before unit tests

It is possible to drop individual keys, column families, and keyspaces, as well as truncating column families through the Thrift API. In some cases, it may be easier to remove all the data directories at the beginning of a unit test. A tool to handle this is inside a contrib sub project. This recipe shows how to build the contrib that contains the data cleaner and then uses it inside a test case.

Getting ready

If the `cassandra-javautills.jar` is not included in the release, the Cassandra source code is needed for this recipe. Follow the steps in *Chapter 9, Coding and Internals, Building Cassandra from source* recipe. This recipe builds on the previous recipe, *Writing unit tests with an embedded Cassandra server*, and enhances it.

How to do it...

1. Build the Cassandra source. Then, change to the `contrib/javautils` directory and run the JAR target:

```
$ cd <cassandra_src>
$ ant
$ cd contrib/javautils
$ ant jar
jar:
    [mkdir] Created dir: /home/edward/cas-trunk/contrib/javautils/
build/classes/META-INF

    [jar] Building jar: /home/edward/cas-trunk/contrib/
javautils/build/cassandra-javautils.jar
```

2. Copy the resulting JAR to the classpath:

```
$ cp <cassandra_src>/contrib/javautils/build/cassandra-javautils.
jar /home/edward/hpcbuild/lib/
```

3. Edit src/test/hpcas/c03/EmbeddedCassandraTest.java and include the CassandraServiceDataCleaner:

```
@BeforeClass
public static void setup() throws Exception {
   CassandraServiceDataCleaner cleaner = new
     CassandraServiceDataCleaner();
   cleaner.prepare();
   cassandra = new EmbeddedCassandraService();
 cassandra.init();
 Thread t = new Thread(cassandra);
 t.setDaemon(true);
 t.start();
}
```

4. Touch a file inside the data directory to test if the cleaner is working:

```
$ touch /tmp/test_data/a
$ ls /tmp/test_data/


a   system
```

5. Run the unit test. The extra file created should be removed:

```
$ ant test
    [junit] Tests run: 1, Failures: 0, Errors: 0
$ ls /tmp/test_data/
system
```

How it works...

Cassandra has several contrib sub projects. The contrib projects are not currently built into the binary distributions. The class needed is part of the javautils contrib project. By building the contrib using ant and then adding the resulting JAR to the classpath, unit tests have a simple way to ensure they always run with a clean state.

Generating Thrift bindings for other languages (C++, PHP, and others)

The low level client for Cassandra is generated using **Thrift**. The Thrift interface descriptor file, found in `<cassandra_home>/interface/cassandra.thrift`, is used to generate code for a long list of programming languages, including .NET, C, Perl, PHP, Ruby, and more. This recipe shows how to download and install Thrift to generate bindings for multiple languages.

Getting ready

A compiler such as GCC and several other development tools are needed to build Thrift.

```
$ yum group install "Development Tools"
```

Generating bindings for languages require additional components installed. For example, generating Ruby binding may require `ruby` and `ruby-devel` packages to be installed. Consult the Thrift documentation for more details.

How to do it...

1. Determine what version of Thrift your Cassandra servers are using and match that version:

   ```
   $ ls <cassandra_home>/lib | grep thrift
   libthrift-0.5.jar
   ```

2. Download a matching version of Thrift and compile it:

   ```
   $ wget http://apache.imghat.com/
   /incubator/thrift/0.5.0-incubating/thrift-0.5.0.tar.gz
   $ tar -xf thrift*.tar.gz
   $ cd thrift*
   $ ./configure
   $ make
   $ sudo make install
   ```

3. Navigate to the directory with the `cassandra.thrift` file. This can be found in either the source or the binary distribution inside the interface folder:

   ```
   $ cd <cassandra_home>/interface
   $ thrift -gen java:hashcode -gen py -o $HOME/thrift-out cassandra.
   thrift
   ```

How it works...

Thrift uses the `cassandra.thrift` file to generate bindings for each language specified using `-gen` arguments. Clients from a variety of different languages can interact with Cassandra. Each of them have access to the same **Remote Procedure Call** (**RPC**) methods provided by the Thrift interface. This allows a PHP web application, a Python batch program, as well as Java applications to access the same functionality!

Using the Cassandra Storage Proxy "Fat Client"

The higher level clients such as Thrift have a more stable API as well as slightly more overhead. These. or even higher level clients such as Hector or Pelops are strongly suggested for most users. Still, a user who requires more access to the Cassandra internals can use the Storage Proxy API directory. The Storage Proxy API is not guaranteed to stay consistent even between minor versions. This recipe shows how to use the Storage Proxy API.

How to do it...

1. Copy the configuration directory into a `sub` folder. Then, edit the listen address and RPC address to an unused IP address:

```
$ cp -r $home/hpcas/apache-cassandra-0.7.0-beta2-1/conf conf-5node
vi conf-5node/cassandra.yaml
listen_address: 127.0.0.10
rpc_address: 127.0.0.10
```

2. Create a file `<hpc_build>/src/java/hpcas/c05/StorageServiceExample.java`:

```
package hpcas.c05;

import java.util.*;
import org.apache.cassandra.db.*;
import org.apache.cassandra.db.filter.QueryPath;
import org.apache.cassandra.db.TimeStampClock;
import org.apache.cassandra.service.StorageProxy;
import org.apache.cassandra.service.StorageService;
import org.apache.cassandra.thrift.ColumnPath;
import org.apache.cassandra.thrift.ConsistencyLevel;

public class StorageServiceExample {
```

3. The StorageService is a static (JVM-wide) class that needs to be initialized. After initialization, we sleep for ten seconds to allow the Gossip protocol to transmit information about the client to other nodes:

```
private static void doInit() throws Exception {
    StorageService.instance.initClient();
    System.out.println("Wait 10 seconds for gossip
initialization");
    Thread.sleep(10000L);
}
```

4. Create a static method that inserts five items. It uses RowMutation objects and inserts them using the StorageProxy.mutate method:

```
private static void testWriting() throws Exception {
    for (int i = 0; i < 2; i++) {
        RowMutation change = new RowMutation("ks33",
("key" + i).getBytes());
        ColumnPath cp = new ColumnPath("cf33")
            .setColumn(("colb").getBytes());
        IClock ic = new TimestampClock(System.currentTimeMillis());
        change.add(new QueryPath(cp), ("value" + i)
            .getBytes("UTF-8"), ic, 0);
        StorageProxy.mutate(Arrays.asList(change),
            ConsistencyLevel.ONE);
        System.out.println("wrote key" + i);
    }
}

/*The testReading() method attempts to read the entries inserted
by the
testWriting() method. */
private static void testReading() throws Exception {
    Collection<byte[]> cols = new ArrayList<byte[]>() ;
    cols.add("colb".getBytes("UTF-8"));
    for (int i = 0; i < 2; i++) {
        List<ReadCommand> commands = new ArrayList<ReadCommand>();
        SliceByNamesReadCommand readCommand =
            new SliceByNamesReadCommand(
                "ks33",
                ("key"+i).getBytes("UTF-8") ,
                new QueryPath("cf33", null, null),
                cols);
        readCommand.setDigestQuery(false);
        commands.add(readCommand);
        List<Row> rows = StorageProxy.readProtocol(commands,
```

```
            ConsistencyLevel.ONE);
        Row row = rows.get(0);
        ColumnFamily cf = row.cf;
        if (cf != null) {
          for (IColumn col : cf.getSortedColumns()) {
            System.out.println(new String(col.name()) + ", "
              + new String(col.value()));
          }
        }
      }
    }
```

5. The `main()` method is the entry point for the application:

    ```
    public static void main(String args[]) throws Exception {
        doInit();
        for (String member : StorageService.instance.getLiveNodes() ){
          System.out.println("live node "+member);
        }
        testWriting();
        testReading();
        StorageService.instance.stopClient();
        System.exit(0);
      }
    }
    ```

6. Make a small driver script `run.sh` with the following content. Change the paths where necessary:

    ```
    CP=dist/lib/hpcas.jar
    for i in lib/*.jar ; do
      CP=$CP:$i
    done
    conf=/home/edward/hpcbuild/conf-5node
    java -cp $CP -Dcassandra.config=file://${conf}/cassandra.yaml \
    -Dstorage-config=$conf hpcas.c05.StorageServiceExample
    ```

7. Run the application:

    $ sh run.sh

    Will sleep for 10 seconds for gossip initialization

    live node 127.0.0.10

    live node 127.0.0.5

    live node 127.0.0.3

    live node 127.0.0.4

    live node 127.0.0.2

```
live node 127.0.0.1
wrote key0
wrote key1
colb, value0
colb, value1
```

How it works...

Using `StorageProxy` and `StorageService` not intended for the average user, using them is closer to running an Embedded Cassandra server than connecting with a client. When a node using `StorageService` joins the cluster, it will not store any data, but it does open up Thrift and storage ports on a particular IP address. Once connected, this API gives you access to more Cassandra internals.

There's more...

A `StorageProxy` instance cannot be open from the same IP as a node in the cluster. Network-wise, the `StorageProxy` has to be able to reach the other nodes as if it were part of the cluster. Also, code in Cassandra is static and not re-entrant. The `StorageService` can be initialized once in the life of the JVM.

Using range scans to find and remove old data

The primary operations used in Cassandra are get and insert operations. In many applications, data can become stale and is no longer needed. In these type of application, a process can be used to iterate all the data on the node using **range scans**. This recipe shows how to use range scans to iterate all the data in a cluster and remove data older than a user-supplied number of seconds.

How to do it...

1. Create a file `<hpcbuild>/src/hpcas/c03/Ranger.java`.

    ```java
    package hpcas.c03;

    import hpcas.c03.FramedConnWrapper;
    import hpcas.c03.Util;
    import java.math.BigInteger;
    import java.util.*;
    import org.apache.cassandra.thrift.*;
    import org.apache.cassandra.utils.FBUtilities;
    ```

```
public class Ranger {
  int size = 0;
  Cassandra.Client client = null;
  FramedConnWrapper fcw = null;

  /*The maximum token in a Cassandra is 2^127. Range scans should
not go past
  this number.*/
  java.math.BigInteger max = new java.math.BigInteger("2").
pow(127);
  java.math.BigInteger start = new java.math.BigInteger("0");
  java.math.BigInteger current = new java.math.BigInteger("0");
  GregorianCalendar cutoff = new GregorianCalendar();

  public void doConnect() throws Exception {
    fcw = new FramedConnWrapper(
            Util.envOrProp("host"),
            Integer.parseInt(Util.envOrProp("port")));
    fcw.open();
    client = fcw.getClient();
  }

  public void runRepair() {
    start = new BigInteger("0");
    current = new BigInteger(start.toString());
    do {
      try {
        doConnect();
        doRange();
        Thread.sleep(1000);
      } catch (Exception e) {
        System.out.println(e);
      }
    } while (size != 0);
  }
  public void doRange() throws Exception {
```

2. One of the parameters needed for `get_range_slices` is a `SlicePredicate`.
   Set the `SlicePredicate` so that it has a large size and it includes any column by
   specifying an empty byte array as the start and finish:

```
SlicePredicate pred = new SlicePredicate();
SliceRange sr = new SliceRange();
sr.setStart(new byte[0]);
sr.setFinish(new byte[0]);
```

```
        sr.setCount(9000);
        pred.setSlice_range(sr);
        ColumnParent parent = new ColumnParent();
        parent.setColumn_family(Util.envOrProp("cf"));
```

A KeyRange is used to select keys for the operation. It can be specified using byte arrays (the keys themselves) or using tokens. This example uses tokens. Like the SlicePredicate, a KeyRange also has a setting for size.

```
        KeyRange kr = new KeyRange();
        kr.setStart_token(this.current.toString());
        kr.setEnd_token(this.max.toString());
        kr.setCount(100);
```

3. Call get_range_slices and pass the results to the handleResults() method:

```
        client.set_keyspace(Util.envOrProp("ks"));
        List<KeySlice> results = client.get_range_slices(
                parent, pred, kr, ConsistencyLevel.ONE);
        this.handleResults(results);
        size = results.size();
    }
```

4. This method iterates through a list of KeySlice objects. For each KeySlice, iterate the columns for that key. If the column is older then the cutoff time removes it:

```
    public void handleResults(List<KeySlice> results) {
        for (KeySlice ks : results) {
            for (ColumnOrSuperColumn columnOrSuper : ks.getColumns()) {
                if (columnOrSuper.isSetColumn() == true) {
                    Column c = columnOrSuper.column;
                    if (c.getTimestamp() < cutoff.getTimeInMillis() * 1000L)
{
                        ColumnPath cp = new ColumnPath();
                        cp.setColumn_family(Util.envOrProp("cf"));
                        cp.setColumn(c.name);
                        try {
                            client.remove(ks.getKey(), cp,
                                System.currentTimeMillis(), ConsistencyLevel.
ONE);
                            System.out.println("Removed " + new String(ks.key)
                                    + " " + new String(c.name));
                        } catch (Exception ex) {
                            System.out.println(ex);
                        }
                    }
                }
            }
        }
```

5. Reset the current variable with the hash of the last key in the `KeySlice`. This causes the next call of `get_range_slices` to iterate into the next set of keys:

```
    this.current = FBUtilities.md5hash(ks.key);
  }
}
public static void main(String[] args) throws Exception {
  Ranger ranger = new Ranger();
  int retentionDays = Integer.parseInt
    (Util.envOrProp("retentionDays"));
  ranger.cutoff.add(GregorianCalendar.DAY_OF_YEAR, -
    retentionDays);
  ranger.runRepair();
  }
}
```

6. Run the program:

```
$cf=cf33 ks=ks33 host=127.0.0.1 port=9160 retentionDays=1 ant run
-DclassToRun=hpcas.c05.Ranger
```

Run:

```
[java] Removed key30 colb
[java] Removed key16 colb
[java] Removed key55 colb
[java] Removed key51 colb
```

How it works...

Whether the cluster is using `RandomPartitioner` or `OrderPreservingPartitioner`, the entire data set has an ordering. Range scans allow you to move through the data set by using the last token or key from the first range scan as the start token for the next range scan.

There's more...

Range scanning can take a long time and be processor intensive. This depends on the settings chosen. Choosing a larger key range size or slice range size causes each operation to read through more data.

There are several ways to reduce the intensity of the program. One is by adding sleep operations in the code. For large clusters, it may be more effective to run several scanning programs on smaller sections of the ring instead of one program. Also, the program can be written to work during low traffic hours.

▶ *Using TTL to create columns with self-deletion times* shows how to automatically clean up old data.

▶ *Iterating all the columns of a large key* if the columns for a key are larger than the slice range size.

Iterating all the columns of a large key

In some designs, a particular row key may have a large number of associated columns. It may be impractical or impossible to retrieve all the columns in a single operation. This recipe shows how to iterate the columns of a key a few columns at a time using a `slice predicate`.

How to do it...

1. Create `<hpc_build>/src/java/hpcas/c03/IterateLargeKey.java`:

```java
package hpcas.c03;
import hpcas.c03.*;
import java.util.List;
import org.apache.cassandra.thrift.*;

public class IterateLargeKey {
  public static void main (String [] args) throws Exception {
    FramedConnWrapper fcw = new FramedConnWrapper
      (Util.envOrProp("host"),
      Integer.parseInt(Util.envOrProp("port")));
    fcw.open();
    fcw.getClient().set_keyspace(Util.envOrProp("ks"));
    ColumnParent parent = new ColumnParent();


    /*Simulate a large list of names under a key "friends" with an
array of names.*/

    byte [] key = "friends".getBytes("UTF-8");
    String [] names = new String [] {"sandy","albert","anthony",
      "bob","chuck"};
    parent.setColumn_family(Util.envOrProp("cf"));


    /*Insert all names as columns.*/
```

```
for (String name : names) {
  Column c = new Column();
  c.setName(name.getBytes());
  c.setTimestamp(System.currentTimeMillis()*1000L);
  c.setValue("".getBytes("UTF-8"));
  fcw.getClient().insert(key, parent, c,
    ConsistencyLevel.QUORUM);
}
```

2. Construct a `SlicePredicate` with count set to 3. The start is set at an empty byte array, which will start the slice at the beginning. Each column family has a column sort order. The default sorting is by byte ordering:

```
SlicePredicate pred = new SlicePredicate();
SliceRange range = new SliceRange();
range.setCount(3);
range.setStart(new byte[0]);
range.setFinish(new byte[0]);
pred.setSlice_range(range);
List<ColumnOrSuperColumn> cols = fcw.getClient().get_slice
        (key, parent, pred, ConsistencyLevel.QUORUM);
while (cols.size()>1 || cols.size()==0){
  for (int i=0;i<cols.size();++i){
    System.out.println( new String( cols.get(i).getColumn()
.getName()));

    /*Start of the SliceRange to the last column in the result
list. */
    range.setStart( cols.get(i).getColumn().getName() );
  }
  cols = fcw.getClient().get_slice
        (key, parent, pred, ConsistencyLevel.QUORUM);
  System.out.println("----");
}
}
}
```

3. Run the application:

```
$ cf=cf33 ks=ks33 host=127.0.0.1 port=9160   ant
-DclassToRun=hpcas.c05.IterateLargeKey
```

```
run:
  [java] albert
  [java] anthony
  [java] bob
```

```
[java]  ----
[java]  bob
[java]  chuck
[java]  sandy
[java]  ----
```

How it works...

The `get_slice` method uses a `SlicePredicate` with `SliceRange` to select columns of a key. The columns of a key are sorted, thus it is possible to move through the list several elements at a time in order. Moving through the list of columns is done by taking the last column seen and using it as the start of the next slice. The last element of the previous slice is the first element of the next slice.

Slicing columns in reverse

The columns of a key are ordered in a Sorted Map structure. When using the `get_slice` to select columns of a row key, the natural ordering of the columns can be leveraged. This recipe shows how to reverse the ordering of the slice results.

Getting ready

This recipe requires the code from the previous recipe, *Iterating all the columns of a large key*.

How to do it...

1. Modify the program written in `<hpc_build>/src/java/hpcas/c03/IterateLargeKey.java` by appending `range.setReversed(true)` to the code:

   ```
   SliceRange range = new SliceRange();
   range.setCount(3);
   range.setStart(new byte[0]);
   range.setFinish(new byte[0]);
   range.setReversed(true);
   ```

2. Run the application:

   ```
   $ cf=cf33 ks=ks33 host=127.0.0.1 port=9160  ant
   -DclassToRun=hpcas.c05.IterateLargeKey run

   run:
       [java]  sandy
       [java]  chuck
       [java]  bob
   ```

```
[java] ----
[java] bob
[java] anthony
[java] albert
[java] ----
```

How it works...

Reversing the order of result columns is useful in several instances. One such instance is when it is desired to fetch the largest column. If the column is a number, it would be the largest number. If the column was a text string, it would be the value that is alphabetically last. If the column was a time stamp, it would be the newest data.

Batch mutations to improve insert performance and code robustness

Batch mutations have several advantages over doing multiple insert operations. Larger messages will result in less network overhead transmitting data between the client and Cassandra. Code is cleaner as well. For example, if code is doing a series of operations, multiple try-catch blocks with retry logic at every step will cause clutter. Instead, with batch mutations a larger list of operations can be built up and submitted. If the mutations fail, it is safe to submit the entire list again as mutations are idempotent due to the time stamp associated with them.

How to do it...

1. Create `<hpc_build>/src/hpcas/c05/BatchMutate.java`:

```java
package hpcas.c05;

import hpcas.c03.FramedConnWrapper;
import hpcas.c03.Util;
import java.util.*;
import org.apache.cassandra.thrift.*;

public class BatchMutate {
  public static void main(String[] args) throws Exception {
```

2. The batch mutation is a large, nested object. The top level map contains the key (byte[]) to a map. The inner map uses a key (string) to represent the column family. The value of the inner map is a list of mutations. An individual mutation can be a list of columns to insert or delete:

```
Map<byte[],Map<String,List<Mutation>>> mutations = new
        HashMap<byte[],Map<String,List<Mutation>>>();
for (String key : new String[]{"ekey", "fkey", "gkey"}) {
    List<Mutation> mutationList = new ArrayList<Mutation>();
    for (int i = 0; i < 2; i++) {
```

3. One mutation is a column with a simple integer in the value side:

```
Mutation xMut = new Mutation();
Column x = new Column();
x.setName(("x"+i).getBytes("UTF-8"));
x.setTimestamp(System.currentTimeMillis() * 1000L);
x.setValue(("" + i).getBytes("UTF-8"));
ColumnOrSuperColumn xcol = new ColumnOrSuperColumn();
xcol.setColumn(x);
xMut.setColumn_or_supercolumn(xcol);
```

4. A second mutation is like the first, except the value is squared:

```
Mutation yMut = new Mutation();
Column y = new Column();
y.setName(("y"+i).getBytes("UTF-8"));
y.setTimestamp(System.currentTimeMillis() * 1000L);
y.setValue(("" + (i * i)).getBytes("UTF-8"));
ColumnOrSuperColumn ycol = new ColumnOrSuperColumn();
ycol.setColumn(y);
yMut.setColumn_or_supercolumn(ycol);
```

5. Add both mutations to the list of mutations:

```
mutationList.add(yMut);
mutationList.add(xMut);
HashMap<String,List<Mutation>> mutationMap =
    new HashMap<String,List<Mutation>>();
```

6. Create a map with the column family name and the mutation list from the previous step:

```
mutationMap.put("cf33", mutationList);
```

7. Put the complete mutation map into the top level mutation object:

```
        mutations.put(key.getBytes("UTF-8"), mutationMap);
    }
}
```

```
FramedConnWrapper fcw = new FramedConnWrapper
  (Util.envOrProp("host"),
        Integer.parseInt(Util.envOrProp("port")));
fcw.open();
fcw.getClient().set_keyspace(Util.envOrProp("ks"));
long start = System.nanoTime();
```

8. Call the `batch_mutate` method to apply all the changes at once:

```
fcw.getClient().batch_mutate
  ( mutations, ConsistencyLevel.QUORUM);
System.out.println("Time taken " +(System.nanoTime() -
start));
  fcw.close();
  }
}
```

9. Run the application:

```
$ cf=cf33 ks=ks33 host=127.0.0.1 port=9160  ant run
-DclassToRun=hpcas.c05.BatchMutate

run:

    [java] Time taken 59809657
```

10. Use the Cassandra cli to confirm the results:

```
$ ${HOME}/hpcas/apache-cassandra-0.7.0-beta2-1/bin/cassandra-cli

[default@unknown] connect localhost/9160


[default@unknown] use   ks33
```

11. Authenticated to keyspace `ks33`:

```
[default@ks33] get cf33['ekey']

=> (column=7931, value=1, timestamp=1291477677622000)
=> (column=7930, value=0, timestamp=1291477677622000)
=> (column=7831, value=1, timestamp=1291477677622000)
=> (column=7830, value=0,  timestamp=1291477677551000)
Returned 4 results.
```

How it works...

Batch mutations are more efficient then doing inserts individually. There are less network round trips and less total data to transfer. Remember that each column has a time stamp. Time stamps are what allow inserts in Cassandra to be idempotent; the update entry with the largest time stamp is the final value of the column. Thus, if a batch insert fails partially, it is safe to replay the entire mutation without the fear of reverting any data that may have changed outside the mutation.

See also...

In *Chapter 10, Libraries and Applications*, the recipe *Doing batch mutations with Hector* shows how the Hector high-level library makes mutations easier.

Using TTL to create columns with self-deletion times

This process of range scanning with `get_range_slices` through data just to find data to remove is intensive. It can lower your cache hit rate, and adds more load to the cluster. An alternative to this is setting the **time-to-live** (**TTL**) property for a column. Once the time-to-live has passed, the column will automatically be removed. This recipe shows how to use the time-to-live property with a mock messaging application to automatically clear old messages.

How to do it...

1. Create `<hpc_build>/src/hpcas/c03/TTLColumns.java` with the following content:

```
package hpcas.c03;

import hpcas.c03.FramedConnWrapper;
import hpcas.c03.Util;
import java.util.List;
import org.apache.cassandra.thrift.*;

public class TTLColumns {
    public static void main(String[] args) throws Exception {
```

2. The user will supply several parameters: who the message is to (`message_to`), the name of the message (`message_name`), the message content (`message_content`), and the time before the message expires (`expire_seconds`):

```
Column x = new Column();
x.setName((Util.envOrProp("message_name")).getBytes("UTF-8"));
x.setTimestamp(System.currentTimeMillis() * 1000L);
x.setValue(Util.envOrProp("message_content").
getBytes("UTF-8"));
    /*set the time-to-live in seconds before the message expires
and is deleted. */
    x.setTtl(Integer.parseInt(Util.envOrProp("expire_seconds")));
    FramedConnWrapper fcw = new FramedConnWrapper
      (Util.envOrProp("host"),
      Integer.parseInt(Util.envOrProp("port")));
```

```
fcw.open();
fcw.getClient().set_keyspace("ks33");
ColumnParent parent = new ColumnParent();
parent.setColumn_family("cf33");
fcw.getClient().insert(
        Util.envOrProp("message_to").getBytes("UTF-8")
        , parent, x, ConsistencyLevel.QUORUM);


/* Use get_slice to return 30 columns for a specific key. This
will return all the
    messages for the key accept those that are past their ttl or
deleted. */

    SlicePredicate predicate = new SlicePredicate();
    SliceRange range = new SliceRange();
    range.setCount(30);
    range.setStart(new byte[0]);
    range.setFinish(new byte[0]);
    predicate.setSlice_range(range);
    List <ColumnOrSuperColumn> results = fcw.getClient().get_
slice(
        Util.envOrProp("message_to").getBytes("UTF-8")
        , parent, predicate, ConsistencyLevel.QUORUM);
    for (ColumnOrSuperColumn result: results){
        System.out.println
        ( "Message name: "+new String(result.column.name) );
        System.out.println
        ( "Message value: "+new String(result.column.value) );
    }
    fcw.close();
    }
}
```

3. Run the program several times. Each time, set a different `message_name` and `message_content`. Each message is set with a 30 second TTL:

```
$ message_to=edward message_name=1st message_content="first
message" \
 expire_seconds=30 host=127.0.0.1 port=9160  ant run \
 -DclassToRun=hpcas.c05.TTLColumns
run:
    [java] Message name: 1st
    [java] Message value: first message
```

```
$ message_to=edward message_name=2nd message_content="second
message" \ expire_seconds=30 host=127.0.0.1 port=9160  ant run
-DclassToRun=hpcas.c05.TTLColumns
```

run:

```
[java] Message name: 1st
[java] Message value: first message
[java] Message name: 2nd
[java] Message value: second message
```

4. Use sleep or just wait before running the command a third time. By then, the first message will have expired:

```
$ sleep 20
$ message_to=edward message_name=3rd \
 message_content="third message" expire_seconds=30 \
host=127.0.0.1  port=9160  ant run -DclassToRun=hpcas.c05.
TTLColumns
```

run:

```
[java] Message name: 2nd
[java] Message value: second message
[java] Message name: 3rd
[java] Message value: third message
```

How it works...

Once a TTL is set, a column past the expiration time will not show up in the results of any get or get_slice request. TTLs use less space then storing the column twice and are more efficient then having to range scan through data to find old entries. TTLs are commonly used in caching use cases.

See also...

▶ *Using range scans to find and remove old data*

▶ Chapter 6, *Schema Design*, the recipe *Using Cassandra for distributed caching*

Working with secondary indexes

The primary ordering and sharding is done by the row key. This makes searching on the value of a key very fast. Columns associated with a row key are sorted by their column name. Secondary indexes allow searching on the values of the columns. This recipe shows how to create and use secondary indexes.

Getting ready

This recipe demonstrates secondary indexes with a limited CRM application. For a given entry, the names of the customers, the states they live in, and their phone numbers will be stored. We create an index on the state column.

```
[default@ks33] create keyspace ks33 with replication_factor=3;

[default@ks33] create column family customers with comparator=UTF8Type
and column_metadata=[

{column_name: customer_name, validation_class:UTF8Type}

,{column_name:state, validation_class:UTF8Type ,index_type:KEYS}];
```

How to do it...

1. Insert sample data into the `customers` column family. Notice two of the users live in the state of New York:

   ```
   [default@ks33] set customers['bobsmith']['state']='New York';

   [default@ks33] set customers['bobsmith']['phone']='914-555-
   5555';[default@ks33] set customers['peterjones']['state']='Texas';

   [default@ks33] set customers['peterjones']['phone']='917-555-
   5555';[default@ks33] set customers['saraarmstrong']['state']='New
   York'; [default@ks33] set customers['saraarmstrong']
   ['phone']='914-555-5555';
   ```

2. The state column is using an equality index. Searches for an exact match state can be done. Ask which users live in 'New York':

   ```
   [default@ks33] get customers where state = 'New York';

   -------------------

   RowKey: saraarmstrong

   => (column=phone, value=3931342d3535352d35353535,
   timestamp=1291575939033000)

   => (column=state, value=New York, timestamp=1291575892195000)

   -------------------

   RowKey: bobsmith

   => (column=phone, value=3931342d3535352d35353535,
   timestamp=1291575717285000)

   => (column=state, value=New York, timestamp=1291575686951000)

   2 Rows Returned.
   ```

How it works...

Secondary indexes allow for optimized searches on column values. Secondary indexes require more disk space as they have to maintain another ordering for data. Cassandra also uses more processing time managing and updating indexes. Secondary indexes are not atomic; they are built and managed in the background.

See also...

Chapter 6, Schema Design, the recipe *Developing secondary data orderings or indexes*.

4

Performance Tuning

In this chapter, you will learn:

- ▶ Choosing an operating system and distribution
- ▶ Choosing a Java Virtual Machine
- ▶ Using a dedicated commit log disk
- ▶ Choosing a high performing RAID level
- ▶ Boosting read performance with the Key Cache
- ▶ Boosting read performance with the Row Cache
- ▶ File system optimization for hard disk performance
- ▶ Tuning concurrent readers and writers for throughput
- ▶ Enabling memory-mapped disk modes
- ▶ Tuning Memtables for write-heavy workloads
- ▶ Setting compaction thresholds
- ▶ Saving memory on 64 bit architectures with compressed pointers
- ▶ Disabling Swap Memory for predictable performance
- ▶ Stopping Cassandra from using SWAP without disabling it system-wide
- ▶ Raising the open file limit to deal with many clients
- ▶ Increasing performance by scaling up
- ▶ Garbage collection tuning to avoid JVM pauses
- ▶ Enabling Network Time Protocol on servers and clients

Introduction

Performance tuning involves optimizing configurations and finding bottlenecks. In this chapter, we present recipes for Cassandra, Java, and system-level tuning.

Choosing an operating system and distribution

The operating system affects software performance greatly. There are some practical points that should affect your decision. This recipe shows the important topics to consider before choosing.

How to do it...

Find an operating system and distribution that has:

- ▶ A supported Java Virtual Machine
- ▶ Java native architecture support
- ▶ File system hard links
- ▶ Package support for Cassandra
- ▶ A large community of users and developers

How it works...

Cassandra runs on Java. Oracle's JVM supports Linux, Solaris, and Windows. Other JVM implementations and ports exist for other operating systems. However, the licensing and maturity of these other JVMs vary.

The Java Native Architecture is a component that allows an application to directly interact with system libraries. Several features of Cassandra use this to avoid using swap, create snapshot files, and optimize performance.

Cassandra has support for RPM and DEB package formats. These packages make it easy to install and run Cassandra.

There's more...

The de facto standard deployment of Cassandra is on 2.6 Linux Kernels. Popular distributions include RedHat Enterprise Linux, CentOS, and Ubuntu. Other operating systems such as Solaris, FreeBSD, or Windows do work, but are less often deployed in production. If you employ a non-typical choice, you may encounter rare bugs or edge cases and are difficult for others to reproduce.

 Other performance recipes in this book assume CentOS 5, a Linux 2.6 Operating systems distribution that is based on Redhat Enterprise Linux.

Choosing a Java Virtual Machine

Cassandra is built using Java. Thus, choosing a version of Java is important to performance. There are several different virtual machines that are compatible with the Java standard. This recipe shows the important factors you should consider when choosing which version of Java to install.

How to do it...

Select a JVM that has:

▶ Java 1.6 compatibility

▶ Low pause garbage collection

▶ Operating system support

▶ Hardware architecture support

▶ Large user and developer community

There's more...

Cassandra requires at minimum a 1.6 compatible JVM. It should support your hardware platform. 64 bit hardware is common and necessary to memory map data files. It should have support for Java Native Architecture and low pause garbage collection.

The Java SE JVM is used for recipes throughout the book. Cassandra has specific code to gather and log garbage collection statistics from the Oracle Java SE JVM. You can download and install the Java SE JDK from `http://www.oracle.com/technetwork/java/javase/downloads/index.html`.

Licensing issues prevents distribution of the Oracle JVM in most RPM repositories. As a result, Oracle offers OpenJDK: `http://openjdk.java.net/`, which is GPLv2 licensed.

See also...

▶ In this chapter, the recipe *Saving memory on 64 bit architectures with compressed pointers*.

▶ In this chapter, the recipe *Garbage collection tuning to avoid JVM pauses*.

Using a dedicated Commit Log disk

Write operations are done sequentially to a commit log on disk and modify a sorted structure in memory called a **Memtable**. When thresholds are reached, a Memtable is flushed to disk in a sorted format called an *SSTable*. After the flush, the **Commit Log** is no longer needed and is deleted. The Commit Log is only read on startup to recover write operations that were never flushed to disk.

Getting ready

For this recipe, your system would need a separate physical disk from your data disk. This disk should be formatted as you would format a normal disk.

How to do it...

1. Use the `df` command to list mounted partitions on your system:

```
$ df -h
Filesystem          Size  Used Avail Use% Mounted on
/dev/sda2           130G   19G  105G  16% /
tmpfs               2.0G   18M  1.9G   1% /dev/shm
/dev/sda3           194M   74M  111M  40% /boot
/dev/sdb1  .........130G    2M  124G   1% /mnt/commitlog
```

2. Ensure the `cassandra` user has ownership of this directory and the directory has appropriate file access permissions:

```
$ chown cassandra:cassandra /mnt/commitlog
```

```
$ chmod 755 /mnt/commitlog
```

3. Edit the configuration file `conf/cassandra.yaml` to set where commit logs will be stored:

   ```
   CommitLogDirectory: /mnt/commitlog
   ```

4. Restart for this change to take effect.

 When moving the commit log directory, make sure to copy the files from the old directory to the new directory before restarting.

How it works...

Having a separate **Commit Log** improves performance for applications with high levels of write activity. It does this by isolating the disk traffic for Commit Log activity from the traffic used for reads as well as flush Memtables and compact **SSTables**.

The Commit Log disk does not need to be large. It only needs to be large enough to hold the **Memtable** data that is unflushed.

Commit logs have sync intervals and this does not block writes. The Commit Log directory and underlying disk need to be fast enough to keep up with write traffic. The speed of this disk is not an issue because the sequential write speed of even a single disk is normally sufficient.

See also...

▶ In this chapter, the recipe *Tuning Memtables for write-heavy workloads*

▶ In this chapter, the recipe *Setting compaction thresholds*

Choosing a high performing RAID level

Cassandra handles replication of data internally. Each **Keyspace** has a user configurable Replication Factor. A **Replication Factor** of two will ensure data is written to two separate nodes. Because Cassandra handles replication, disk systems can be optimized for more performance versus redundancy. This recipe shows which RAID levels are commonly used with Cassandra.

Getting ready

The fastest option for reads and writes is **RAID-0**, calling **striping**. A single disk failure in a **RAID-0** results in complete data loss for that node. This configuration allows 100 percent of the storage capacity of the disks in the array.

RAID-1 typically uses two disks and mirrors data to both disks. This option does not speed up writing, but reads can normally be striped. Because data is copied to both disks, the storage capacity is 50 percent the total capacity of the disk.

RAID-5 requires at least three disks. It can survive a single disk failure However, a failed disk will result in degraded performance. The parity information in this configuration reduces your overall storage.

RAID-10 requires at least four disks. RAID-10 is a stripe and a mirror. It typically performs better then RAID-5 in reads and writes and can survive multiple disk failures. You get 50 percent of the storage capacity of your disks using this RAID level.

Just a Bunch Of Disks (**JBOD**) can be used because Cassandra allows multiple data directories. This configuration allows for 100 percent of disk utilization. However, it is hard to balance out hotspots across the disks and is rarely deployed.

How to do it...

1. Have spare hardware available.
2. Consider the risk of disk failure and the downtime associated with one.
3. Consider the disk space lost to RAID redundancy.

How it works...

In a large enough cluster, failures are the norm not the exception. Having spare hardware is always a good idea. In a hardware failure, the performance of a node may be degraded or it might be entirely offline. For small clusters, the performance lost can be significant.

There's more...

While RAID cards offload processing, RAID can be done with software as well. With the multiple options of RAID types, levels, and disks, having tools to determine which configurations work the best are available.

Software v/s hardware RAID

Modern Linux distributions provide support for **software RAID** levels 0, 1, 5, and more. **Hardware RAID** is provided by cards that offload CPU processing and perform better than software RAID. RAID cards vary in cost, performance, and feature set. Read specifications carefully because not all RAID cards support all RAID levels.

Disk performance testing

Disk performance tools such as **Bonnie++**: `http://www.coker.com.au/bonnie++/`, or IOZone: `http://www.iozone.org/` can be used to test the performance of your disk system.

See also...

In *Chapter 12, Collecting and Analyzing Performance Statistics*, the recipe *Monitoring disk utilization and having a performance baseline*.

File system optimization for hard disk performance

The file system for a device as well as the mount options chosen affect performance. Several file system options exist, including (but not limited to) EXT, JFS, and XFS. The most commonly deployed is EXT. Most modern distributions of Linux have support for EXT4, which has impressive performance numbers and stability. This recipe will show how to format and mount an EXT4 file system.

Getting ready

Make sure your system supports EXT4. Most modern Linux distributions do. A quick check is to look for `/sbin/mkfs.ext4` on your system.

How to do it...

1. Format a device, in this example `/dev/sda1` as an `ext4` file system:

   ```
   $ mke2fs -t ext4 /dev/sda1
   ```

2. To configure your `ext4` file system for the highest performance, with a small risk to data integrity in the event of a failure, edit `/etc/fstab` enabling the following mount options:

   ```
   noatime,barriers=0,data=writeback,nobh
   ```

3. To configure your `ext4` file system for strong performance, while making less data integrity sacrifices, enable the following mount options:

   ```
   noatime,barriers=1,data=journal,commit=30
   ```

4. You can apply mount options without having to `unmount` by using the remount option. However, some changes might require a complete unmount and remount:

   ```
   $ mount -o remount /var
   ```

How it works...

Noatime does not update **inode** information each time it is read. Since access time information is not used by Cassandra and reads are frequent, this option should be used.

Barriers=0 disables write barriers. Write barriers enforce proper on-disk ordering of journal commits, making volatile disk write caches safe to use, with some performance penalty. If your disks are battery-backed in one way or another, disabling barriers may safely improve performance.

The commit=x option syncs all data and metadata every 'X' seconds. The default commit time is five seconds. Making this longer can increase performance. This option only applies to journal mode.

With data=writeback, unlike the default ordered mode, the ordering of metadata and file data writes are not preserved. In the event of a crash, old data can appear in files. Cassandra data files are typically write once and written in a linear fashion. Thus, writeback may not be as large of a problem as would be an application that edits files in place. This mode is considered to have the best raw performance.

Boosting read performance with the Key Cache

The **Key Cache** stores keys and their locations in each **SStable** in heap memory. Since keys are typically small, you can store a large cache without using much RAM. This recipe shows how to enable the Key Cache for a **Column Family**.

Using fixed size settings versus percentage

Key cache size can be set as an absolute value or a percentage between 0 and 1. In most cases, you want to use an absolute size as percentages grow with your data and change your memory profile.

Getting ready

Ensure the Cassandra service is not close to the memory limit by using nodetool info. This value should be sampled over time because JVM garbage collection is a background process on a separate thread.

```
$ bin/nodetool --host 127.0.0.1 --port 8080 info | grep Heap
   Heap Memory (MB) : 5302.99 / 12261.00
```

How to do it...

1. Set the Key Cache size for `"Keyspace1 Standard1"` to `200001` entries per SSTable:

```
$ bin/nodetool --host 127.0.0.1 --port 8080 setcachecapacity
Keyspace1 Standard1 200001 0
```

Specifying cache size as an absolute value

The value can either be an absolute value or a double between 0 and 1 (inclusive on both ends) denoting what fraction should be cached. Using a percentage is generally not suggested because table growth results are increasing memory used. Use `nodetool cfstats` to see the effectiveness of the Key Cache. Remember, the cache hit rate may not be high right away. The larger the cache, the longer it will take to warm up. Once the **Key cache size** reaches the **Key cache capacity**, you should have a good idea of the hit rate.

```
$ bin/nodetool --host 127.0.0.1  --port 8080 cfstats
Column Family: Standard1
...
Key cache capacity: 200001
Key cache size: 200001
Key cache hit rate: 0.625
```

2. Make the changes permanent by updating the `column family` metadata with the CLI:

```
$ <cassandra_home>/bin/cassandra-cli -h 127.0.0.1 -p 9160

Connected to: "Test Cluster" on 127.0.0.1/9160

[default@unknown] use Keyspace1;

Authenticated to keyspace: Keyspace1;

[default@football] update column family Standard1 with keys_
cached=200001;

91861a85-5e0f-11e0-a61f-e700f669bcfc

Waiting for schema agreement...

... schemas agree across the cluster
```

How it works

Each cache hit results in less disk activity. A high key cache hit ratio makes searches less intensive, freeing resources for other operations.

There's more...

When using the Key Cache, set aside enough RAM to be used for the OS Virtual File System cache. Heap memory controlled with the Xmx JVM option should only be a portion of your total system memory. A ratio of half JVM to free memory is suggested as a good starting point. This is suggested because key cache works well in tandem with the VFS cache, and for the VFS cache to be effective, memory must be free for the Operating System to use.

 Cassandra 0.8.X and a higher version has a setting `compaction_preheat_key_cache` which defaults to true. This setting migrates caches so that after compaction, the key cache is not cold. Set this to false when using large key caches.

See also...

The next recipe, *Boosting Read Performance with the Row Cache* shows how to enable the row cache that stores key and all associated columns.

In this chapter, the recipe for *JVM tuning to avoid system pauses* describes how Xmx memory should typically be used with Key Cache.

In *Chapter 12*, the recipe *Profiling the effectiveness of caches with cache graphs.*

Boosting read performance with the Row Cache

The **Row Cache** stores a key and all its associated columns in memory. Using the Row Cache can save two or more seeks per request. The benefit of the Row Cache is that a request can be served entirely from memory without accessing the disk. This can allow for a high rate of low latency reads. This recipe shows how to enable the Row Cache.

How to do it...

1. Ensure the Cassandra service is not close to the memory limit by using `nodetool info`. This value should be sampled over time because JVM garbage collection is a background process on a separate thread:

   ```
   $ bin/nodetool --host 127.0.0.1 --port 8080 info | grep Heap
   Heap Memory (MB) : 5302.99 / 12261.00
   ```

2. Set the Row Cache size for `Keyspace1 Standard1` to `200005` entries:

   ```
   $ bin/nodetool -h 127.0.0.1 -p 8080 setcachecapacity Keyspace1
   Standard1 0 200005
   ```

This change only takes effect on the server you have specified. You will have to run this command for each server.

3. Use `nodetool cfstats` to see the effectiveness of the Row Cache. Remember, the cache hit rate will not be high right away. The larger the cache, the longer it will take to 'warm' up. Once the **Row Cache Size** reaches the **Row Cache Capacity**, you should have a good idea of the hit rate. Recent hit rate shows the value since the last time the information was polled:

```
$ bin/nodetool --host 127.0.0.1  --port 8080 cfstats
    Column Family: Standard1
    ...
    Row cache capacity: 200005
    Row cache size: 200005
    Row cache hit rate: 0.6973947895791583
```

4. Make the change permanent on each node in the cluster by updating the **Colum Family**. **Meta Data** using the command-line interface: $ <cassandra_home>/bin/ cassandra-cli -h 127.0.0.1 -p 9160:

```
Connected to: "Test Cluster" on 127.0.0.1/9160
[default@unknown] use Keyspace1;
Authenticated to keyspace: Keyspace1;
[default@football] update column family Standard1 with rows_
cached=200005;
91861a85-5e0f-11e0-a61f-e700f669bcfc
Waiting for schema agreement...
... schemas agree across the cluster
```

How it works...

The `nodetool setcachecapacity` command reconfigures the cache size on a single node for testing. The `nodetool cfstats` is used to determine how effective the cache is. Once the cache settings are optimal, the `cassandra-cli` can be used to change the column metadata definitions across all nodes in the cluster.

There's more...

Row Cache requires more memory than the equivalent sized key cache. However, accessing memory is significantly faster than accessing the hard disk even if the disk read is completely from the VFS cache.

There are times where it can be problematic to use the Row Cache. One such situation is when keys have a large number of associated columns. Another instance is when the values inside columns are very large. Columns with a high write-to-read ratio are also not good candidates for the Row Cache. These scenarios move a lot of data into and out of the heap causing **memory pressure**. Also, sizing the cache can be difficult since the cache is based on the number of items, not the size of the items.

Disabling Swap Memory for predictable performance

Many users of Cassandra choose it for low latency read-and-write performance. **Swap Memory** and Swapping presents a challenge to Java and Cassandra. Even if the operative system is not low on memory, it may decide to swap parts of memory, called **pages**, to disk. When these pages need to be accessed, they will have to be read in from a disk, which takes significantly longer than if they were still in main memory. **Swapping** leads to unpredictable performance. This recipe shows how to disable Swap Memory entirely.

How to do it...

1. Run the swapoff command as the root user:

    ```
    $ swapoff -a
    ```

2. Edit the /etc/fstab file. Find any lines with swap in column two or three and place a # character in the first column to comment them out:

    ```
    #/dev/sda2   swap   swap   defaults   0 0
    ```

How it works...

The swapoff command disables all swap memory that may be currently in use. Editing the /etc/fstab file ensures swap will not be reactivated on operating system startup.

See also...

The next recipe, *Stopping Cassandra from using swap without disabling it system-wide* to see an alternative to turning off all swap memory.

Stopping Cassandra from using swap without disabling it system-wide

Disabling Swap Memory system-wide may not always be desirable. For example, if the system is not dedicated to running Cassandra, other processes on the system may benefit from Swap Memory. This recipe shows how to install the Java Native Architecture, which allows Java to lock itself in memory making it inevitable.

Getting ready

You will need to have the **Java Native Access (JNA)** JAR found at `https://jna.dev.java.net/`. For this recipe, Cassandra must run as the root user.

How to do it...

1. Place the `jna.jar` and `platform.jar` in the `<cassandra_home>/lib` directory:

   ```
   $cp jna.jar platform.jar /tmp/hpcas/apache-cassandra-0.7.0-
   beta1-10/lib
   ```

2. Enable `memory_locking_policy` in `cassandra.yaml`:

   ```
   memory_locking_policy: required
   ```

3. Restart your Cassandra instance.

4. Confirm this configuration has taken effect by checking to see if a large portion of memory is `Unevictable`:

   ```
   $ grep Unevictable /proc/meminfo
   ```

   ```
   Unevictable:         1024 Kb
   ```

Enabling Memory Mapped Disk modes

Cassandra has the capability to use **Memory Mapped File IO**. Memory mapped file IO is more efficient for reading and writing than **Standard IO**.

Getting ready

Disable **Swap** before enabling **Memory Mapped IO**. Do this by following either the *Disabling Swap Memory for predictable performance* or the *Stopping Cassandra from using Swap without disabling it system-wide* recipes in this chapter.

How to do it...

1. Check if the operating system is 64 bit using the `uname` command:

    ```
    $ uname -m
    x86_64
    ```

2. Edit the `<cassandra_home>/cassandra.yaml` file and turn disk access mode to `mmap`:

    ```
    disk_access_mode: mmap
    ```

    If the operating system is not 64 bit it cannot efficiently memory map large files. However, it can memory map the smaller index files.

    ```
    disk_access_mode: mmap_index_only
    ```

How it works...

Memory mapping makes disk access more efficient. However, the larger the data, index, and bloom filter file, the more heap memory is required. The alternative to `mmap` and `mmap_index_only` is `standard`, which uses direct IO.

Tuning Memtables for write-heavy workloads

Cassandra is designed so that all disk write operations are serial. Write operations are written to a sorted structure in memory called a **Memtable** (and to a **Commit Log** only used to replay writes on startup). When a Memtable reaches threshold criteria it is flushed to disk. The criteria for flushing is listed below:

Variable	Description
`memtable_flush_after_mins`	The maximum time to leave a dirty memtable unflushed (Default 60)
`memtable_throughput_in_mb`	Size of the Memtable in memory before it is flushed (Default 64)
`memtable_operations_in_millions`	Number of objects in millions in the Memtable before it is flushed (Default 0.3)

A flush writes the **Memtable** to its on-disk representation: a **Sorted String Table** (**SSTable**). A background process called **Compaction** merges smaller SSTables together. This recipe shows how to modify the Memtable settings so they will flush less often.

How to do it...

Change the Memtable settings using the `cassandra` command-line interface:

```
$ <cassandra_home>/bin/cassandra-cli -h 127.0.0.1 -p 9160
Connected to: "Test Cluster" on 127.0.0.1/9160
[default@unknown] use Keyspace1;
Authenticated to keyspace: Keyspace1;
[default@football] update column family Standard1 with memtable_
operations=.5 and memtable_throughput=128 and memtable_flush_after=45;
91861a85-5e0f-11e0-a61f-e700f669bcfc
Waiting for schema agreement...
... schemas agree across the cluster
```

How it works...

Each column family has individual Memtable settings. Setting the flush settings larger causes Memtables to flush less often. For workloads where the same column is repeatedly modified, large Memtables will absorb multiple writes, thus saving writes to disk. Less flushing and therefore less compacting should make the **VFS Cache** (**Virtual File System Cache**) more effective.

There's more...

Larger Memtable settings result in more **Heap Memory** dedicated to Memtables. Consider your settings carefully if you have many Column Families as each Column Family has its own Memtable. When Cassandra is storing many column families, managing Memtables settings on a per column family basis can be difficult. Cassandra 0.8.X has the knob `memtable_total_space_in_mb`. When all memtables use more memory than this, value with the largest memtable will be flushed.

See also...

In *Chapter 12, Collecting and Analysing Performance Statistics*, the recipe *Using Memtable graphs to profile when and why they flush*.

Saving memory on 64 bit architectures with compressed pointers

In the Java Virtual Machine, an **Ordinary Object Pointer (OOP)** is a managed pointer to an object. An OOP is normally the same size as the machine pointer. When modern CPU architectures moved from 32 bit to 64 bit, the result was a larger Java **Heap Size** due to growth of pointer size. Compressed OOPs replaces some of the OOPs with managed pointers. These compressed pointers result in smaller heap sizes. This recipe shows how to enable compressed OOPs.

 More detail on compressed pointers can be found at `http://download-llnw.oracle.com/javase/7/docs/technotes/guides/vm/compressedOops.html`.

Getting ready

This option may not be available on all JVMs. The Oracle JVM has supported this option since version 1.6.0_14.

How to do it...

1. Edit the `conf/cassandra-env.sh` file by adding this line:

    ```
    JVM_OPTS="$JVM_OPTS -XX:+UseCompressedOops"
    ```

2. Restart the Cassandra instance.

How it works...

Using less memory benefits the system overall as the system bus has less data to shuffle. Less memory usage means more memory is available for use as **Key Cache**, **Row Cache**, and **Memtables**. Each request allocates temporary objects, so better memory usage equates to a higher theoretical maximum request rate.

Tuning concurrent readers and writers for throughput

Cassandra is coded using **staged event-driven architecture (SEDA)**. SEDA architectures address the challenges of concurrent, multi-threaded applications by breaking the application into stages. Each stage is an event queue. Messages enter a stage and an event handler is called. This recipe will show you how to tune the **Concurrent Reader** and **Concurrent Writer** stages.

How to do it...

1. Determine the number of CPU cores on your system:

```
$ cat /proc/cpu
...
processor  : 15
siblings   : 8
core id    : 3
cpu cores  : 4
```

Processors are numbered 0 to (X-1). In the example, we have 16 cores. It is common to calculate the number of Concurrent Readers by taking the number of cores and multiplying it by two. This can be set in cassandra.yaml:

```
ConcurrentReaders: 32
```

Concurrent Writers should be set equal to or higher then Concurrent Readers:

```
ConcurrentWriters: 48
```

You can change these values at runtime through JMX. Navigate to the **org.apache.cassadra.concurrent** heading in the left pane. Locate **ROW-READ-STAGE** and select **Attributes**, and change the **CorePoolSize** by entering in the textbox on the right.

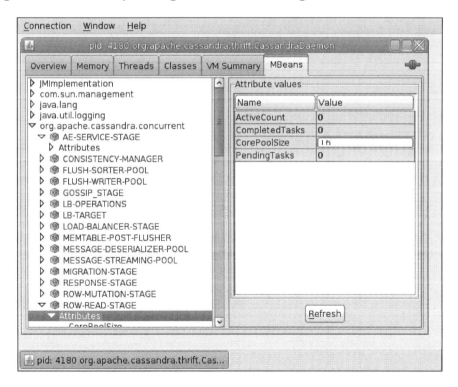

How it works...

The Concurrent Readers and Concurrent Writers control the maximum number of **threads** allocated to a particular stage. Reads are typically IO intensive. In cases where data size exceeds main memory, this normally makes the disk the bottleneck for reads rather than number of read threads. Writes or **Row Mutations** update a Memtable and a Commit Log. Writes do not have to make in-place changes to data files. Thus, Cassandra supports high write concurrency. Raising these values beyond the limits of your hardware causes more contention and decreases performance.

Setting compaction thresholds

Cassandra does not do in-place writes or updates. Rather, it uses a log structured format. Writes are done to Memtables, which are periodically flushed to disk as **SSTables**. As a result of this approach, the number of SSTables grows over time.

Having multiple SSTables causes read operations to be less efficient as columns for an associated key may be spread over multiple SSTables. Cassandra uses **Compaction** to merge multiple SSTables into a single larger one. This recipe shows how to adjust two compaction settings: MinCompactionThreshold and MaxCompactionThreshold.

How to do it...

1. Use nodetool to list the current compaction thresholds:

    ```
    $ bin/nodetool -h 127.0.0.1 -p 8080 getcompactionthreshold
    ```

2. Current compaction threshold: Min=4, Max=32

3. Next, change the min compaction threshold to 5 and the max compaction threshold to 30:

    ```
    $ bin/nodetool -h 127.0.0.1 -p 8080 setcompactionthreshold 5 30
    $ bin/nodetool -h 127.0.0.1 -p 8080 getcompactionthreshold
    ```

4. Current compaction threshold: Min=5, Max=30.

5. Update the column family metadata to make this change permanent across the cluster:

    ```
    $ <cassandra_home>/bin/cassandra-cli -h 127.0.0.1 -p 9160
    [default@unknown] use Keyspace1;
    Authenticated to keyspace: Keyspace1
    update column family Standard1 with min_compaction_threshold=5 and
    max_compaction_threshold=30;
    a83a1706-5e18-11e0-a61f-e700f669bcfc
    Waiting for schema agreement...
    ... schemas agree across the cluster
    ```

How it works...

MinCompactionThreshold is the minimum number of like-sized SSTables that will be compacted at a time. Raising MinCompactionThreshold causes compaction to happen less often, but when it does, more tables are compacted.

MaxCompactionThreshold controls the maximum number of SSTables that exist before a minor compaction is forced.

There's more...

Compaction thresholds are closely related to Memtable thresholds. Memtable settings affect the size quantity of SSTables. Ensure the two are configured with respect to each other. Cassandra 0.8.X and up has a setting compaction_throughput_mb_per_sec which throttles the rate of compaction. The setting concurrent_compactors controls how many compaction threads can run at once.

See also...

- ▶ Disabling Compaction for bulk loads
- ▶ In this chapter, the recipe *Tuning Memtables for write-heavy workloads*

Garbage collection tuning to avoid JVM pauses

The **JVM** has a variety of options that drastically affect how it operates. For applications such as SWING Graphical User Interface applications, periodic application **Garbage Collections** are not a large issue. Server applications use large quantities of memory, perform rapid object allocation/deallocation, and are very sensitive to **JVM pauses**. This recipe shows how to tune JVM settings to limit (and hopefully remove) JVM pauses.

How to do it...

1. Ensure you have set MAX_HEAP_SIZE (-Xmx) in conf/cassandra-env.sh.

2. Determine how much physical memory your system has by searching through the /proc/meminfo file:

```
$ grep MemTotal /proc/meminfo
    MemTotal:        4012320 kB
```

A good starting point is to use half your free memory. Do not include swap in this calculation since it is suggested to disable swap anyway.

```
MAX_HEAP_SIZE="2G"
```

3. Ensure these options are set in `<cassandra_home>/conf/cassandra.env` vs. `cassandra-env.sh`:

```
JVM_OPTS="$JVM_OPTS -Xss128k"
JVM_OPTS="$JVM_OPTS -XX:+UseParNewGC"
JVM_OPTS="$JVM_OPTS -XX:+UseConcMarkSweepGC"
JVM_OPTS="$JVM_OPTS -XX:+CMSParallelRemarkEnabled"
JVM_OPTS="$JVM_OPTS -XX:CMSInitiatingOccupancyFraction=75"
JVM_OPTS="$JVM_OPTS -XX:+UseCMSInitiatingOccupancyOnly"
```

4. Restart for these changes to take effect.

How it works...

The `ConcurrentMarkSweep` is a garbage collector designed to avoid stop-the-world pauses in the JVM. It does this by using multiple threads to mark objects to be garbage collected in parallel. `CMSParallelRemarkEnabled` lowers remarking pauses.

Concurrent Mark Sweep uses heuristics to decide when to start a concurrent collection. The heuristics are not aggressive enough, especially under heavy load. Using the `UseCMSInitiatingOccupancyOnly` option will result in CMS running concurrently as soon as the **Old Geneneration** is `CMSInitiatingOccupancyFraction` percent full.

`ParNewGC` (or the parallel young generation collector) is important to Cassandra. Cassandra allocates temporary objects during operation, and being able to process the young generation quickly stops these objects from being promoted to the older generations.

There's more...

The JVM options in this recipe are a suggested starting point. Each workload may require additional tuning.

Large memory systems

One situation where the standard advice does not apply is systems with large amounts of memory. Because Java actively manages memory and garbage collections, large heaps represent a challenge for the JVM. Heaps around 20 GB start to show diminishing returns. In these situations you have some options:

▶ Set a ceiling on Xmx around 16 GB and let the operating system VFS cache the rest
▶ Run multiple instances of Cassandra per machine, but be sure to carefully assign token ranges so that a range and its replicas are not served all from a single node.

See also...

In *Chapter 1, Getting Started* the recipe *Insight into Cassandra with JConsole* shows how to use JConsole to view Java memory usage.

There's more

The **Garbage-First garbage collector** (**G1**) is a next generation collector designed to work for medium-to-large machines with large heaps. More information on the G1 garbage collector is available at `http://research.sun.com/jtech/pubs/04-g1-paper-ismm.pdf`.

Raising the open file limit to deal with many clients

Each client connection, as well as the connections between servers in the cluster, uses socket resources. Each socket requires a file descriptor. Serving requests requires reading and writing multiple files. The defaults for a Unix/Linux system limit the number of open files. This recipe shows how to raise the open file limit to serve multiple connections under high load.

How to do it...

1. Edit `/etc/security/limits.conf`. The default limit for the number of files is typically `1024`. You can raise this to any power of 2:

```
* soft     nofile          16384
* hard     nofile          32768
```

2. Start a new shell and run the `ulimit` command:

```
$$ ulimit -a
core file size          (blocks, -c) 0
data seg size           (kbytes, -d) unlimited
scheduling priority             (-e) 0
file size               (blocks, -f) unlimited
pending signals                 (-i) 147456
max locked memory       (kbytes, -l) 32
max memory size         (kbytes, -m) unlimited
open files                      (-n) 16384
pipe size            (512 bytes, -p) 8
POSIX message queues     (bytes, -q) 819200
real-time priority              (-r) 0
stack size              (kbytes, -s) 10240
```

```
cpu time              (seconds, -t)  unlimited
max user processes            (-u)  147456
virtual memory        (kbytes, -v)  unlimited
file locks                    (-x)  unlimited
```

How it works...

The soft limit is a warning threshold. When the hard limit is reached, the system will deny the process the ability to open more files. This results in exceptions that usually shutdown the Cassandra process.

There's more...

You should raise your open files above the default. However, there are other ways to keep the number of sockets low. Client should not be opening a socket per request. They should issue multiple requests over the same connection or they should be using a **Connection Pooling** implementation such as Hector.

Increasing performance by scaling up

Cassandra is designed to be scaled out by adding more nodes to the cluster. Scaling up is done by enhancing each node.

How to do it...

Scale up by:

- ▶ Adding more RAM
- ▶ Bonding networking cards
- ▶ Upgrading hard disks to SCSI or SSD
- ▶ Growing the disk array

How it works...

Adding RAM is a simple way to scale out. RAM can be allocated to the Java heap to be used for caches or Memtables. RAM not directly allocated to a process can be used by the disk cache. VFS cache is very effective at speeding up disk access. Keep in mind that motherboards have a limited number of slots, but higher density DIMMs are more expensive.

Network capacity can be upgraded. If your system has multiple network cards, they can be bonded together to double their performance. Larger servers may even be able to utilize 10 gigabit Ethernet.

Disk performance is an important factor for Cassandra. Faster seeking disks give better write performance. SCSI systems will perform better than SATA. **Solid State Drives** (**SSD**) do not have physical parts and can seek extremely quickly. However, they are still new and more costly then spinning disks.

Enabling Network Time Protocol on servers and clients

Network Time Protocol (**NTP**) is a distributed hierarchical system used to keep system clocks in sync. Clients to Cassandra require NTP because clients need to set the **timestamp** filed of an insert themselves. Servers running Cassandra require the correct time as well as they need to correctly evaluate if the lifetime of a tombstone or time-to-live column has passed. This recipe shows how to set up Network Time Protocol.

Getting ready

It is ideal to have one or two NTP servers locally (on the same subnet or in the same LAN network) synchronizing to **NTP server pools** on the Internet. This is preferred over having each server sync to the **NTP server pools** individually.

How to do it...

1. Install NTP using the system package manager:

   ```
   $ yum install ntp
   ```

2. Review the configurations in `/etc/ntp.conf`. Remove the public servers and replace with internal servers where appropriate:

   ```
   server ntp1.mynetwork.pvt
   server ntp2.mynetwork.pvt
   ```

   The NTP service will not sync a clock that is drastically out of sync with the contacted server. Use run `ntpdate` to initially synchronize.

   $ ntpdate ntp1.mynetwork.pvt

3. Enable `ntpd` and ensure it starts on bootup:

   $ /etc/init.d/ntpd start
   $ chckconfig ntpd on

How it works...

The NTP Daemon runs continuously and sends messages to its configured NTP servers. It uses the reply information as well as the calculated latency involved in transmitting that data to adjust or "groom" the clock. Running NTP helps to stop clocks from drifting. This is especially useful under high load where CPUs tend to drift more.

5

Consistency, Availability, and Partition Tolerance with Cassandra

In this chapter, you will learn:

- ▶ Working with the formula for strong consistency
- ▶ Supplying the timestamp value with write requests
- ▶ Disabling the hinted handoff mechanism
- ▶ Adjusting read repair chance for less intensive data reads
- ▶ Confirming schema agreement across a cluster
- ▶ Adjusting replication factor to work with quorum
- ▶ Using write consistency ONE, read consistency ONE for low latency operations
- ▶ Using write consistency QUORUM, read consistency QUORUM for strong consistency
- ▶ Mixing levels write consistency QUORUM, read consistency ONE
- ▶ Choosing consistency over availability consistency ALL
- ▶ Choosing availability over consistency with write consistency ANY
- ▶ Demonstrating how consistency is not a lock or a transaction

Introduction

Distributed systems such as Cassandra face challenges that single-system data stores do not have to face. The CAP theorem describes distributed systems with respect to consistency, availability, and partition tolerance. Achieving all three features simultaneously is impossible. Distributed systems can at best achieve two out of three. Cassandra has a versatile data model that allows the user to choose the aspects of CAP enforced per request.

 Go to `http://www.cs.berkeley.edu/~brewer/cs262b-2004/` `PODC-keynote.pdf` to learn more about the CAP theorem.

The recipes in this chapter require multiple Cassandra nodes to execute. In *Chapter 1, Getting Started*, the recipe *Scripting a multiple instance installation* will quickly set up the prerequisites.

Working with the formula for strong consistency

Cassandra provides consistency when the read replica count (R) plus write replica count (W) is greater than the replication factor (N).

R + W > N

Based on the replication factor and the number of live nodes, some consistency levels may not be achievable. Cassandra allows users to submit consistency level per request, allowing the user to trade-off between consistency, performance, and failed node tolerance.

Getting ready

The table describes the strength of consistency based on the levels chosen for read and write operations.

	Read.ONE	Read.QUORUM	Read.ALL
Write.ZERO*	Weak	Weak	Weak
Write.ANY	Weak	Weak	Weak
Write.ONE	Weak	Weak	Strong
Write.QUORUM	Weak	Strong	Strong
Write.ALL	Strong	Strong	Strong

* Write.ZERO has been removed from Cassandra 0.7.X and up.

How to do it...

1. Create a file `<hpc_build>/src/hpcas/c05/StrongConsistency.java`:

```java
package hpcas.c05;
import org.apache.cassandra.thrift.*;

public class StrongConsistency {

    public static void main (String [] args) throws Exception{
        long start=System.currentTimeMillis();
```

Users of this application will specify a host and port to connect to Cassandra with. The program also requires a value from the user that will be written to a column.

```java
        String host = Util.envOrProp("host") ;
        String sport = Util.envOrProp("port");
        String colValue = Util.envOrProp("columnValue");
        if (host==null || sport==null ||colValue == null){
            System.out.println("Cassandra Fail: specify host port
columnValue");
            System.exit(1);
        }
        int port = Integer.parseInt(sport);
        FramedConnWrapper fcw = new FramedConnWrapper(host,port);
        fcw.open();
        Cassandra.Client client = fcw.getClient();
```

2. Check if a keyspace named `newKeyspace` exists. If not, create it, and a column family inside it named `newCf`. Set the replication factor to 5:

```java
        if (!Util.listKeyspaces(client).contains("newKeyspace") ) {

            KsDef newKs = Util.createSimpleKSandCF("newKeyspace",
    "newCf", 5);
            client.system_add_keyspace(newKs);
            Thread.sleep(2000); //wait for schema agreement
        }

        /*Setup a column to be inserted.*/

        client.set_keyspace("newKeyspace");
        ColumnParent cp= new ColumnParent();
        cp.setColumn_family("newCf");
        Column c = new Column();
```

```
c.setName("mycolumn".getBytes("UTF-8"));
c.setValue(colValue.getBytes("UTF-8"));
c.setTimestamp(System.currentTimeMillis()*1000L);
try {
```

3. Insert at `ConstistencyLevel.ALL`. With the replication factor defined previously as 5, all five nodes in the cluster must be up for this write to succeed without exception:

```
        client.insert ("test".getBytes(), cp, c,
ConsistencyLevel.ALL );
        } catch (UnavailableException ex){
            System.err.println("Ensure all nodes are up");
            ex.printStackTrace();
        } try {
            fcw.close();
        }
        long end=System.currentTimeMillis();
        System.out.println("Time taken " + (end-start));
    }
}
```

Down a node in our cluster by killing it, and use nodetool to confirm its status.

```
$ bin/nodetool -h 127.0.0.1 -p 8080 ring | grep Down
127.0.0.17        Down      Normal    25.81 KB
```

4. Run the application:

```
$ host=127.0.0.1 port=9160 columnValue=testme ant
-DclassToRun=hpcas.c03.StrongConsistency   run
run:
    [java] Ensure all nodes are up
    [java] UnavailableException()
    [java] Time taken 305
```

5. Start up the down node and run the application again:

```
$ host=127.0.0.1 port=9160 columnValue=insertmeto ant
-DclassToRun=hpcas.c03.StrongConsistency run
run:
    [java] Time taken 274
```

How it works...

First, the program detects if the required keyspace and column family exists. If they do not exist they will be created. The replication factor of this keyspace is set to five, so the write must succeed on five nodes, otherwise an exception will be returned to the user.

All of the needed parameters except for the `colVal` are specified by the users at the start of the program. The write operation will either succeed and continue to the next line in the program or take the exception branch if a problem arises.

See also...

▶ In *Chapter 8, Multiple Datacenter Deployment*, several recipes focus on other consistency levels.

▶ Consistency is not a substitute for transaction processing. In *Chapter 3, Application Programmer Interface* we should know how to use transactional style locking using Cages.

Supplying the timestamp value with write requests

Each column has a user-supplied timestamp. When two columns for a row key have the same name, the timestamps of the columns are compared and the value of the column with the highest timestamp is the final value. This recipe shows how to set the timestamp of a column.

How to do it...

Create a column, calculate the current time, multiply by 1,000, and then pass the result to the `setTimestamp` method.

```
Column c = new Column();
c.setName("mycolumn".getBytes("UTF-8"));
c.setValue(colValue.getBytes("UTF-8"));
c.setTimestamp(System.currentTimeMillis()*1000L);
```

How it works...

The timestamp is used to enforce the idempotent behavior of a column. The column with the highest timestamp is the final value. This is useful in situations where a write operation may be received out of order. A column with a smaller timestamp will not overwrite a column with a larger timestamp.

There's more...

The timestamp column does not have to be a numeric representation of a date and time. It is a 64 bit integer that is used to resolve conflicts, and the user is free to choose any value. Using microsecond precision is suggested. Other options are incrementing the previous value or use an auto-increment value from another source. Remember that a delete operation creates a tombstone that will need to have a higher timestamp than the current data to remove it.

Disabling the hinted handoff mechanism

Cassandra determines which nodes data should be written to using the row key (and the replication factor, partition, strategy, and options). If a node that should receive a write is down, a hint is written to another node. When the downed node comes back online, the hints are redelivered to it. Hinted handoff is designed for dealing with temporary outages. Long-term outages can be a problem as storing hints on other nodes can begin to negatively impact their performance. This recipe shows how to disable hinted handoff.

 Hinted handoff writes do not count towards the strong consistency calculation discussed in the section *Working with the formula for strong consistency*.

How to do it...

Open `<cassandra_home>/conf/cassandra.yaml` in a text editor and set the `hinted_handoff_enabled` variable to `false`:

```
hinted_handoff_enabled: false
```

How it works...

With hinted handoff disabled, hints will not be stored. If there are failures, data could remain out of sync until it is repaired either with anti-entropy repair or read repair. This could result in stale reads depending on the read consistency level chosen, especially when using `Read.ONE`.

There's more...

When hinted handoff is enabled, two variables fine-tune how it operates:

- `max_hint_window_in_ms`

  The option `max_hint_window_in_ms` describes how long a downed node should have hints accumulated for it. This is used to ensure that a node that is down for extended periods of time will not cause other nodes to store hints indefinitely.

▶ `hinted_handoff_throttle_delay_in_ms`

This option adds small delays in between each hinted handoff row that is delivered. This is helpful in two ways: first, the revived node is not overloaded with a burst of hinted handoff messages. Secondly, the sending node does not consume a large amount of resources trying to deliver the hinted messages.

Adjusting read repair chance for less intensive data reads

Read consistency levels `QUORUM` and `ALL` are always synchronized before data is returned to the client. Data read at consistency level `ONE` uses a different code path. As soon as a natural endpoint finds data, it is returned to the client. In the background, a **read repair** can be initiated. Read repair keeps data consistent by comparing and updating the data across all the replicas. Each column family has a `read_repair_chance` property that controls the chance of a read repair being triggered. This recipe shows how to adjust `read_repair_chance` for better performance.

Getting ready

A quick way to set read repair chance is by using the CLI.

```
update column family XXX with read_repair_chance=.5
```

The following recipe manipulates the value using a program to demonstrate the functionality in the API.

How to do it...

1. Create a Java program in the project directory `<hpc_build>/src/hpcas/c05/ChangeReadRepairChance.java`:

```
package hpcas.c05;

import org.apache.cassandra.thrift.*;

public class ChangeReadRepairChance {

  public static void main(String[] args) throws Exception {
    String host = Util.envOrProp("host");
    String sport = Util.envOrProp("port");
    String ksname = Util.envOrProp("ks");
    String cfname = Util.envOrProp("cf");
```

```
String chance = Util.envOrProp("chance");

/*Ensure that read repair chance is between 0 and 1
inclusive.*/
double chan = Double.parseDouble(chance);
if (chan >1.0D || chan <0.0D){
  System.out.println("Chance must be >= 0 and <= 1");
  System.exit(2);
}
int port = Integer.parseInt(sport);
FramedConnWrapper fcw = new FramedConnWrapper(host, port);
fcw.open();
Cassandra.Client client = fcw.getClient();
```

2. Use the `describe_keyspace` method to find a keyspace by the user-specified name. Each keyspace has a list of `CfDef`, or column family definition, objects. Iterate the list looking for the user-specified column family:

```
KsDef ks = client.describe_keyspace(ksname);
for (CfDef cf: ks.cf_defs){
  if (cf.getName().equals(cfname)){
    System.out.println("Current Read repair chance"
      + cf.getRead_repair_chance());
```

3. Set the client to the keyspace in which the column family is a part of. Update the `CfDef` and use the `system_update_column_family` method to modify the schema:

```
        if (chan!=cf.getRead_repair_chance()){
          cf.setRead_repair_chance(chan);
          client.set_keyspace(ksname);
          client.system_update_column_family(cf);
          System.out.println("set Read repair chance to "+chan);
        }
      }
    }
    fcw.close();
  }
}
```

4. Start the application passing it the required environment variables, including the keyspace, column family, and the chance:

```
$ host=127.0.0.1 port=9160 ks=ks33 cf=cf33 chance=0.5 \
ant -DclassToRun=hpcas.c03.ChangeReadRepairChance run
run:
    [java] Current Read repair chance 0.4
    [java] set Read repair chance to 0.5
```

How it works...

Lowering `read_repair_chance` will result in less read traffic across the cluster. Setting it to 0.0 and using read consistency level ONE will reduce the reads across the cluster by 1/replication factor. If data is requested multiple times, the savings are cumulative.

There's more...

Setting `read_repair_chance` to 0.0 can be problematic as data will stay out of sync until it is written again or anti-entropy repair is run. Disabling `read_repair_chance` and hinted handoff greatly increases the risk of data being out of sync. Use a percentage that is appropriate for your requirements.

See also...

In this chapter, the recipe *Disabling hinted handoff*.

Confirming schema agreement across the cluster

Cassandra is a peer-to-peer distributed system and schema changes will propagate quickly, but not instantly, to all nodes. This recipe shows how to check that all nodes are at the same schema level. This is helpful for applications that need to create keyspaces and column families and write to them once they are available on all nodes.

How to do it...

1. Create a file `<hpc_build>hpcas/c05/ConfirmSchemaAgreement.java`:

```java
package hpcas.c05;
import java.util.*;
import org.apache.cassandra.thrift.Cassandra;

public class ConfirmSchemaAgreement {

    public static void main(String[] args) throws Exception {
        String host = Util.envOrProp("host");
        String sport = Util.envOrProp("port");
        if (host == null || sport == null ) {
          System.out.println("Cassandra Fail: specify host port");
          System.exit(1);
        }
```

```
int port = Integer.parseInt(sport);
FramedConnWrapper fcw = new FramedConnWrapper(host, port);
fcw.open();
Cassandra.Client client = fcw.getClient();
```

2. Call describe_schema_versions() and save the returned map. This map is a list of the schema ID, and a list of all nodes that are using that ID. Two nested loops are used to display all the information inside this structure:

```
Map<String,List<String>> sv =client.describe_schema_
versions();
    for (Map.Entry<String,List<String>> mapEntry: sv.entrySet()){
        System.out.println("key:"+mapEntry.getKey());
        for (String listForKey : mapEntry.getValue()){
          System.out.println("\t"+listForKey);
        }
    }
}
```

If the numbers of keys in the map is greater than one, two versions of the schema are currently present in the cluster and the changes are not completely propagated.

```
if (sv.size()>1) {
    System.out.println("Schemas are not in agreement on all
nodes.");
    } else {
    System.out.println("Schemas are in agreement for all
nodes");
    }
    fcw.close();
  }
}
```

3. Run the application:

```
$ host=127.0.0.1 port=9160 ant -DclassToRun=hpcas.c03.
ConfirmSchemaAgreement run
run:
    [java] key:c3f38ebc-e1c5-11df-95a0-e700f669bcfc
    [java]    127.0.0.2
    [java]    127.0.0.3
    [java]    127.0.0.4
    [java]    127.0.0.5
    [java]    127.0.0.1
    [java] Schema is in agreement for all nodes
```

How it works...

Each time a schema changing operation is issued, an ID is calculated. The `describe_schema_versions` method returns the schema ID for each cluster node. If only one key in the schema map exists, all nodes in the cluster are at the same schema version.

There's more...

A schema change has to propagate to every node in the cluster. To avoid issues, it is best not to make too many rapid schema changes or make changes when nodes in the cluster are down.

Adjusting replication factor to work with quorum

A **quorum** is the number of nodes that need to be in agreement to reach a consensus. The formula to determine the nodes needed for a quorum is:

`NodesNeededForQuorum = ReplicationFactor / 2 + 1`

When using a replication factor of one, data only exists on a single node and it is always consistent, but not redundant. When using a replication factor of two or higher, operations at level quorum are used to achieve consistency. This recipe shows how to create keyspaces at different replication levels and how quorum operations work at different replication levels.

How to do it...

Writing an application that inserts ten columns using quorum.

1. Create a file `<hpc_build>/src/hpcas/c05/ShowQuorum.java`:

   ```
   package hpcas.c05;
   import org.apache.cassandra.thrift.*;

   public class ShowQuorum {
       public static void main(String[] args) throws Exception {
   ```

2. Collect five mandatory values from the user. Host and port are required to connect to the cluster. `ksname`, `cfname`, and `replication` allows the user to specify the column family that will be created and written to:

   ```
   String host = Util.envOrProp("host");
   String sport = Util.envOrProp("port");
   String ksname = Util.envOrProp("ks");
   String cfname = Util.envOrProp("cf");
   ```

```
String replication = Util.envOrProp("replication");
if (host == null || sport == null || ksname == null
    || cfname == null || replication == null) {
  System.out.println("Cassandra Fail: specify host port ksname
cfname");
    System.exit(1);
}
int rep = Integer.parseInt(replication);
int port = Integer.parseInt(sport);
FramedConnWrapper fcw = new FramedConnWrapper(host, port);
fcw.open();
Cassandra.Client client = fcw.getClient();

/*Use the listKeyspaces() to determine if the column family
already exists. If the
target does not exist create it. */
if (!Util.listKeyspaces(client).contains(ksname)) {
  KsDef newKs = Util.createSimpleKSandCF(ksname, cfname, rep);
  client.system_add_keyspace(newKs);
  Thread.sleep(3000);
}

/*Set up the object to be inserted. */
ColumnParent cp = new ColumnParent();
client.set_keyspace(ksname);
cp.setColumn_family(cfname);
Column c = new Column();
c.setTimestamp(System.currentTimeMillis());

/* Declare two accumulators to record how many inserts pass
and fail. */
int k2pass = 0;
int k2fail = 0;
for (int i = 0; i < 10; ++i) {
  byte[] data = (i + "").getBytes("UTF-8");
  c.setName(data);
  c.setValue(data);
  try {
    client.insert(data, cp, c, ConsistencyLevel.QUORUM);
    k2pass++;
  /* Trap likely exceptions and increment the failure counter
if they happen */
  } catch (TimedOutException ex) {
    System.out.println(ex);
    k2fail++;
  } catch (UnavailableException ex) {
    System.out.println(ex); k2fail++;
  }
```

```
        }
      System.out.println("inserts ok:" + k2pass);
      System.out.println("inserts fail:" + k2fail);
   }
 }
```

3. Assure all nodes in the cluster are UP. Run the application supplying a keyspace name of `ks22`, a column family named `cf22`, and a replication factor of two:

```
$ host=127.0.0.1 port=9160 ks=ks22 cf=cf22 replication=2 ant
-DclassToRun=hpcas.c03.ShowQuorum run:
run:
      [java] inserts ok:10
      [java] inserts fail:0
```

4. Again, run the application with a keyspace name of `ks33` and a column family name of `cf33` with a replication factor of 3:

```
$ host=127.0.0.1 port=9160 ks=ks33 cf=cf33 replication=3 \
ant -DclassToRun=hpcas.c03.ShowQuorum run
run:
      [java] inserts ok:10
      [java] inserts fail:0
```

5. Stop one of the nodes and confirm it is down using nodetool:

```
$ <cassandra_home>/bin/nodetool -h 127.0.0.1 -p 8001 ring | grep
Down
127.0.0.5        Down    Normal
```

6. Run the programs again:

```
$ host=127.0.0.1 port=9160 ks=ks22 cf=cf22 replication=2 \
ant -DclassToRun=hpcas.c03.ShowQuorum run
run:
      [java] inserts ok:9
      [java] inserts fail:1
```

```
$ host=127.0.0.1 port=9160 ks=ks33 cf=cf33 replication=3 \
ant -DclassToRun=hpcas.c03.ShowQuorum run
run:
      [java] inserts ok:10
      [java] inserts fail:0
```

How it works...

With a replication factor of three, consistency level QUORUM requires two of its three natural endpoints UP for an operation not to throw an UnavailableException. Additionally, the operation can throw a TimedOutException if the nodes are UP according to cluster gossip, but do not respond in a timely fashion.

When replication factor is two, QUORUM is equal to ALL. This is because QUORUM requires a majority. This majority is only possible with replication factor of two when both nodes are UP.

See also...

Using write consistency QUORUM, read consistency QUROUM for strong consistency recipe in this chapter to see the performance characteristics with using QUORUM.

Using write consistency ONE, read consistency ONE for low latency operations

Consistency level ONE is the lowest latency consistency level available for clients to read and write with. It is low latency because the operation is acknowledgment to the client by only one of the natural endpoints for the data. This recipe shows how to use consistency level ONE, and what the CAP trade-offs are for using this level.

How to do it...

1. Refer to the getLevel(String) method of <hpc_build>/src/hpcas/c03/ Util.java. This will be used to map user-supplied strings to their associated Java **enum**:

```
public static ConsistencyLevel getLevel(String read) {
    return ConsistencyLevel.valueOf(read);
}
```

2. Create <hpc_build>src/hpcas/c05/ConsistencyPerformanceTester.java:

```
package hpcas.c03;

import java.util.*;
import org.apache.cassandra.thrift.*;

public class ConsistencyPerformanceTester {

    public static void main(String[] args) throws Exception {
        String readLevel = Util.envOrProp("readLevel");
```

```
   String writeLevel = Util.envOrProp("writeLevel");
   String hostList = Util.envOrProp("hostList");
   String sport = Util.envOrProp("port");
   int inserts = Integer.parseInt(Util.envOrProp("inserts"));
   boolean retryRead = (Util.envOrProp("retryRead") != null) ;
   if (readLevel == null || writeLevel == null || hostList ==
null
         || sport == null ) {
      System.out.println("Params: readLevel writeLevel hostList
port inserts ");
      System.exit(1);
  }
```

This application connects to multiple cluster nodes. Users will supply a host list and internally the application will open a connection to each.

```
   List<String> nodes = Arrays.asList(hostList.split(","));
   List<FramedConnWrapper> clients = new
ArrayList<FramedConnWrapper>();
   for (String node : nodes) {
      FramedConnWrapper fcw = new FramedConnWrapper(node,
        Integer.parseInt(sport));
      fcw.open();
      fcw.getClient().set_keyspace(Util.envOrProp("ks"));
      clients.add(fcw);
   }
   ColumnParent parent = new ColumnParent();
   parent.setColumn_family(Util.envOrProp("cf"));
   ColumnPath path = new ColumnPath();
   path.setColumn_family(Util.envOrProp("cf"));
   path.setColumn("acol".getBytes("UTF-8"));

   /*Declare two accumulators to keep track get requests that
return no data.*/
   int notFoundCount = 0;
   int notFoundCount2 = 0;
   Random generator = new Random();
   long startTime = System.nanoTime();
   for (int j = 0; j < inserts; j++) {
     byte[] key = (generator.nextInt() + "").getBytes("UTF-8");
     Column dat = new Column();
     dat.setTimestamp(System.currentTimeMillis());
     dat.setName("acol".getBytes("UTF-8"));
     dat.setValue(key);
```

3. Connect to the first node to insert the data. Inserts can be done to any node in the cluster as the request will be proxied to its proper destinations. Then, use a random number generator to select a random node from the pool and attempt to read the key that was just written. If the column has not reached the node yet, a `NotFoundException` is thrown:

```
        clients.get(0).getClient().insert(key, parent, dat, Util.
getLevel(writeLevel));
        try {
          clients.get(generator.nextInt(nodes.size() - 1) + 1)
                  .getClient().get(key, path, Util.
getLevel(readLevel));
        } catch (NotFoundException nfe) {
          notFoundCount++;
          if (retryRead){
            try {
                clients.get(generator.nextInt(nodes.size() - 1)+1)
                      .getClient().get(key, path, Util.
getLevel(readLevel));
            } catch (NotFoundException nfe2) {
                Thread.sleep(10);
                notFoundCount2++;
            }
          }
        }
      }
```

4. Calculate the time of the program run using the `System.nanoTime()` method. Then, display the counters collected during the run of the program:

```
        long end = System.nanoTime()-startTime;
        System.out.println("insertCount:" + inserts + "
NotFoundCount:"
                + notFoundCount+" NotFoundCount2: "+notFoundCount2
          + " nanos:"+end);


        /*Close up all connections to the cluster by iterating the
list of connections .*/

        for (FramedConnWrapper client : clients) {
          client.close();
        }
      }
    }
```

5. Run the application doing 10,000 inserts at write consistency ONE and read consistency ONE:

```
$ hostList=127.0.0.1,127.0.0.2,127.0.0.3,127.0.0.4,127.0.0.5
port=9160 \
ks=ks33 cf=cf33 inserts=10000 readLevel=ONE writeLevel=ONE \
ant -DclassToRun=hpcas.c03.ConsistencyPerformanceTester run
run:
      [java] insertCount:10000 NotFoundCount:117 NotFoundCount2: 0
nanos:18638128979
```

6. Retry the application, this time specifying the `retryRead` environment variable:

```
$ hostList=127.0.0.1,127.0.0.2,127.0.0.3,127.0.0.4,127.0.0.5
port=9160 \
ks=ks33 cf=cf33 inserts=10000 readLevel=one writeLevel=ONE
retryRead=yes \
ant -DclassToRun=hpcas.c03.ConsistencyPerformanceTester run
run:
      [java] insertCount:10000 NotFoundCount:86 NotFoundCount2: 3
nanos:20087524941
```

How it works...

This application shows that using consistency level ONE for write and read operations results in **eventual consistency**. Because ONE has the lowest consistency guarantee, in the first run of the application, 117 of the inserts had not propagated to the other replicas before a `get` request for that data was issued. In the next run with the `retryRead` option enabled, only three keys were not found. The data would eventually arrive at the destination, but there is no guarantee how long it will take.

The following diagram illustrates a client reading from a node before a write has propagated to it:

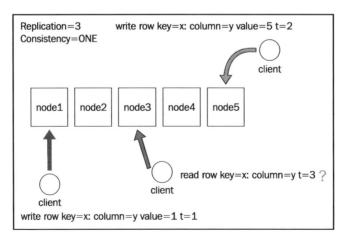

There's more...

Historically, there have been several misconceptions around eventual consistency. It is important to understand that "eventual" can be small deltas in time. From the output above, using Cassandra at the weakest level only caused a stale read 117/100000 times in a contrived scenario designed to detect it. The term **tunable consistency** is often used to describe Cassandra as the consistency is chosen on a per request basis.

Using write consistency QUORUM, read consistency QUORUM for strong consistency

Writing and reading at QUORUM level allows strong consistency. When combined with a replication factor of three or higher, QUORUM operations still succeed even when some of the nodes are down. Using quorum is favored in many cases because it brings consistency, good performance, and failure tolerance. This recipe demonstrates the features of QUORUM.

Getting ready

This recipe requires the application from the last recipe: *Using write consistency ONE, read consistency ONE for low latency operations*. This requires a keyspace and a column family to work with.

How to do it...

1. Create a list of all hosts in the cluster. Set readLevel and writeLevel to QUORUM and run the ConsistencyPerformanceTester application:

   ```
   $ hostList=127.0.0.1,127.0.0.2,127.0.0.3,127.0.0.4,127.0.0.5
   port=9160 \
   ks=ks33 cf=cf33 inserts=10000 readLevel=QUORUM writeLevel=QUORUM \
   ant -DclassToRun=hpcas.c03.ConsistencyPerformanceTester run
   run:
        [java] insertCount:10000 NotFoundCount:0 NotFoundCount2: 0
   nanos:24894699808
   ```

2. Down a node and confirm it is down using nodetool:

   ```
   $ <casandra_home>/bin/nodetool -h 127.0.0.1 -p 8080 ring | grep
   Down
   127.0.0.3        Down    Normal   69.83 KB
   ```

3. Take the downed host out of the hostList and run the application again:

   ```
   $ hostList=127.0.0.1,127.0.0.2,127.0.0.4,127.0.0.5 port=9160 \
   ks=ks33 cf=cf33 inserts=10000 readLevel=QUORUM writeLevel=QUORUM \
   ```

```
ant -DclassToRun=hpcas.c03.ConsistencyPerformanceTester run
run:
      [java] insertCount:10000 NotFoundCount:0 NotFoundCount2: 0
nanos:25773869616
```

How it works...

When reading and writing at QUORUM data, consistency is strong. Using this combination, the NotFoundCount counter should always be 0 unless enough nodes in your cluster are down that a quorum cannot be achieved. While reading at QUORUM, clients are blocked until a majority confirms the data is consistent. This means the read time is longer than that of reading at ONE.

The following diagram illustrates how reading and writing at QUORUM ensures clients always have a consistent view of data:

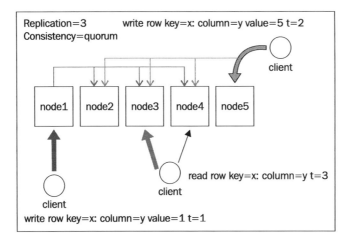

Mixing levels write consistency QUORUM, read consistency ONE

Since the read operations are typically more intensive than write operations, read-heavy applications try to optimize reads in any way possible. This recipe shows performance advantages and the consistency trade-off for this combination of quorum levels.

Trading off consistency for performance may not be an acceptable solution. Consider other techniques for enhancing performance before giving up on consistency.

Getting ready

Complete the code in the recipe *Using write consistency ONE, read consistency ONE for low latency operations*.

How to do it...

Run the `ConsistencyPerformanceTester` application, using a `readLevel` of ONE and a `writeLevel` of QUORUM:

```
$ hostList=127.0.0.1,127.0.0.2,127.0.0.4,127.0.0.5,127.0.0.3 port=9160 \
ks=ks33 cf=cf33 inserts=10000 readLevel=ONE writeLevel=QUORUM \
ant -DclassToRun=hpcas.c03.ConsistencyPerformanceTester run
run:
     [java] insertCount:10000 NotFoundCount:64 NotFoundCount2: 0
nanos:21594606710
```

How it works...

Read operations are more intensive than write operations especially as the data per node increases. The run of the program shows the performance of this combination is strong. However, due to eventual consistency, this combination can result in stale reads if data is read from a natural endpoint quickly before the write was replicated to it. Since QUORUM acknowledges the write on two nodes, the `NotFoundCount` would be lower than if the data was written at ONE.

Choosing consistency over availability consistency ALL

Using the consistency level ALL always has strong consistency regardless of what other level it is paired with, with one important exception: writing at ANY and reading at ALL is not strongly consistent. This recipe uses the ALL level and demonstrates trade-offs.

How to do it...

1. Run the `ConsistencyPerformanceTester` with the `writeLevel` of ALL and the `readLevel` of ONE:

```
$ hostList=127.0.0.1,127.0.0.2,127.0.0.4,127.0.0.5,127.0.0.3
port=9160 \
ks=ks33 cf=cf33 inserts=10000 readLevel=ONE writeLevel=ALL \
```

```
ant -DclassToRun=hpcas.c03.ConsistencyPerformanceTester run
run:
      [java] insertCount:10000 NotFoundCount:0 NotFoundCount2: 0
nanos:20558351612
```

2. Remove the downed node from the host list and run the application again:

```
$ <cassandra_home>/bin/nodetool -h 127.0.0.1 -p 8080 ring | grep
Down
  127.0.0.3      Down    Normal   10.25 MB
$ hostList=127.0.0.1,127.0.0.2,127.0.0.4,127.0.0.5 port=9160 \
ks=ks33 cf=cf33 inserts=10000 readLevel=ONE writeLevel=ALL \
ant -DclassToRun=hpcas.c03.ConsistencyPerformanceTester run
run:
      [java] insertCount:10000 NotFoundCount:8727 NotFoundCount2: 0
nanos:10301708949 exceptions 8727
```

How it works...

The drawback of using ALL is any node failure will cause operations involving that node to fail. Failures will return an UnavailableException or TimedOutException to the client. From the example, the high **exceptions** count shows many writes fail when even a single node is down. This example shows how rigid ALL is. Normal operation cannot continue even with a single node being down.

Choosing availability over consistency with write consistency ANY

Some use cases may wish for Cassandra to accept writes even if all the natural endpoint nodes are down. Cassandra has a consistency level that can be only used for write operations called ANY. When using ANY, the write is delivered to any node in the cluster to be redelivered later via the hinted handoff mechanism. This recipe shows how to use the ANY level.

How to do it...

1. Ensure one or more cluster nodes are down:

```
$ <cassandra_home>/bin/nodetool -h 127.0.0.1 -p 8080 ring | grep
Down
  127.0.0.3      Down    Normal   10.25 MB
  127.0.0.5      Down    Normal   487.03 KB
```

2. Take the downed host out of the host list and set the `writeLevel` to ANY and run the `ConsistencyPerformanceTester`:

```
$ hostList=127.0.0.1,127.0.0.2,127.0.0.4 port=9160 \
ks=ks33 cf=cf33 inserts=10000 readLevel=ONE writeLevel=ANY \
ant -DclassToRun=hpcas.c03.ConsistencyPerformanceTester run
run:
      [java] insertCount:10000 NotFoundCount:271 NotFoundCount2: 0
nanos:12797227510 exceptions:0
```

3. Using nodetool, look for a node with **Active** or **Pending** tasks in the **HINTED_POOL** stage:

```
$ <cassandra_home>/bin/nodetool -h 127.0.0.1 -p 8080 tpstats |
grep HINTED
            Active       Pending        Total
HINTED_POOL                 1             3              9
```

How it works...

The ANY consistency level will always accept write operations. The number of NotFoundCount events shows that the consistency is unpredictable when using this level for writing regardless of the level used for reading. This level is best used for applications that do not want to miss write operations, do not care about the consistency of data, and do not care about delivery delays.

Demonstrating how consistency is not a lock or a transaction

Consistency is not equivalent to a transaction or locking. The classic way to illustrate this functionality is with a counter that needs to be manipulated by multiple threads at once. This recipe demonstrates how Cassandra works in these scenarios.

How to do it...

1. Create `<hpc_build>src/java/hpcas/c05/ShowConcurrency.java`:

```
package hpcas.c05;
import hpcas.c03.*;
import java.util.*;
import org.apache.cassandra.thrift.*;
public class ShowConcurrency implements Runnable {
  String host;
  int port;
  int inserts;
```

```java
  public ShowConcurrency(String host, int port, int inserts) {
    this.host = host;
    this.port = port;
    this.inserts = inserts;
  }


  /*getValue() reads a number from a specific key and column. */
  public static int getValue(Cassandra.Client client) throws
Exception {
    client.set_keyspace("ks33");
    ColumnPath cp = new ColumnPath();
    cp.setColumn_family("cf33");
    cp.setColumn("count_col".getBytes("UTF-8"));
    ColumnOrSuperColumn col = client.get("count_key".
getBytes("UTF-8"), cp, ConsistencyLevel.QUORUM);
    int x = Integer.parseInt(new String(col.column.getValue()));
    System.out.println("read " + x);
    return x;
  }


  /*setValue() sets a specific key and column to the specified
integer value. */
  public static void setValue(Cassandra.Client client, int x)
throws Exception {
      client.set_keyspace("ks33");
  ColumnParent parent = new ColumnParent();
  parent.setColumn_family("cf33");
  Column c = new Column();
  c.setName("count_col".getBytes("UTF-8"));
  c.setValue((x + "").getBytes("UTF-8"));
  c.setTimestamp(System.nanoTime());
  client.insert("count_key".getBytes("UTF-8"), parent, c,
      ConsistencyLevel.QUORUM);
  System.out.println("wrote " + x);
  }


  /*Threading in Java requires overriding the run method. The
thread attempts to
 read a value, increment it locally, and then write it back
several times. */
 public void run() {
    try {
    FramedConnWrapper fcw = new FramedConnWrapper(host, port);
    fcw.open();
    Cassandra.Client client = fcw.getClient();
    client.set_keyspace("ks33");
```

```
        for (int i = 0; i < inserts; i++) {
            int x = getValue(client);
            x++;
            setValue(client, x);
        }
         fcw.close();
        } catch (Exception ex) {
          System.out.println(ex);
        }
    }


    /*Along with connection information of host and port, users must
supply the
    number of threads and the number of inserts per thread */

    public static void main(String[] args) throws Exception {
        String host = Util.envOrProp("host");
        int port = Integer.parseInt(Util.envOrProp("port"));
        int inserts = Integer.parseInt(Util.envOrProp("inserts"));
        int threads = Integer.parseInt(Util.envOrProp("threads"));
        FramedConnWrapper fcw = new FramedConnWrapper(host, port);
        fcw.open();
        Cassandra.Client client = fcw.getClient();

        /*truncate the column family and set the initial value of the
counter to 0 */

        client.set_keyspace("ks33");
        client.truncate("cf33");
        Thread.sleep(1000);
        setValue(client, 0);
        int start = getValue(client);
        System.out.println("The start value is " + start);
        /*Create a thread group to manage all the
        application threads as a single entity */

        ThreadGroup group = new ThreadGroup("readWrite");
        for (int i = 0; i < threads; ++i) {
            ShowConcurrency sc = new ShowConcurrency(host, port,
inserts);
            Thread t = new Thread(group, sc);
            t.start();
        }
```

```
    /* sleep until the activeCount() method of thread group is 0
*/

    while (group.activeCount() > 0) {
      Thread.sleep(1000);
    }

    /* print out the final value of the counter.*/
    int x = getValue(client);
    System.out.println("The final value is " + x);
    }
}
```

2. Run the application doing 70 inserts from one thread:

```
$ host=127.0.0.1 port=9160 inserts=70 threads=1 ant
-DclassToRun=hpcas.c04.ShowConcurrency run
     [java] read 68
     [java] wrote 69
     [java] read 69
     [java] wrote 70
     [java] read 70
     [java] The final value is 70
```

3. Run the program again specifying 70 inserts from three threads:

```
$host=127.0.0.1 port=9160 inserts=70 threads=3 ant
-DclassToRun=hpcas.c04.ShowConcurrency run
     [java] read 97
     [java] read 97
     [java] wrote 98
     [java] wrote 98
     [java] read 98
     [java] wrote 99
     [java] read 99
     [java] wrote 100
     [java] read 100
     [java] The final value is 100
```

How it works...

For the first run of the program, one thread does 70 inserts. As expected, the final value of the counter is 70. The second run uses three threads doing 70 inserts. The expected final value of the counter would be 210. However, in our example run, the final value was 100. On examination of the output, multiple threads read the value as 97 and updated it to 98. This happened because multiple clients are operating on the column simultaneously and have no way to lock the value so it cannot be read or changed by others.

See also...

In *Chapter 10, Third-party Libraries and Applications*, the recipes *Setting up Zookeeper to support Cages for transactional locking* and *Using Cages to implement an atomic read and set*.

6

Schema Design

In this chapter, you will learn the following recipes:

- ▶ Saving disk space by using small column names
- ▶ Serializing data into large columns for smaller index sizes
- ▶ Storing time series data effectively
- ▶ Using different replication factors per keyspace
- ▶ Hybrid Random Partitioner using Order Preserving Partitioner
- ▶ Using Super Columns for nested maps
- ▶ Storing large objects
- ▶ Using Cassandra for distributed caching
- ▶ Storing large or infrequently accessed data in a separate column family
- ▶ Storing and searching edge graph data in Cassandra
- ▶ Developing secondary data orderings or indexes

Introduction

A critical component of performance understands how to utilize the data model that Cassandra provides. The recipes in this chapter show ways by which data can be modeled to be stored and accessed efficiently when using Cassandra.

Saving disk space by using small column names

The columns associated with a key are stored in a sorted map data structure. This is different than data stores that use column separators or fixed width rows. One advantage of this is that all entries can have differing columns. However, due to this design the column names and values need to be stored on disk for each key. This recipe demonstrates the advantages of using smaller column names.

How to do it...

1. Create a file `src/hpcas/c06/ColumnSize.java`:

```java
package hpcas.c06;
import hpcas.c03.*;
import java.nio.ByteBuffer;
import org.apache.cassandra.thrift.*;

public class ColumnSize {
  public static void main(String[] args) throws Exception {
    FramedConnWrapper fcw = new FramedConnWrapper(
            Util.envOrProp("host"),
            Integer.parseInt(Util.envOrProp("port")));
    fcw.open();
    Cassandra.Client client = fcw.getClient();
    client.set_keyspace(Util.envOrProp("ks"));
    ColumnParent parent = new ColumnParent();
    parent.setColumn_family(Util.envOrProp("cf"));
    Column column = new Column();
```

2. The name of the column comes from the user. This allows us to demonstrate how the column name affects the overall size of data files:

```java
    column.setName(Util.envOrProp("colname").getBytes("UTF-8"));
    column.setValue("1".getBytes("UTF-8"));
    for (int i=0;i<20000;i++){
      client.insert(ByteBuffer.wrap((i+"").getBytes("UTF-8")),
      parent, column,
            ConsistencyLevel.QUORUM);
    }
    fcw.close();
  }
}
```

3. Run the `ColSize` application specifying a `colname` that is a large string:

```
$ cf=cf33 ks=ks33 colname=thisisabigcolumnnameandlookout
host=127.0.0.2 port=9160 ant -DclassToRun=hpcas.c06.ColumnSize run
$ <cassandra_home>/bin/nodetool -h 127.0.0.1 -p 8080 flush ks33
$ cd $HOME/hpcas/data/1/ks33 ls -lah
total 2.4M
-rw-rw-r--. 1 edward edward 2.2M Jan  3 05:10 cf33-e-1-Data.db
-rw-rw-r--. 1 edward edward  25K Jan  3 05:10 cf33-e-1-Filter.db
-rw-rw-r--. 1 edward edward 186K Jan  3 05:10 cf33-e-1-Index.db
-rw-rw-r--. 1 edward edward 4.8K Jan  3 05:10 cf33-e-1-Statistics.
db
```

4. Run the `ColumnSize` application again, this time specifying a column name of just a single character `s`:

```
$ cf=cf33 ks=ks33 colname=s host=127.0.0.2 port=9160 ant
-DclassToRun=hpcas.c06.ColumnSize run
```

5. Flush the data to the disk and use the `ls` command to display file size information:

```
$ <cassandra_home>/bin/nodetool -h 127.0.0.1 -p 8080 flush ks33
$ ls -lah $HOME/edward/hpcas/data/1/ks33/
total 916K
-rw-rw-r--. 1 edward edward 804K Jan  3 05:19 cf33-e-1-Data.db
-rw-rw-r--. 1 edward edward  11K Jan  3 05:19 cf33-e-1-Filter.db
-rw-rw-r--. 1 edward edward  83K Jan  3 05:19 cf33-e-1-Index.db
-rw-rw-r--. 1 edward edward 4.8K Jan  3 05:19 cf33-e-1-Statistics.
db
```

How it works...

A column is stored as a tuple of name, value, and timestamp. Larger column names require more disk space to store. These larger columns also use more memory inside key caches, row caches, and Memtables. The savings using smaller column names can be significant when the size of a column name is a large portion of the column size.

Serializing data into large columns for smaller index sizes

If all or most of the data for a key will be read with each request, it may be better to serialize all the columns of a key into a single column. This recipe will use delimited text as an alternative to storing multiple columns under the same key.

How to do it...

1. Create `src/hpcas/c06/LargeColumns.java`:

```java
package hpcas.c06;
import hpcas.c03.*;
import java.nio.ByteBuffer;
import org.apache.cassandra.thrift.*;

public class LargeColumns {
  static class Car {
    String make, model; int year;
    public Car(String make, String model, int year) {
      this.make = make;this.model = model; this.year = year;
    }
```

2. Serialize this object into three pipe delimited fields. The first column represents a serialization version:

```java
    public String toString() {
      return "v1|" + make + "|" + model + "|" + year;
    }
  }

  public static void main(String[] args) throws Exception {
    FramedConnWrapper fcw = new FramedConnWrapper
    (Util.envOrProp("host"),
  Integer.parseInt
    (Util.envOrProp("port")));
    fcw.open();
    Cassandra.Client client = fcw.getClient();
    client.set_keyspace("parking");
    Car myCar = new Car("lincoln", "towncar", 99);
    ByteBuffer ownerName = ByteBuffer.wrap
    ("Stacey".getBytes("UTF-8"));
```

3. Inserting this object calling the `toString()` method and store the result directly:

```
client.insert(ownerName, Util.simpleColumnParent("parking"),
    Util.simpleColumn("car", myCar.toString()),
ConsistencyLevel.ONE);
    fcw.close();
  }
}
```

4. Use the CLI to see that the data is stored in a single column:

[default@parking] assume parking validator as ascii;

[default@parking] assume parking comparator as ascii;

[default@parking] list parking;

RowKey: Stacey

**=> (column=car, value=v1|lincoln|towncar|99,
timestamp=120959663165400)**

How it works...

Each column is a tuple consisting of a column name, a column value, and a timestamp. When column sizes are very small, the overhead of the **tuple** can be significant. Beyond the data size of the column, index overhead exists as well. This method reduces overhead in some cases, but can use more storage in others. This can happen if this data is updated often as each update will be the entire row rather than a small column.

stacey	column=car, value=v1|lincoln|towncar|99, timestamp=120959663165400

There's more...

Other popular serialization solutions are JSON, Protocol Buffers, and YAML. For complex objects, it is also possible to use `java.beans.XMLBeanEncoder` or Java serialization using the `java.io.Serializable` interface.

Storing time series data effectively

Modeling time series information has wide appeal. Typically, **Network Management Systems (NMS)** use time series data to store system performance information. This type of storage is useful for trending statistics over time such as the weather or stock market prices. This recipe shows how to take advantage of the distributed nature of Cassandra while using a **Comparator** to organize numeric data inside a column.

How to do it...

1. Create the file `<hpc_build>/src/java/hpcas/c06/TimeSeries.java`:

```
package hpcas.c06;

import java.nio.ByteBuffer;
import hpcas.c03.*;
import java.io.ByteArrayOutputStream;
import java.io.DataOutputStream;
import java.text.SimpleDateFormat;
import java.util.GregorianCalendar;
import org.apache.cassandra.thrift.*;

public class TimeSeries {
```

The `DateFormat` classes allow calendar information to be displayed in a user-defined format. The date format is used to group data into the same key.

```
  public static SimpleDateFormat format = new
SimpleDateFormat("yyyy.MM.dd");
```

The `Counter` class stores generic descriptor information as well as numeric data about the state of the counter.

```
  public static class Counter {
    String host,object,instance,value;
    long time;
    public Counter(String host, String object, String instance,
          String value, long time){
      this.host=host; this.object = object; this.
instance=instance;
      this.value=value; this.time=time;
    }
```

Many of the fields of the counter will be formed into a **Composite Key**. Building a composite key results in `Counter` objects that are distinct from each other without having to generate ids.

```
    public ByteBuffer keyName() throws Exception {
      GregorianCalendar gc = new GregorianCalendar();
      gc.setTimeInMillis(time);
      ByteBuffer name = ByteBuffer.wrap(
          (host+"/"+object+"/"+instance+"/"
      +format.format(gc.getTime()))
          .getBytes("UTF-8") );
      return name;
    }
```

To work with the **Long Comparator** and have it sort data by time inside a column properly, write `Long` values directly out to the byte outputs.

```java
public Column getColumn() throws Exception {
    Column c = new Column();
    ByteArrayOutputStream bos = new ByteArrayOutputStream();
    DataOutputStream dos = new DataOutputStream(bos);
    dos.writeLong(time);
    dos.flush();
    c.setName( bos.toByteArray() );
    c.setValue((value+"").getBytes("UTF-8"));
    return c;
}
}
public static void main(String [] args) throws Exception{
    FramedConnWrapper fcw = new
        FramedConnWrapper( Util.envOrProp("host"),
            Integer.parseInt(Util.envOrProp("port")));
    fcw.open();
    Cassandra.Client client = fcw.getClient();
    client.set_keyspace("perfdata");
```

2. Use `System.getCurrentlTimeMillis()` to retrieve clock information from the system. Create a second time five minutes in the future:

```java
long now = System.currentTimeMillis();
long future = now + (60L*1000L*5L);
ColumnParent parent = Util.simpleColumnParent("perfdata");
```

3. Use the `Counter` class and its utility methods to write two counters. These counters represent the CPU usage of a fictitious processor core:

```java
Counter s1t1 = new Counter("server1", "cpu","core1","20",now );
    client.insert(s1t1.keyName(), parent, s1t1.getColumn(),
ConsistencyLevel.ONE);
    Counter s1t2 = new Counter("server1",
"cpu","core1","25",future );
    client.insert(s1t2.keyName(), parent, s1t2.getColumn(),
ConsistencyLevel.ONE);
    fcw.close();
}
}
```

4. Create the required keyspace and column family. Make sure to set the comparator to `LongType`:

    ```
    [default@unknown] create keyspace perfdata;

    [default@unknown] use perfdata;

    [default@perfdata] create column family perfdata with
    comparator='LongType';
    ```

5. List the `perfdata` column:

    ```
    [default@perfdata] assume perfdata validator as ascii;

    [default@perfdata] list perfdata;

    RowKey: server1/cpu/core1/2011.01.03
    => (column=1294109019835, value=20, timestamp=0)
    => (column=1294109319835, value=25, timestamp=0)
    1 Row Returned.
    ```

How it works...

The ability to construct long composite keys combined with the sharding capabilities of the data model provides a horizontally scalable storage system for performance counters. Comparators allow the column data to be ordered in a user-defined manner since data in Cassandra is a `byte []`.

Using Super Columns for nested maps

Super Columns are columns where the value is a sorted map of keys and values. This is different than a standard column where the value is a byte array. Super Columns add another level of nesting, allowing storage of more complex objects without encoding data into composite columns. For this recipe, we use a Super Column to store information about movies and reviews of the movie.

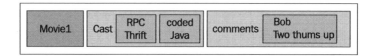

How to do it...

1. Create a keyspace and column family named `moviereview`:

    [default@unknown] create keyspace moviereview;

    [default@unknown] use moviereview;

Authenticated to keyspace: moviereview

[default@moviereview] create column family moviereview with column_ type='Super';

2. Create a file `src/hpcas/c06/MovieReview.java`:

```
package hpcas.c06;
import hpcas.c03.*;
import java.nio.ByteBuffer;
import org.apache.cassandra.thrift.*;

public class MovieReview {
  public static void main (String [] args) throws Exception {
    FramedConnWrapper fcw = new
     FramedConnWrapper( Util.envOrProp("host"),
          Integer.parseInt(Util.envOrProp("port")));
    fcw.open();
    Cassandra.Client client = fcw.getClient();
    client.set_keyspace("moviereview");
    ByteBuffer movieName = ByteBuffer.wrap(
          "Cassandra to the Future".getBytes("UTF-8") );
```

3. Create a `ColumnParent` instance and set the super column property to `reviews`. Then, use the parent to insert two columns that represent two reviews of the movie:

```
        ColumnParent review = new ColumnParent();
        review.setColumn_family("moviereview");
        review.setSuper_column("reviews".getBytes("UTF-8"));
        client.insert(movieName, review,
          Util.simpleColumn("bob", "Great movie!"), ConsistencyLevel.
          ONE);
        client.insert(movieName, review,
          Util.simpleColumn("suzy", "I'm speechless."),
          ConsistencyLevel.ONE);
        ColumnParent movieInfo = new ColumnParent();
        movieInfo.setColumn_family("moviereview");
```

4. Insert two columns into the `cast` super column:

```
        movieInfo.setSuper_column("cast".getBytes("UTF-8"));
        client.insert(movieName, movieInfo,
                Util.simpleColumn("written in", "java"),
ConsistencyLevel.ONE);
        client.insert(movieName, movieInfo,
                Util.simpleColumn("RPC by", "thrift"),
ConsistencyLevel.ONE);
        System.out.println("Reviews for: "+new String(movieName.
array(),"UTF-8"));
```

5. Set the super column property of a `ColumnPath` to `cast` and use it to extract all the data from that super column:

```
ColumnPath cp = new ColumnPath();
cp.setColumn_family("moviereview");
cp.setSuper_column("cast".getBytes("UTF-8"));
System.out.println("--Starring--");
ColumnOrSuperColumn sc = client.get(movieName, cp,
ConsistencyLevel.ONE);
   for (Column member : sc.super_column.columns){
      System.out.println( new String (member.getName(),"UTF-8")
   +" : "
 + new String(member.getValue(),"UTF-8"));
      }
   System.out.println("--what people are saying--");
   cp.setSuper_column("reviews".getBytes("UTF-8"));
   ColumnOrSuperColumn reviews = client.get(movieName, cp,
ConsistencyLevel.ONE);
   for (Column member : reviews.super_column.columns){
      System.out.println( new String (member.getName(),"UTF-8")
   +" : "
 +new String(member.getValue(),"UTF-8"));
      }
   fcw.close();
   }
}
```

6. Run the application:

```
$ host=127.0.0.1 port=9160 ant -DclassToRun=hpcas.c06.MovieReview
run
run:
      [java] Reviews for: Cassandra to the Future
      [java] --Staring--
      [java] RPC by : thrift
      [java] written in : java
      [java] --what people are saying--
      [java] bob : Great movie!
      [java] suzy : I'm speechless.
```

How it works...

Super Columns provide another level of associated arrays in the value of the column. This can be used as an alternative to generating composite column keys. This recipe uses two Super Columns: `cast` to store actors in the movie, and `reviews` to store comments on what the users thought of the movie. Super Columns allow us to store this information without using multiple Standard Column Families or composite keys.

There's more...

Operations on Super Columns involve de-serializing the entire Super Column. Because of the de-serialization overhead, avoid storing a large number of sub columns in a Super Column family column.

Using a lower Replication Factor for disk space saving and performance enhancements

The **Replication Factor** can be set on keyspace (not per column family). The chosen Replication Factor has several implications. The higher the Replication Factor, the more nodes data is stored on and the more fault tolerant your cluster is. A larger Replication Factor means the storage capacity of the cluster is diminished. A higher Replication Factor also means write and read operations take more resources on more hardware.

How to do it...

Create a keyspace named `bulkload` with a replication factor of 2.

```
[default@unknown] connect localhost/9160;

Connected to: "Test Cluster" on localhost/9160

[default@unknown] create keyspace bulkload with strategy_options =
[{replication_factor:1}];
```

Between versions 0.7.X and 0.8.X the replication factor moved from a property of `KsDef` to a parameter of the `stratefy_options`. The 0.7.X syntax is:

```
    [default@unknown] create keyspace bulkload with replication_factor=2;
```

How it works...

Using a Replication Factor of 2 for the `bulkload` keyspace uses less disk space and uses less resources, creating less overall utilization. This results in a performance gain at the cost of some redundancy.

There's more...

At a Replication Factor of 2, **Consistency Level Quorum** is the same as **Consistency Level All**. This is because Quorum requires a majority that cannot be achieved with one of two replicas.

See also...

- ▶ See the *Using nodetool cleanup* recipe in *Chapter 7, Administration* when lowering the replication of an existing keyspace.
- ▶ The *Running nodetool repair* in *Chapter 7, Administration* when raising the replication factor of an existing keyspace.
- ▶ In the *multi-datacenter deployment* chapter we visit larger Replication Factors needed for multiple datacenter deployments.

Hybrid Random Partitioner using Order Preserving Partitioner

An important decision when setting up your cluster is choosing a **Partitioner.** Two common choices are the **Random Partitioner** (**RP**) and the **Order Preserving Partitioner** (**OPP**).

The Random Partitioner hashes the user supplied key and uses the result to place this data on nodes in the cluster. The hash function distributes the data roughly evenly across the cluster in a pseudo random order.

The Order Preserving Partitioner uses the key itself to determine which nodes on the cluster the data should be stored on. This stores the keys in order, which allows ordered **Range Scans** on keys. If the keys do not have an even distribution, nodes can become unbalanced and some will have more data than others.

This recipe shows how to use an Order Preserving Partitioner and hash the values on the client side, achieving a similar effect to the Random Partitioner.

Getting ready

The partitioner used is a global setting that can only be set when the cluster is first initialized. To change the partitioner, you must remove all data in your cluster and start again.

How to do it...

In `conf/cassandra.yaml`

```
partitioner: org.apache.cassandra.dht.OrderPreservingPartitioner:
```

1. Create `src/hpcas/c06/HybridDemo.java`:

```
package hpcas.c06;
import hpcas.c03.*;
import java.math.BigInteger;
import java.nio.ByteBuffer;
import org.apache.cassandra.thrift.*;
import org.apache.cassandra.utils.FBUtilities;public class
HybridDemo {
    public static void main(String[] args) throws Exception {
        FramedConnWrapper fcw = new FramedConnWrapper( Util.
envOrProp("host"),
                Integer.parseInt(Util.envOrProp("port")));
        fcw.open();
        Cassandra.Client client = fcw.getClient();
```

2. Use the `describe_keyspace` method and compare the result to the expected class name for the `OrderPreservingPartitioner` and exit if the result does not match:

```
if ( ! client.describe_partitioner().equals(
            "org.apache.cassandra.dht.
OrderPreservingPartitioner")){
        System.out.println("You are not using
OrderPreservingPartitioner." +
 "You are using "
+client.describe_partitioner());
        System.exit(1);
    }
```

3. Check for the existence of the `phonebook` keyspace. If it does not exist, create a keyspace and a column family for `phonebook` and `user`:

```
if ( ! Util.listKeyspaces(client).contains("phonebook") ) {
    client.system_add_keyspace(
            Util.createSimpleKSandCF("phonebook", "phonebook",
3)        );
    client.system_add_keyspace(
      Util.createSimpleKSandCF("user", "user", 3));
    Thread.sleep(1000);
}
```

4. Next, insert entries into the `phonebook` column family. Notice the key used for the insert is the name unaltered:

```
String [] names = new String [] {"al", "bob", "cindy"};
for ( String name : names ){
  client.set_keyspace("phonebook");
  client.insert(ByteBuffer.wrap( name.getBytes("UTF-8")),
        Util.simpleColumnParent("phonebook"),
        Util.simpleColumn("phone", "555-555-555"),
ConsistencyLevel.ONE);
```

5. Use the `FButilities.md5hash` method to generate an **md5 checksum**. Left pad the name with two characters from the hash:

```
client.set_keyspace("user");
    BigInteger i = FBUtilities.md5hash(ByteBuffer.wrap
      (name.getBytes("UTF-8")));
    StringBuilder sb = new
     StringBuilder(i.toString().substring(0,2));
    sb.append(name);
    client.insert(ByteBuffer.wrap(sb.toString().
getBytes("UTF-8")),
            Util.simpleColumnParent("user"),
            Util.simpleColumn("password", "secret"),
ConsistencyLevel.ONE);
    }
  fcw.close();
  }
}
```

6. Connect to Cassandra using the `cassandra-cli`. Change to the `phonebook` keyspace with the `use` command, and then use the `list` command to range scan through the `phonebook` column family:

```
$<cassandra_home>/bin/cassandra-cli

[default] use phonebook;

[default@phonebook] list phonebook;

Using default limit of 100

-------------------

RowKey: al

=> (column=70686f6e65, value=3535352d3535352d353535,
timestamp=12307009989944)

-------------------

RowKey: bob
```

```
=> (column=70686f6e65, value=3535352d3535352d353535,
timestamp=12307242917168)

-------------------

RowKey: cindy

=> (column=70686f6e65, value=3535352d3535352d353535,
timestamp=12307245916538)


3 Rows Returned.
```

7. Change to the user keyspace and list the user column family:

```
[default] use user;

[default@user] list user;

Using default limit of 100

-------------------

RowKey: 12bob

=> (column=70617373776f7264, value=736563726574,
timestamp=12556213919473)

-------------------

RowKey: 13al

=> (column=70617373776f7264, value=736563726574,
timestamp=12556210336153)

-------------------

RowKey: 68cindy

=> (column=70617373776f7264, value=736563726574,
timestamp=12556258382038)


3 Rows Returned.
```

How it works...

By generating an MD5 check-sum from the key, we randomize which node the data for that key will be stored on. This achieves a similar effect to that of using RandomPartitioner. Range scans performed on the phonebook column family return results in alphabetical order. Range scans performed on the user column family return data in a pseudo random order, which should balance data across the cluster as the RandomPartitioner would.

There's more...

Choosing a partitioner is an important decision that cannot be changed. To experiment with this option, using a multiple node cluster in your test environment can help determine the distribution of your row keys.

Scripting a multiple instance installation with OOP

Modify the recipe in *Chapter 1, Scripting a multiple instance installation* to create a test cluster using the `OrderPreservingPartitioner` by adding the highlighted text below.

Copy the file `scripts/ch1/multiple_instances.sh` to `scripts/ch6/multiple_instances_ordered.sh` and make the highlighted changes.

```
    sed -i "s|8080|800${i}|g" ${TAR_EXTRACTS_TO}-${i}/conf/cassandra-
env.sh
      RP= org.apache.cassandra.dht.RandomPartitioner

      OPP= org.apache.cassandra.dht. OrderPreservingPartitioner

      sed -i "s|${RP}|${OPP}|g" \
      ${TAR_EXTRACTS_TO}-${i}/conf/cassandra.yaml
done
popd
```

Using different hash algorithms

This recipe used the `md5hash()` method used internally by Cassandra. Different algorithms can be used that may be less computationally expensive while still achieving good entropy.

Storing large objects

The row data stored in Cassandra is typically smaller in size, between a few bytes to a few thousand bytes. Some use cases may wish to store entire file or binary data that could be megabytes or gigabytes in size. Storing large files with a single set operation is difficult. This is because the underlying transport layer does not have streaming capability and is designed around smaller objects. This recipe demonstrates how to store large objects or files by breaking them up into small parts and storing the parts across multiple columns of a single key.

How to do it...

1. Create a file `src/hpcas/c06/LargeFile.java`.

```
package hpcas.c06;
import hpcas.c03.*;
import java.io.*;
```

```
import java.nio.ByteBuffer;
import java.text.DecimalFormat;
import org.apache.cassandra.thrift.*;

public class LargeFile {
```

2. By default, we use a block size of 128 bytes. This can be much larger, but the request cannot be larger than the frame size, which default to 16 MB:

```
private static final int block_size = 128;
public static void main(String[] args) throws Exception {
    FramedConnWrapper fcw = new FramedConnWrapper(
            Util.envOrProp("host"),
            Integer.parseInt(Util.envOrProp("port")));
```

3. Open an input stream to this file to the user specified file:

```
File f = new File(Util.envOrProp("thefile"));
ByteBuffer fileName =ByteBuffer.wrap(f.toString()
.getBytes("UTF-8"));
BufferedInputStream inputStream =
        new BufferedInputStream(new FileInputStream(f));
byte buffer[] = new byte[block_size];
fcw.open();
Cassandra.Client client = fcw.getClient();
client.set_keyspace("filedata");
int read = 0; int blockCount=0;
DecimalFormat format = new DecimalFormat("00000");
ColumnParent cp = new ColumnParent();
cp.setColumn_family("filedata");
```

4. Begin reading data from the file one `buffer` at a time. For each buffer being read, increment the `blockCount` variable. Use the `blockCount` as the name of the column and fill the value with the `buffer`:

```
do {
    read = inputStream.read(buffer);
    if(read != -1) {
        Column block = new Column();
        block.setValue(buffer);
        block.setName(format.format(blockCount++)
.getBytes("UTF-8"));
        client.insert(fileName, cp, block, ConsistencyLevel.ONE);
    }
} while (read != -1);
inputStream.close();
fcw.close();
}
}
```

5. Create the `filedata` keyspace and column family:

```
[default@moviereview] create keyspace filedata;

[default@moviereview] use filedata;

Authenticated to keyspace: filedata

[default@filedata] create column family filedata;
```

6. Run the application (it produces no output):

```
$ thefile=/home/edward/encrypt/hpcbuild/run.sh host=127.0.0.1
port=9160 ant -DclassToRun=hpcas.c06.LargeFile run
```

7. As long as the file loaded was not a binary file, the CLI can be configured to display the data as `ascii`:

```
[default@filedata] assume filedata comparator as ascii;

[default@filedata] assume filedata validator as ascii;
```

8. List the column family to display the contents of the file:

```
[default@filedata] list filedata;

Using default limit of 100

RowKey: /home/edward/encrypt/hpcbuild/run.sh

=> (column=00000, value=CP=dist/lib/hpcas.jar

for i in lib/*.jar ; do

  CP=$CP:$i

done

#conf=/home/edward/hpcas/apache-cassandra-0.7.0-beta2-1/conf
...
```

How it works...

Rather than attempting to store a file under a single key and column, the file is broken up into smaller pieces and stored across multiple columns. This is done because the transport protocol has to buffer objects completely in memory to transmit them, and because the frame size for that transport is smaller than some files.

There's more...

This approach stores all the blocks of a file under a single row key and thus on a single set of nodes. Another possible design may be to store the blocks of the file in different row keys. This will spread the blocks of a single file across multiple nodes.

Using Cassandra for distributed caching

Cassandra has several variables that can be configured for each keyspace and column family that drastically change the profile of how it operates. In typical caching use cases, the amount of write and update traffic is low compared to the amount of read traffic. Additionally, the size of the data may be relatively small. This recipe shows how to set up a keyspace and column family for this type of workload.

How to do it...

1. Create a keyspace with a high replication factor (assume this is a 10-node cluster):

   ```
   $ <cassandra_home>/bin/cassandra-cli
   [default] create keyspace cache with replication_factor=10;
   [default] use cache;
   ```

2. Create a column family with a low `read_repair_chance` and settings `rows_cached` to 100000:

   ```
   [default@cache] create column family cache with read_repair_
   chance=.05 and rows_cached=100000;
   ```

Clients should read at consistency level ONE.

How it works...

With a replication factor of 10, each write uses resources on each node. This does not scale writes because each node must maintain a copy of all the data in the keyspace. Because `read_repair_chance` is set to a low value, read repairs will rarely be triggered as long as clients use consistency level ONE on read operations. By increasing replication factor and reading at ONE, more nodes can be used to serve the same data set. This is useful when common data is read intensely.

Storing large or infrequently accessed data in a separate column family

In many cases it is suggested to store all data related to a key in a single column family. This allows applications to fetch data by having to seek only a single key. This is not always the best option, however, and this recipe demonstrates a case where storing the data in two separate column families is preferred.

For this recipe, assume the source data to be inserted as the following table:

id	height	age	weight	quote (infrequently accessed)
bsmith	71"	32	160	Always bear in mind that your own resolution to succeed is more important than any other. -Abraham Lincoln
tjones	66"	17	140	All mankind is divided into three classes: those that are immovable, those that are movable, and those that move. -Benjamin Franklin

How to do it...

Write the data across two column families.

```
[default@unknown] create keyspace user_info  with strategy_options =
[{replication_factor:3}];
[default@unknown] create column family user_info with rows_cached=5000;
[default@unknown] use user_info;
[default@user_info] set user_info['bsmith']['height']='71';
[default@user_info] set user_info['bsmith']['age']='32';
[default@user_info] set user_info['bsmith']['weight']='160';
[default@unknown] create keyspace extra_info  with strategy_options =
[{replication_factor:2}]
[default@user_info] use extra_info;
[default@user_info] create columnfamily extra_info with keys_cached=5000;
[default@user_info] set extra_info['bsmith']['quote']='Always bear in
mind....';
```

How it works...

For the example data, of the five columns that need to be stored, the `quote` data is many times larger than all the other columns combined. Since this data is not accessed as frequently as the other columns, it is stored in the `extra_info` column family.

This design has several advantages. Each keyspace has a different replication factor. The `extra_info` family uses a lower replication factor, which saves disk space. For the other `user_info` keyspace, the standard replication factor of 3 was chosen.

Each keyspace is a folder

Each keyspace corresponds to a folder under the data directory. These folders can be separate physical disks.

Also, by separating the data into two column families, two separate caching policies are utilized. The `user_info` has a small and predictable row size and a row cache was used. The `extra_info` data can have an unpredictable size, thus the key cache was used.

Storing and searching edge graph data in Cassandra

Graph databases are used to store structures based on data from graph theory. Graph databases have a concept of nodes that are entries and edges that connect one node to another. Typically, graph databases are used to determine data that is closely related, as in the following image:

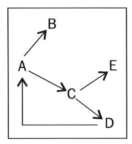

This recipe shows how to use, store, and traverse a simple graph database.

Getting ready

Create a keyspace and column family to store the graph data and insert some sample data into it.

```
[default@unknown] connect localhost/9160;
[default@unknown] create keyspace graph;
[default@unknown] use graph;
[default@graph] create column family graph;
[default@graph] set graph['a']['b']='';
[default@graph] set graph['a']['c']='';
[default@graph] set graph['c']['d']='';
[default@graph] set graph['d']['a']='';
[default@graph] set graph['c']['e']='';
```

How to do it...

1. Create `<hpc_build>/src/hpcas/c06/Graph.java`:

```
package hpcas.c06;

import hpcas.c03.FramedConnWrapper;
import hpcas.c03.Util;
import java.nio.ByteBuffer;
import java.util.*;

import org.apache.cassandra.thrift.*;

public class Graph {
  FramedConnWrapper fcw;
  Cassandra.Client client;

  public Graph(String host,int port) throws Exception {
    fcw = new FramedConnWrapper(host, port);
    fcw.open();
    client = fcw.getClient();
    client.set_keyspace("graph");
  }
```

Graph traversal is done with a recursive method. Recursive methods commonly have a long signature because they need to pass data between calls. Creating a **kickoff** method with a smaller signature is suggested.

```
public void traverse(int depth, byte[] start) {
  Set<String> seen = new HashSet<String>();
  traverse(depth, start, seen, 0);
}
```

To traverse a graph, a few pieces of information are needed: the first is a starting point, the next a stopping condition, and the third a list of already seen nodes to prevent cycles, and a depth counter to control how many recursions. Notice that this method is declared `private`. The only way to call it is through the kickoff method defined previously.

```
private void traverse(int depth, byte[] start,
        Set<String> seen, int currentLevel) {
  if (currentLevel>depth)
    return;
  for (int j=0;j<currentLevel;j++)
    System.out.print("\t");
  System.out.println(new String (start));
  if (seen.contains(new String(start))){
```

```
        for (int j=0;j<currentLevel;j++)
          System.out.print("\t");
        System.out.println("loop detected");
        return;
      }
      seen.add( new String(start));
      ColumnParent cp = new ColumnParent();
      cp.setColumn_family("graph");
      SlicePredicate predicate = new SlicePredicate();
      SliceRange sr = new SliceRange();
      sr.setStart(new byte[0]);
      sr.setFinish(new byte[0]);
      sr.setCount(10000);
      predicate.setSlice_range(sr);
      try {
        List<ColumnOrSuperColumn> results = client.get_slice
        (ByteBuffer.wrap(start), cp, predicate, ConsistencyLevel.
  ONE);
        for ( ColumnOrSuperColumn c : results) {
          traverse(depth, c.column.getName(),seen,currentLevel+1);
        }
      } catch (Exception ex) {
        System.out.println(ex);
      }
    }

  public static void main(String[] args) throws Exception {
    Graph g = new Graph(Util.envOrProp("host")
            , Integer.parseInt(Util.envOrProp("port")));
    g.traverse(Integer.parseInt( Util.envOrProp("depth") )
            ,Util.envOrProp("startAt").getBytes());
  }
}
```

2. Run the application, supplying a node to start at using the startAt parameter and a depth for recursion into the graph:

```
$ startAt=a depth=5 host=127.0.0.1 port=9160 ant
-DclassToRun=hpcas.c06.Graph run

run:

    [java] a
    [java]     b
    [java]     c
```

```
[java]          d
[java]           a
[java]           loop detected
[java]          e
```

How it works...

The edge data between elements is one dimensional—A -> B does not mean B->A. Each node is a single column, the row key is the name of the node, each column is the name of a node this node is related to, and the value is unneeded and left empty.

Inside the recursive `traverse` method, `getSlice` is called against the start node. It returns the key, if it exists, and the columns returned are the related nodes. If the related node does not exist in the set of already seen nodes, and the max depth has not been exceeded, a recursive called will be done using the related node.

Developing secondary data orderings or indexes

The row key determines which nodes the data is stored on. The row key is also used to locate the data on disk in the underlying data files. These factors make searching by row key optimal. The columns of a row key are sorted by the column name, making searching for specific columns inside a specific key optimal. At times, one or more ordering of data may be required. Storing data multiple times in different ways can be done to support different requests. This recipe shows how to create two orderings of a mailbox—the first being efficient to search messages by time, and another to search messages by user.

Getting ready

Create the required keyspace and column families for this recipe.

```
[default@unknown] create keyspace mail;

[default@unknown] use mail;

[default@mail] create column family subject with comparator='LongType';

[default@mail] create column family fromIndex with comparator='LongType';
```

How to do it...

1. Create `scr/hpcas/c06/SecondaryIndex.java`:

```java
package hpcas.c06;

import hpcas.c03.*;
import java.io.*;
import java.nio.ByteBuffer;
import java.util.List;
import java.util.concurrent.atomic.AtomicInteger;
import org.apache.cassandra.thrift.*;

public class SecondaryIndex {

  private FramedConnWrapper fcw;
  private Cassandra.Client client;

  private static ColumnParent subjectParent =new ColumnParent();
  private static ColumnParent fromParent = new ColumnParent();
  private static AtomicInteger ai = new AtomicInteger();

  static {
    subjectParent.setColumn_family("subject");
    fromParent.setColumn_family("fromIndex");
  }

  public SecondaryIndex(String host, int port) {
    fcw = new FramedConnWrapper(host, port);
    try {
      fcw.open();
    } catch (Exception ex) {
      System.out.println(ex);
    }
    client = fcw.getClient();
  }
```

A message is inserted into two separate column families. The `subject` column family uses the mailbox name as a row key and orders the columns by a message ID. The `fromIndex` column family is also ordered by the message ID, but uses a composite key of the sender and the receiver as the row key.

```java
  public void sendMessage(String to,String subject, String body,
String from) {
    Column message = new Column();
    byte [] messageId = getId();
```

```
      message.setName(messageId);
      message.setValue(subject.getBytes());

      Column index = new Column();
      index.setName(messageId);
      index.setValue(subject.getBytes());
      try {
        client.set_keyspace("mail");
        client.insert(ByteBuffer.wrap(to.getBytes()), subjectParent,
message, ConsistencyLevel.ONE);
        client.insert(ByteBuffer.wrap((to +"/"+ from).getBytes()),
fromParent, index, ConsistencyLevel.ONE);
      } catch (Exception ex) {
        System.err.println(ex);
      }
    }
```

The `searchFrom` method is used to quickly locate messages to and from some specific users.

```
    public void searchFrom(String mailbox, String from){
      SlicePredicate predicate = new SlicePredicate();
      SliceRange sr = new SliceRange();
      sr.setCount(1000);
      sr.setReversed(true);
      sr.setStart(new byte[0]);
      sr.setFinish(new byte[0]);
      predicate.setSlice_range(sr);
      try {
        client.set_keyspace("mail");
        List<ColumnOrSuperColumn> results=client.get_slice(
                ByteBuffer.wrap((mailbox + "/" + from).getBytes()),
                fromParent, predicate, ConsistencyLevel.ONE);
        for (ColumnOrSuperColumn c : results){
          System.out.println( new String(c.column.getValue()) );
        }
      } catch (Exception ex) {
        System.err.println(ex);
      }
    }
```

This method generates message IDs.

```
    public byte [] getId()  {
      ByteArrayOutputStream bos = new ByteArrayOutputStream();
      DataOutputStream dos = new DataOutputStream(bos);
      try {
```

```
            dos.writeLong((long) ai.getAndAdd(1));
            dos.flush();
        } catch (IOException ex){ System.out.println(ex);}
        return  bos.toByteArray() ;
    }

    public static void main(String[] args) throws Exception {
        SecondaryIndex si = new SecondaryIndex(
                Util.envOrProp("host"),
                Integer.parseInt(Util.envOrProp("port")));
        si.sendMessage("bob@site.pvt","Have you seen my tennis
racket?",
                "Let me know if you find it.","kelly@example.pvt");
        si.sendMessage("bob@site.pvt","Check out my new book!",
                "It is called High Performance Cassandra."
        ,"edward@example.pvt");
        si.sendMessage("bob@site.pvt","Nevermind about the racket",
                "I found it in the car","kelly@example.pvt");
        si.searchFrom(Util.envOrProp("to"),Util.envOrProp("from"));
    }
}
```

2. Run the program from the command line searching for messages to and from specific users:

```
$ host=127.0.0.1 port=9160 to=bob@site.pvt from=edward@example.pvt
ant -DclassToRun=hpcas.c06.SecondaryIndex run

run:
    [java] Check out my new book!
```

How it works...

This recipe stores data from messages in two separate columns families. Storing data in multiple times increases the overall disk usage. However, the cost can be justified because the data can be stored in a way that is optimal for specific requests. The `subject` column family is useful for looking up messages for a user by time. The `fromIndex` column family is designed to help find messages from a specific user.

See also...

In *Chapter 3, Application Programmer Interface* the recipe *Working with secondary indexes*.

7
Administration

In this chapter, you will learn the following recipes:

- ▶ Defining seed nodes for Gossip Communication
- ▶ Nodetool Move: Moving a node to a specific ring location
- ▶ Nodetool Remove: Removing a downed node
- ▶ Nodetool Decomission: Removing a live node
- ▶ Joining nodes quickly with auto_bootstrap set to false
- ▶ Copying SSTables as an auto_bootstrap alternative
- ▶ Nodetool Repair: When to use anti-entropy repair
- ▶ Nodetool Drain: Stable files on upgrade
- ▶ Lowering gc_grace for faster tombstone cleanup
- ▶ Scheduling Major Compaction
- ▶ Using nodetool snapshot for backups
- ▶ Clearing snapshots with nodetool clearsnapshot
- ▶ Restoring from a snapshot
- ▶ Exporting data to JSON with sstable2json
- ▶ Nodetool cleanup: Removing excess data
- ▶ Nodetool Compact: Defragment data and remove deleted data from disk

Defining seed nodes for Gossip Communication

Cassandra has no single point of failure or master nodes. Instead, it uses an internal process called **Gossip** to communicate changes about the topology of the **Ring** between nodes. **Seeds** are a list that a node attempts to contact on startup to begin gossiping. This recipe shows how to define seed nodes.

Getting ready

The technique for defining Seeds can vary based on the type and size of your deployment. This recipe describes the process for simple deployments using `org.apache.Cassandra.locator.SimpleStrategy`. For multiple datacenter deployments, place one or more seed in each datacenter, refer to *Chapter 8, Multiple Datacenter Deployments*.

How to do it...

For the cluster of ten nodes: `cassandra01.domain.pvt (10.0.0.1)` - `cassandra10.domain.pvt (10.0.0.10)`

1. Open `<cassandra_home>/conf/cassandra.yaml` and locate the **seeds** section.

   ```
   seeds:
       -   10.0.0.1
       -   10.0.0.2
   ```

2. Make this change to each node in the cluster. Restart Cassandra for this change to take effect.

There's more

Seeds are easy to configure. However, there are a few subtle things to keep in mind when configuring them.

IP vs Hostname

It is suggested to use an IP address instead of a hostname in the seed list. This should allow the cluster to continue functioning even with DNS issues since Cassandra communicates exclusively by IP address.

Keep the seed list synchronized

The seed list should be the same for every node in your deployment. This is not a strict requirement for the gossip protocol to work, but there are cases during failures where using different nodes can cause strange results. Consider using a configuration management tool such as Puppet to keep configuration files in sync.

Seed nodes do not auto bootstrap

At least one seed node needs to be specified during initial deployment. Seed nodes will not auto bootstrap. For a joining node to receive data from other nodes, do not include its hostname or IP in its seed list. After it has bootstrapped and joined the cluster, it can be put in any seed list for any node, including itself.

Choosing the correct number of seed nodes

The number of seed nodes should be some factor of the cluster size. Nodes starting up will attempt to contact all configured seed nodes to learn about the topology of the cluster. Ensure at least one seed is running at all times. For deployments of less than ten, two or three seed nodes are sufficient. For larger clusters, more may be needed.

Nodetool Move: Moving a node to a specific ring location

Cassandra uses a **Consistent Hashing** to divide the data in a cluster between nodes. Each node has an **Initial Token** that represents its logical position on the **ring** and what data it should hold. There are many situations where a node is not placed at an optimal position in the ring. This may be because of the addition or removal of other nodes. It also may be because while using `OrderPreservingPartitioner`, hotspots can naturally develop due to uneven key distribution. This recipe shows how to use `nodetool move` to adjust a node's position.

Getting ready

Use the recipe *Calculating Correct Initial Tokens* from *Chapter 1* to determine what the ideal tokens should be.

How to do it...

1. Run `nodetool ring` and determine how unbalanced the cluster is:

```
$ <cassandra_home>/bin/nodetool -h localhost -p 8001 ring
Address          Load           Owns     Token

127.0.0.3        Up     Normal   10.43 KB        29.84%   48084680596
54490950691536852350993814
```

```
127.0.0.4        Up      Normal   10.43 KB          34.04%  10599911091
74803633547458635908541720046
127.0.0.5        Up      Normal   10.43 KB           9.82%  12270622935
72125582338719014391201388764
127.0.0.1        Up      Normal   10.43 KB           5.90%  13275039505
54640412217788744207874723292
127.0.0.2        Up      Normal   10.43 KB          20.40%  16745517058
8521173062172773965470038351
```

2. Notice that in the **Owns** column, some nodes own larger portions of the ring than others. Run the `InitialTokens` application and see what the ideal tokens should be:

```
$ tokens=5 ant -DclassToRun=hpcas.c01.InitialTokens run
run:
    [java] 0
    [java] 34028236692093846346337460743176821145
    [java] 68056473384187692692674921486353642290
    [java] 102084710076281539039012382229530463435
    [java] 136112946768375385385349842972707284580
```

Consider a token carefully

Unless the number of nodes in the cluster is growing by exactly double, not specifying the `InitialToken` will likely result in a non-optimal number being picked. The node on top of the list should have a token of **0**. Instead, it has **48084680596544909506915368523509938144**. Use the move command to move two nodes.

Moving large amounts of data can take a long time

The more data a node has on it, the longer an operation such as move will take. Also, these operations are intensive and are best done at times of low traffic.

```
$<cassandra_home>/bin/nodetool -h 127.0.0.1 -p 8001 move 0
$<cassandra_home>/bin/nodetool -h 127.0.0.2 -p 8002 move 340282366
92093846346337460743176821145
```

3. Run `nodetool ring` after the `nodetool move` operations have completed:

```
$ <cassandra_home>/bin/nodetool -h 127.0.0.1 -p 8001 ring
Address          Status State   Load          Owns      Token
127.0.0.1        Up      Normal   17.58 KB      27.88%   0
127.0.0.2        Up      Normal   12.57 KB      20.00%   34028236692
09384634633746074317682114 5
...
```

How it works...

Nodetool Move is a one-step way to accomplish the two-part process of removing and adding a node. It combines a **Nodetool Decomission** with an **AutoBootstrap** startup.

Behind the scenes, `nodetool move` causes the node to move data to other nodes before leaving the cluster. The node then re-joins at the location specified by the user. Other nodes compute data that belongs on the rejoined node and transmit that data back to it.

In the example, using `nodetool move` corrects imbalances of data across the cluster. Before the move, the first two nodes owned **29 percent** and **34 percent**. After the move, they owned **27 percent** and **20 percent**. Once all the proper move operations are complete, the owned percentage would be **20 percent** across all nodes. It is important to keep clusters as close to balanced as possible.

Nodetool Remove: Removing a downed node

If a node fails, it is not assumed lost forever. The other nodes in the cluster become aware that it is down through gossip. If enabled, the other nodes will store **Hinted Handoff** messages, which are writes destined to downed system. They will attempt to re-deliver the hinted messages when they detect the destination node is up again. If a node is lost forever, either because of hardware failure or because it is no longer needed, the administrator must actively acknowledge the failure using `nodetool removetoken`.

How to do it...

1. Determine the token of the node to be removed. The node must be in the Down state:

    ```
    $<cassandra_home>/bin/nodetool -h 127.0.0.1 -p 8001 ring
    Address          Status State   Load           Owns     Token
                                                             12270622935721255823
    3871901439120138764
    127.0.0.1        Up      Normal  17.58 KB       27.88%   0
    127.0.0.2        Up      Normal  12.57 KB       20.00%   34028236692
    09384634633746074 3176821145
    127.0.0.3        Up      Normal  20.51 KB       8.26%    48084680596
    5449095069153685235 09938144
    127.0.0.4        Up      Normal  20.51 KB       34.04%   10599911091
    7480363354745863590854172046
    127.0.0.5        Down    Normal  20.51 KB       9.82%    12270622935
    721255823387 1901439120138764
    ```

2. Use the `nodetool removetoken` command to remove the node in the Down state **127.0.0.5**:

    ```
    $<cassandra_home>/bin/nodetool -h 127.0.0.1 -p 8001 removetoken 12
    270622935721255823387 1901439120138764
    ```

The `nodetool removetoken` operation can take some
time. You can run the command again with the optional
`status` argument at that end to see the progress.

3. Run `nodetool ring` again. When the removal is complete, the list should be one
    element shorter:

```
$ <cassandra_home>/bin/nodetool -h 127.0.0.1 -p 8001 ring
Address           Status State   Load          Owns    Token
                                              105999110917480363354 7458
63590854172046
127.0.0.1         Up     Normal  17.58 KB      37.70%  0
127.0.0.2         Up     Normal  12.57 KB      20.00%  340...
127.0.0.3         Up     Normal  20.51 KB      8.26%   480...
127.0.0.4         Up     Normal  20.51 KB      34.04%  105...
```

How it works...

Each keyspace has a configurable **Replication Factor.** When a node is removed, Cassandra
begins actively replicating the missing data until it is all stored on the number of nodes
specified by the replication factor.

See also...

The `nodetool removetoken` command can only be run on a node in the `Down` state. The
next recipe, *Nodetool Decommission: Removing a live node* shows how to remove a node in
the `Up` state.

Nodetool Decommission: Removing a live node

Decommission is the process for which a node in the `UP` state is removed. This recipe shows
how to use `nodetool decommission`.

How to do it...

1. Use `nodetool ring` and find the **Address** of a node to remove:

```
$ <cassandra_home>/bin/nodetool -h 127.0.0.1 -p 8001 ring
Address           Status State   Load          Owns    Token
127.0.0.1         Up     Normal  17.58 KB      37.70%  0
```

```
127.0.0.2        Up      Normal   12.57 KB         20.00%   340...
127.0.0.3        Up      Normal   20.51 KB         8.26%    480...
127.0.0.4        Up      Normal   20.51 KB         34.04%   105...
```

2. Select node **127.0.0.3** for decommission and remove it with `nodetool decomission`.

 Be careful not to confuse `decommission` with `removetoken`. The host `nodetool` connects to with `nodetool decommission` will be the one removed. With `removetoken`, the node with the specified token will be removed.

```
$<cassandra_home>/bin/nodetool -h 127.0.0.3 -p 8003 decommission
```

Depending on the amount of data in your cluster, this operation can take a long time. The machine first **anti-compacts** the data it has and then **streams** the data to the node that will now be responsible for that data. Use `nodetool ring` over time and the decommissioned host will eventually vanish from your list. Review the logs of the nodes to see how the compaction and streaming are progressing. You can also use `nodetool compactionstats` and `nodetool streams` to view the progress.

```
$<cassandra_home>/bin/nodetool -h 127.0.0.1 -p 8001 ring
Address          Status State   Load             Owns     Token
127.0.0.1        Up     Normal  22.56 KB         37.70%   0
127.0.0.2        Up     Normal  17.55 KB         20.00%   340...
127.0.0.4        Up     Normal  12.53 KB         42.30%   105...
```

How it works...

`Nodetool decommission` has the same effect as `Nodetool remove`, but is more efficient because the node leaving the cluster helps calculate and transmit the data that will need to be moved to other nodes before leaving.

Joining nodes quickly with auto_bootstrap set to false

By default, the nodes of a cluster have `auto_bootstrap` set to false. With this setting when a node starts up, it does not begin migrating data to itself from other nodes. This recipe shows how to use this setting and explains the caveats that come with it.

Generating SSH keys for password-less interaction

Several recipes in this chapter will use password-less access to the **OpenSSL** tools such as `ssh`, `scp`, and `rsync`. This recipe shows how to generate a **public private SSH key** pair.

How to do it...

1. On a clean node that has not bootstraped, edit `<cassandra_home>/conf/cassandra.yaml`:

   `auto_bootstrap: false`

2. Start the instance.

How it works...

With `auto_bootstrap` set to `false`, the node joins the cluster immediately and starts serving requests. Setting `auto_bootstrap` to `true` means other nodes in the cluster recompute and transfer data for the new node before it comes online.

There's more...

The data of a node that did not `auto_bootstrap` can be populated in several ways:

Normal write traffic

After the node is joined, it is responsible for a part of the **Token Ring**. Write operations will be delivered to this node as normal. This keeps newly written data in sync, but does nothing for already existing data that this node is now responsible for.

Read Repair

Read operations trigger the **Read Repair** process. The **Natural Endpoints** for the data are compared and the most recent timestamp is the final value. Out of sync copies are updated. For read repair to deliver the consistent data, applications must be reading at consistency level `Quorum` or higher. Reading at `One` causes the first read to return an empty or stale result and the data is repaired after the result is returned to the client.

Anti-Entropy Repair

Anti-Entropy Repair is an intensive process that calculates the differences between data on nodes and then streams the differing data between nodes. The anti-entropy repair ends up being more computational work on the cluster than joining a node using auto-bootstrap. Thus, auto-bootstrap is preferred.

How to do it...

1. Generate an SSH public private key pair. When prompted for a passphrase, leave it empty:

```
$ ssh-keygen
Generating public/private rsa key pair.
Enter file in which to save the key (/root/.ssh/id_rsa):
Enter passphrase (empty for no passphrase):
Enter same passphrase again:
Your identification has been saved in /root/.ssh/id_rsa.
Your public key has been saved in /root/.ssh/id_rsa.pub.
The key fingerprint is:
XX:XX:XX:XX:XX:XX:XX:XX:XX:XX:XX:XX:XX:XX:XX:XX user@host
```

2. Use `rsync` to transfer the key to the destination server:

```
$ rsync ~/.ssh/id_rsa.pub root@cassandra05-new:~/
```

3. Append the public key to the `authorized_keys` file and ensure the permissions are strong. SSH typically denies access if the ownership of its configuration files are too weak:

```
$ ssh root@cassandra05-new
root@cassandra05-new password:
$ cat id_rsa.pub >> ~/.ssh/authorized_keys
$ chmod 700 ~/.ssh
$ chmod 600 .ssh/authorized_keys
$ exit
```

If done correctly, connecting to the destination server with `ssh`, `rsync`, and `scp` should not require a password.

How it works...

SSH key pairs allow an alternative to password-based authentication. This ability to run commands on remote machines makes it a fast and simple solution for ad-hoc distributed computing. It is commonly used to run commands on remote computers typically from non-interactive jobs such as rsync-based backups through cron.

These is more

Even though SSH keys are cryptographically secure, they do represent a security risk as they can be used to move from one server to the next or execute remote commands. If a machine is compromised, a key with no passphrase would allow a user to spring to another server. It is highly advised to limit commands an SSH key can execute. See the SSH manual pages for information on restricting these keys.

Copying the data directory to new hardware

The Bootstrap and Anti Entropy Repair processes are generally the best ways to move data to new nodes. In some cases, it is more efficient to move data around with a file copy tool such as `rsync`. This method is efficient when doing a one-to-one move from old hardware to new hardware.

Getting ready

For this example, assume the node `cassandra05` is being replaced by `cassandra05-new` and the Cassandra data directory is `/var/lib/cassandra`. This recipe requires an SSH Server and SSH Client, but any method of transferring binary data such as FTP is sufficient.

How to do it...

1. Create an executable script `/root/sync.sh` that uses the `rsync` command:

    ```
    nohup rsync -av --delete  --progress /v
    ar/lib/cassandra/data \ root@cassandra05-new:/var/lib/cassandra/
    2> /tmp/sync.err \
    1> /tmp/sync.out &

    $ chmod a+x /root/sync.sh
    $ sh /root/sync.sh
    ```

2. On the source server, `cassandra05`, stop the Cassandra process and run the sync again. It will take much less time than the first run because `rsync` only transfers changes in the files. Disable Cassandra so it will not be accidentally started again:

    ```
    $ /etc/init.d/cassandra stop
    $ sh /root/sync.sh
    $ chkconfig cassandra off
    ```

3. Switch the host names and IP addresses of the machines. On the new machine, start Cassandra. Use `nodetool ring` to ensure the cluster is up:

How it works...

The `rsync` command is an intelligent copy tool that calculates rolling check sums and only transfers new or changed parts of files. One of the advantages of `rsync` is that runs after the first one only need to transfer changes. This is ideal for the structured log format of Cassandra's SSTable. The second and third sync may take only seconds!

This technique requires less computation and data movement compared to the process of `nodetool decommission`, new node bootstrap, and then subsequent `nodetool cleanup`. However, it is slightly more intensive on the administrative side. This method is best used when the volume of data per node is very large. As far as the other nodes in the cluster know, the node was offline for a few minutes and is now restarted. They are unaware that the data, IP, and host name moved to new hardware.

There's more

`rsync` has a myriad of options that can change how it works. One option is the ability to exclude data that does not need to be copied with expressions.

```
--exclude='*snapshot*' --exclude='*CommitLog*'
```

The `bwlimit` knob throttles the network usage and, in effect, the disk usage. This can be used so that the added disk activity will not diminish the serving capabilities of the node.

```
--bwlimit=4000
```

A node join using external data copy methods

Cassandra uses `Consistent Hashing` to decide which nodes data should be stored on. When a new node joins the cluster, it becomes responsible for a section of data. That data is calculated and transferred to that node during the bootstrap process. That transferred data is always a subset of data on the node `logicall` right in the ring. One way to achieve a node join is to transfer the data yourself and then run cleanup on both nodes.

Getting ready

Review the *Generating SSH Keys for password-less interaction* recipe for moving data between different physical nodes.

How to do it...

1. Use the `nodetool ring` tool to locate a section of the ring with the most data:

```
$ <cassandra_home>/bin/nodetool -h 127.0.0.1 -p 8001 ring
```

Address	Status State	Load	Owns	Token
				10599911091748036335
4745863590854172046				

```
127.0.0.1          Up        Normal   79.42 KB        37.70%  0

127.0.0.2          Up        Normal   77.55 KB        20.00%  34028236692
09384634633746074317682145

127.0.0.4          Up        Normal   72.53 KB        42.30%  10599911091
74803633547458635908541720 46
```

The node `127.0.0.4` owns 42 percent of the ring. To relieve this imbalance, the joining node should be inserted between `127.0.0.2` and `127.0.0.4`.

2. Insert `127.0.0.5` at `70000000000000000000000000000000000000000`, which will divide that range roughly in half. Edit the `<cassandra_home>/conf/cassandra.yaml` for the 127.0.0.5, the destination node:

    ```
    initial_token: 70000000000000000000000000000000000000000
    ```

    ```
    auto_bootstrap: false
    ```

3. Use `rsync` to copy data from `127.0.0.4` to `127.0.0.5` and either exclude the `system keyspace` or remove it from the destination after the copy:

    ```
    $ rsync -av --delete  --progress    --exclude='*system*' \
    /v
    ar/lib/cassandra/data \ root@127.0.0.5:/var/lib/cassandra/
    ```

4. Start the node and confirm it has correctly joined the cluster using `nodetool ring`:

    ```
    $<cassandra_home>/bin/nodetool -h 127.0.0.1 -p 8001 ring
    ```

Address	Status	State	Load	Owns	Token
127.0.0.1	Up	Normal	79.42 KB	37.70%	
127.0.0.2	Up	Normal	77.55 KB	20.00%	
127.0.0.5	Up	Normal	51.9 KB	33.18%	
127.0.0.4	Up	Normal	72.53 KB	9.12%	

    Just as with auto-bootstrap, some nodes in the cluster are now carrying extra data that they are no longer responsible for. Use `nodetool cleanup` to remove data that is no longer served by other nodes.

    ```
    $<cassandra_home>/bin/nodetool -h 127.0.0.4 -p 8004 cleanup
    ```

How it works...

This technique uses `rsync` to carry out roughly the same process of an auto-bootstrap. The built-in Cassandra bootstrap is the ideal solution in most situations. This solution can be faster particularly if the node is under heavy usage as normally Cassandra would have to use resources to anti-compact and stream the data. Unlike the bootstrap process, `rsync` can be stopped and restarted.

Nodetool Repair: When to use anti-entropy repair

Anti-Entropy Repair, also called **Anti-Entropy Service** or **AES**, is a process where nodes compare their data and ensure data is replicated properly and up-to-date. This recipe explains how to do an anti-entropy repair and the conditions for which it should be ran.

How to do it...

Use `nodetool repair` against a node to be repaired.

```
$<cassandra_home>/bin/nodetool -h 127.0.0.1 -p 8001 repair
```

How it works...

Anti-entropy repair is intensive for disk, CPU, and network resources. It is optimal to run this at times of low traffic. It can create excess copies of data on your nodes. If the storage on nodes grows significantly as a result of AES, use `nodetool compact`. Major compaction should remove duplicate data that resulted from the repair.

There's more...

Anti-entropy-repair should be run on a schedule that matches equal to or lower than the setting for `gc_grace_seconds`. There are also other situations when this operation should be run.

Raising the Replication Factor

If the **Replication Factor** of a Column Family is raised from two to three, data previously stored on two nodes should now be stored on three nodes. Read repair fixes this over time but AES should be run to ensure the node has the proper data as quickly as possible.

Joining nodes without auto-bootstrap

If a node without auto-bootstrap starts with no data, AES will ensure this node gets populated with the correct data.

Loss of corrupted files

If data files such as SSTables, Indexes, Commit Logs, or Bloom Filters are lost or corrupt, AES fixes this by re-synchronizing with other nodes. This is more effective than removing and rejoining the node again.

Nodetool Drain: Stable files on upgrade

Cassandra is designed to be **fail-fast**. It is designed without elaborate shutdown procedures to be resilient and start up properly even after an unplanned shutdown. Sending the daemon process a standard kill should shut the node down properly. A special **Nodetool** operation called **Drain** exists as an alternative to the standard **kill**. This recipe shows how to use drain and under what circumstances it should be used.

How to do it...

1. Use the `nodetool drain` command to shut down a selected node:

    ```
    $ <cassandra_home>/bin/nodetool -h 127.0.0.1 -p 8001 drain
    ```

    Drain can be almost instantaneous or can take a long time depending on the **Commit Log** and **Memtable** settings. Check for the presence of the final message to ensure the drain is complete.

    ```
    $ tail -5 /var/log/cassandra
    ```

2. Use kill to terminate the process:

    ```
    $ kill <cassandra_pid>
    ```

    Future versions of drain may self-terminate and remove the need to run kill.

How it works...

The drain operation stops the nodes from accepting requests. It flushes the Commit Logs to Memtables and then flushes Memtables to SSTables on disk. The next time a node starts up it will not need to re-read its commit logs since those will be empty. This option was originally added to the 0.6.X series in preparation for 0.7.X, which has incompatible Commit Log formats. Users who are paranoid about losing a write should use drain as the log actively acknowledges a clean shutdown.

Lowering gc_grace for faster tombstone cleanup

The SSTable format does not do in-place deletes. Instead, a delete is another write entry known as a **tombstone**. During the compaction process, old versions of columns as well as their tombstones older then GCGraceSeconds can finally be removed. Changing the GCGracePeriod has implications. This recipe shows how to lower GCGraceSeconds and what this change implies.

How to do it...

From the CLI, issue the update column family operation and change the grace seconds time.

```
[default@ks1] update column family cf1 with gc_grace=4000000;
```

How it works...

The default for gc_grace is ten days. Lowering this value is important for data sets that are completely rewritten often. The worst case scenario would be a data set that is completely rewritten every day as the disk would hold many tombstones or old data with newer versions in other SSTables. Lowering this setting to three days allows compactions to reclaim the disk space sooner. Also, it allows some lead time; if an outage happens on a Friday night, you will hopefully be able to enjoy your weekend before dealing with the troubled node.

There's more...

One of the drawbacks of lowering gc_grace deals with data resurrection. Cassandra is a distributed system, and distributed deletes have a complex lifecycle of their own.

Data resurrection

Envision a three-node cluster with nodes A, B, C, a Replication Factor of three, and gc_grace set to one day. On Friday night, node A suffers a power supply failure. The cluster continues on without it. On Saturday, a key X is deleted and Tombstones are written to node B and node C. On Sunday, node B and node C compactions remove all data and Tombstones for key X. Monday morning: node A is repaired and turned on. A read comes into node A for key X. Key X does exist on node A and it happily returns it to the client and Read Repair (if enabled) would recreate the key on nodes B and C!

If a node is shutdown longer than `gc_grace`, you must rebootstrap it to avoid resurrecting deleted data like previously described!

Scheduling Major Compaction

Because **SSTables** are written once and not modified, delete operations are implemented as a special write called a **Tombstone**. A Tombstone is a marker that signifies a column is deleted. **Compaction** is a process that merges multiple SSTables together, rows Tombstoned are removed, while other rows are moved to the same location on disk for more efficiency. After the compaction is done, the source tables are deleted.

Normal Compaction can remove all traces of a key if the Tombstone is older than the `gc_grace` and if the **Bloom Filters** confirm that the key exists in no other SSTables. During **Major Compaction**, all SSTables are merged. Data that is marked as deleted and older than GCGracePeriod will not be present in the new SSTable.

SSTables normally compact only when there are a few like-sized tables. This means that data can still be resident on disk long after it is deleted, waiting for compaction to finally remove it. This recipe shows how to run Major Compaction on a schedule forcing the removal of Tombstones.

How to do it...

1. Create a file `scripts/ch7/ major_compaction_launcher.sh`:

```sh
#!/bin/sh
DELAY_SECONDS=86400
NODE_TOOL=/usr/local/cassandra/bin/nodetool
JMX_PORT=8080
for i in server1 server2 server3 server4 ; do
  ${NODE_TOOL} --host ${i} --port ${JMX_PORT} compact
  echo "compacting ${i}"
  sleep $DELAY_SECONDS
done
```

2. Set the script to be executable, then use the `nohup` command to run the script detached from the console:

```
$ chmod a+x  major_compaction_launcher.sh
$ nohup major_compaction_launcher.sh &
```

How it works...

Compaction is a disk, memory, and CPU-intensive process. The more data to be compacted, the longer this process takes. In a cluster of many nodes, the compaction of a few nodes at a time is absorbed. This script uses a list supplied by the user. It compacts a node, then it sleeps, and then it compacts the next in the list. The `nohup` command detached the process from this way as the user closing that terminal does not stop the script from running.

There's more...

Normally, users will have access to an enterprise-wide task scheduler or configuration management system. For those using Puppet for configuration management, it can handle randomizing when compaction runs.

```
$aminute = fqdn_rand(60)
$ahour = fqdn_rand(24)
$awday = fqdn_rand(7)

cron { "compact":
command => "/usr/local/cassandra/bin/nodetool -h localhost -p 8585
compact",
user => root,
hour => $ahour,
minute => $aminute,
weekday => $awday
}
```

Using nodetool snapshot for backups

One of the benefits of the write-once data file format of Cassandra is that a point in time snapshot backup of data is easy to achieve. Snapshot makes hard-links of files in the data directory to a subfolder. These files are not removed until the snapshot is cleared. This recipe shows how to create snapshots.

Getting ready

List the directory responsible for your keyspaces.

```
$ ls -lh /home/edward/hpcas/data/1/football/
total 48K

-rw-rw-r--. 1 edward edward  111 Mar 25 17:23 teams-f-1-Data.db
-rw-rw-r--. 1 edward edward   16 Mar 25 17:23 teams-f-1-Filter.db
-rw-rw-r--. 1 edward edward   16 Mar 25 17:23 teams-f-1-Index.db
-rw-rw-r--. 1 edward edward 4.2K Mar 25 17:23 teams-f-1-Statistics.db
```

How to do it...

1. Run the snapshot command:

   ```
   $ <cassandra_home>/bin/nodetool -h 127.0.0.1 -p 8001 snapshot
   ```

2. Confirm the snapshot worked. Inside the data directory, a snapshot/<timestamp> folder should exist. The files inside the directory are hard-linked from the data directory at the time of a snapshot .$ ls -lhR /home/edward/hpcas/data/1/ football:

   ```
   /home/edward/hpcas/data/1/football/:
   total 44K
   drwxrwxr-x. 3 edward edward 4.0K Apr 24 12:01 snapshots
   -rw-rw-r--. 2 edward edward  111 Mar 25 17:23 teams-f-1-Data.db
   -rw-rw-r--. 2 edward edward   16 Mar 25 17:23 teams-f-1-Filter.db
   -rw-rw-r--. 2 edward edward   16 Mar 25 17:23 teams-f-1-Index.db
   -rw-rw-r--. 2 edward edward 4.2K Mar 25 17:23 teams-f-1-
   Statistics.db

   /home/edward/hpcas/data/1/football/snapshots:
   total 4.0K
   drwxrwxr-x. 2 edward edward 4.0K Apr 24 12:01 1303660885180

   /home/edward/hpcas/data/1/football/snapshots/1303660885180:
   total 40K
   -rw-rw-r--. 2 edward edward  111 Mar 25 17:23 teams-f-1-Data.db
   -rw-rw-r--. 2 edward edward   16 Mar 25 17:23 teams-f-1-Filter.db
   -rw-rw-r--. 2 edward edward   16 Mar 25 17:23 teams-f-1-Index.db
   -rw-rw-r--. 2 edward edward 4.2K Mar 25 17:23 teams-f-1-
   Statistics.db
   ```

How it works...

Cassandra uses a structured log format for data. SSTables are written once and never edited until they are compacted into other tables and removed. Snapshots maintain a folder with hard links to the original SSTables at the time of the snapshot. These files will not be removed until the snapshots are cleared. Multiple snapshots can be taken.

There's more...

Many common backup tools do incremental or differential backup. This can easily be used to back up Cassandra's data files to a remote system.

See also...

The next recipe, *Clearing snapshots with nodetool clearsnapshot*.

Clearing snapshots with nodetool clearsnapshot

Snapshots are used to make point in time backups of data on a specific node. Each time a snapshot is taken, a folder with hard links to data files are made. When multiple data files are compacted, the old files are no longer needed. However, if snapshots still exist with references to the files, they can now be removed. This recipe shows how to clear all snapshots.

Getting ready

Check for existing snapshots in your Cassandra data directory. If you need to create one, refer to the previous recipe, *Using nodetool snapshot for backups*.

```
$ ls -lh /home/edward/hpcas/data/1/football/snapshots/
total 8.0K
drwxrwxr-x. 2 edward edward 4.0K Apr 24 12:01 1303660885180
drwxrwxr-x. 2 edward edward 4.0K Apr 24 22:50 1303699830608
```

How to do it...

1. Use the `nodetool clearsnapshot` command to remove all existing snapshots:

   ```
   $ <cassandra_home>/bin/nodetool -h 127.0.0.1 -p 8001 clearsnapshot
   ```

2. Check to make sure the snapshot directory has been removed:

   ```
   $ ls -lh /home/edward/hpcas/data/1/football/snapshots/
   ls: cannot access /home/edward/hpcas/data/1/football/snapshots/:
   No such file or directory
   ```

How it works...

The `nodetool clearsnapshot` feature removes all existing snapshot directories and unlinks all the files in them. This allows the data files to be removed and the space to be freed for new data.

Restoring from a snapshot

A snapshot is a copy of the Cassandra data files at a point in time. These files can be the results of a snapshot command or another backup method. This recipe shows how to restore a snapshot.

How to do it...

1. List the Cassandra data directory:

```
$ ls -lh /home/edward/hpcas/data/1/football/
total 40K
drwxrwxr-x. 3 edward edward 4.0K Apr 24 23:20 snapshots
-rw-rw-r--. 1 edward edward  111 Mar 25 20:05 teams-f-2-Data.db
-rw-rw-r--. 1 edward edward   16 Mar 25 20:05 teams-f-2-Filter.db
-rw-rw-r--. 1 edward edward   16 Mar 25 20:05 teams-f-2-Index.db
-rw-rw-r--. 1 edward edward 4.2K Mar 25 20:05 teams-f-2-
Statistics.db
```

2. Stop Cassandra and remove the files from that directory:

```
$ rm /home/edward/hpcas/data/1/football/*.db
```

3. Copy the data from the snapshot directory into the data directory:

```
$ cp snapshots/1303701623423/* /home/edward/hpcas/data/1/football/
$ ls -lh /home/edward/hpcas/data/1/football/
total 44K
drwxrwxr-x. 3 edward edward 4.0K Apr 24 23:20 snapshots
-rw-rw-r--. 1 edward edward  111 Apr 24 23:29 teams-f-1-Data.db
-rw-rw-r--. 1 edward edward   16 Apr 24 23:29 teams-f-1-Filter.db
-rw-rw-r--. 1 edward edward   16 Apr 24 23:29 teams-f-1-Index.db
-rw-rw-r--. 1 edward edward 4.2K Apr 24 23:29 teams-f-1-
Statistics.db
```

4. Start Cassandra.

How it works...

On startup, Cassandra scans its data directories for data files and loads them for serving. By stopping the server and changing the files in the directory, restarting Cassandra will begin serving the data from those files.

There's more...

Data is typically stored on more than a single node. Read operations will read repair and update data. Multiple nodes will have to be restored at once so that updates are not reapplied.

Exporting data to JSON with sstable2json

Exporting data can be used as a backup or to move data to another system. This recipe shows how to use the `sstable2json` tool for exporting data.

How to do it...

Use the `sstable2json` tool to display the data in an SSTable.

```
$ <cassandra_home>/bin/sstable2json /home/edward/hpcas/data/1/football/
teams-f-1-Data.db
{
"4769616e7473": [["41686d6164204272616473686177",
"52427c41686d6164204272616473686177c313233357c343133", 0, false]]
}
```

How it works...

This tool exports the binary data of an `sstable` to a JSON format that can be read by other tools.

There's more...

`Sstable2json` has several options that can help it be used for troubleshooting as well as exporting data.

Extracting specific keys

`Sstable2json` can extract one or more specific keys using `-k` arguments.

```
$ <cassandra_home>/bin/sstable2json /home/edward/hpcas/data/1/football/
teams-f-1-Data.db -k 4769616e7473
```

Excluding specific keys

`Sstable2json` can exclude certain rows using `-x` arguments.

```
$ <cassandra_home>/bin/sstable2json /home/edward/hpcas/data/1/football/
teams-f-1-Data.db -x 4769616e7473
```

Saving the exported JSON to a file

Send the output to standard out to save the results.

```
$ <cassandra_home>/bin/sstable2json /home/edward/hpcas/data/1/football/
teams-f-1-Data.db > /tmp/json.txt
```

Using the xxd command to decode hex values

When a column is row stored only as bytes with no comparator or validator, it is displayed as hex. If the system has the xxd tool, you can decode these.

```
$ echo 4769616e7473 | xxd -r -p
Giants
$ echo 41686d6164204272616473686177 | xxd -r -p
Ahmad Bradshaw
```

Nodetool cleanup: Removing excess data

When a node is added to a Cassandra cluster or an existing node is moved to a new position on the token ring, other systems still retain copies of data they are not responsible for. Nodetool cleanup removes data that does not belong on this node.

How to do it...

Use the IP and JMX port as arguments to nodetool cleanup.

```
$ <cassandra_home>/bin/nodetool -h 127.0.0.1 -p 8001 cleanup
```

Keyspace and Column Family are optional arguments

If called with no arguments, cleanup is run on all keyspaces and column families. The keyspace and column family can be specified at the end of the command to limit the data cleaned up.

How it works...

Cleanup is a special type of compaction that removes data that does not belong on the node. Cleanup is intensive because it has to examine large portions of the data on disk.

There's more...

There are two reasons where running cleanup is required. They are as follows:

Topology changes

The first and most common reason cleanup is needed is a node being added or moved from the token ring. These changes cause the nodes that some data in the cluster belong to shift. Cassandra was designed not to automatically remove data from the old location. The reasoning behind this logic is that if a node has faulty hardware, it will likely fail quickly and keeping the data in the old place for some protects against this.

Hinted handoff and write consistency ANY

The second reason where cleanup is needed is when using hinted handoff and write consistency ANY. During a write, if all the nodes data belongs on are down, a write can be delivered to any node in the cluster. This write will be re-delivered later to the node in which it belongs. No process is in place to remove the hinted handoff data automatically.

See also...

▶ In this chapter, *Nodetool Compact: Defragment data and remove deleted data from disk*

▶ In *Chapter 5, Consistency, Availability, and Partition Tolerance with Cassandra,* the recipe *Choosing availability over consistency write consistency ANY*

Nodetool Compact: Defragment data and remove deleted data from disk

The data files in Cassandra are stored in a structured log format. This design choice has many consequences. Row keys with columns written over time can be spread across many data files. Frequently updated columns may be stored multiple times on disk. The process that merges these tables over time is called compaction. Compaction happens normally as new data files are created. This recipe shows how to force a major compaction that combines multiple data files into a single one.

How to do it...

Use the IP and JMX port as arguments to `nodetool compact`.

```
$ <cassandra_home>/bin/nodetool -h 127.0.0.1 -p 8001 compact
```

Keyspace and Column Family are optional arguments

If called with no arguments, compact is run for all keyspaces and column families. The `keyspace` and `column family` can be specified at the end of the command to limit the data compacted.

How it works...

Major compaction joins multiple data files into a single one. If a row was fragmented across multiple physical data files, it will now be in a single file, which should make reading more efficient. Delete records called tombstones that are past. The `gc_grace` are removed along with their data they mark as deleted, which shrinks the size of the data files.

See also...

In this chapter, *Lowering gc_grace for faster tombstone cleanup*.

8
Multiple Datacenter Deployments

In this chapter, you will learn the following recipes:

- ▶ Changing debugging to determine where read operations are being routed
- ▶ Using IPTables to simulate complex network scenarios in a local environment
- ▶ Choosing IP addresses to work with RackInferringSnitch
- ▶ Scripting a multiple datacenter installation
- ▶ Specifying Rack and Datacenter configuration with a property file snitch
- ▶ Troubleshooting dynamic snitch using JConsole
- ▶ Quorum operations in multi-datacenter environments
- ▶ Using traceroute to troubleshoot latency between datacenters
- ▶ Ensuring bandwidth between switches in multiple rack environments
- ▶ Increasing rpc_timeout for dealing with latency across datacenters
- ▶ Changing consistency level from the CLI to test various consistency levels with multiple datacenter deployments
- ▶ Using the consistency levels TWO and THREE
- ▶ Calculating Ideal Initial Tokens for use with Network Topology Strategy and Random Partitioner

The tunable consistency model of Cassandra extends beyond a single datacenter to complex multiple datacenter scenarios. This chapter discusses the features inside Cassandra that are designed for this type of deployment.

Changing debugging to determine where read operations are being routed

Cassandra replicates data to multiple nodes; because of this, a read operation can be served by multiple nodes. If a read at QUORUM or higher is submitted, a Read Repair is executed, and the read operation will involve more than a single server. In a simple flat network which nodes have chosen for digest reads, are not of much consequence. However, in multiple datacenter or multiple switch environments, having a read cross a switch or a slower WAN link between datacenters can add milliseconds of latency. This recipe shows how to debug the read path to see if reads are being routed as expected.

How to do it...

1. Edit `<cassandra_home>/conf/log4j-server.properties` and set the logger to debug, then restart the Cassandra process:

   ```
   log4j.rootLogger=DEBUG,stdout,R
   ```

2. On one display, use the tail -f `<cassandra_log_dir>/system.log` to follow the Cassandra log:

   ```
   DEBUG 06:07:35,060 insert writing local
   RowMutation(keyspace='ks1', key='65', modifications=[cf1])
   DEBUG 06:07:35,062 applying mutation of row 65
   ```

3. In another display, open an instance of the Cassandra CLI and use it to insert data. Remember, when using `RandomPartitioner`, try different keys until log events display on the node you are monitoring:

   ```
   [default@ks1] set cf1['e']['mycolumn']='value';
   Value inserted.
   ```

4. Fetch the column using the CLI:

   ```
   [default@ks1] get cf1['e']['mycolumn'];
   ```

   Debugging messages should be displayed in the log.

   ```
   DEBUG 06:08:35,917 weakread reading SliceByNamesReadComman
   d(table='ks1', key=65, columnParent='QueryPath(columnFami
   lyName='cf1', superColumnName='null', columnName='null')',
   columns=[6d79636f6c756d6e,]) locally
   . . .
   DEBUG 06:08:35,919 weakreadlocal reading SliceByNamesReadCo
   mmand(table='ks1', key=65, columnParent='QueryPath(columnFa
   milyName='cf1', superColumnName='null', columnName='null')',
   columns=[6d79636f6c756d6e,])
   ```

How it works...

Changing the logging property level to DEBUG causes Cassandra to print information as it is handling reads internally. This is helpful when troubleshooting a snitch or when using the consistency levels such as LOCAL_QUORUM or EACH_QUORUM, which route requests based on network topologies.

See also...

Later in this chapter, the recipe *Quorum operations in multiple datacenter environments* describes a scenario where being able to troubleshoot the read path is critical to performance.

Using IPTables to simulate complex network scenarios in a local environment

While it is possible to simulate network failures by shutting down Cassandra instances, another failure you may wish to simulate is a failure that partitions your network. A failure in which multiple systems are UP but cannot communicate with each other is commonly referred to as a **split brain** scenario. This state could happen if the uplink between switches fails or the connectivity between two datacenters is lost.

Getting ready

When editing any firewall, it is important to have a backup copy. Testing on a remote machine is risky as an incorrect configuration could render your system unreachable.

How to do it...

1. Review your `iptables` configuration found in `/etc/sysconfig/iptables`. Typically, an IPTables configuration accepts loopback traffic:

    ```
    :RH-Firewall-1-INPUT - [0:0]
    -A INPUT -j RH-Firewall-1-INPUT
    -A FORWARD -j RH-Firewall-1-INPUT
    -A RH-Firewall-1-INPUT -i lo -j ACCEPT
    ```

2. Remove the highlighted rule and restart IPTables. This should prevent instances of Cassandra on your machine from communicating with each other:

    ```
    #/etc/init.d/iptables restart
    ```

3. Add a rule to allow a Cassandra instance running on `10.0.1.1` communicate to `10.0.1.2`:

```
-A RH-Firewall-1-INPUT -m state --state NEW -s 10.0.1.1 -d
10.0.1.2 -j ACCEPT
```

How it works...

IPTables is a complete firewall that is a standard part of current Linux kernel. It has extensible rules that can permit or deny traffic based on many attributes, including, but not limited to, source IP, destination IP, source port, and destination port. This recipe uses the traffic blocking features to simulate network failures, which can be used to test how Cassandra will operate with network failures.

Choosing IP addresses to work with RackInferringSnitch

A *snitch* is Cassandra's way of mapping a node to a physical location in the network. It helps determine the location of a node relative to another node in order to ensure efficient request routing. The `RackInferringSnitch` can only be used if your network IP allocation is divided along octets in your IP address.

Getting ready

The following network diagram demonstrates a network layout that would be ideal for `RackInferringSnitch`.

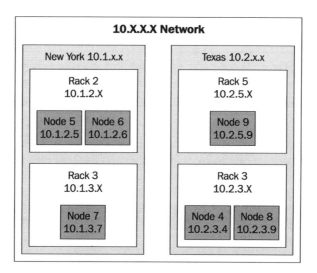

How to do it...

1. In the `<cassandra_home>/conf/cassandra.yaml` file:

   `endpoint_snitch: org.apache.cassandra.locator.RackInferringSnitch`

2. Restart the Cassandra instance for this change to take effect.

How it works...

The `RackInferringSnitch` requires no extra configuration as long as your network adheres to a specific network subnetting scheme. In this scheme, the first octet, `Y.X.X.X`, is the private network number 10. The second octet, `X.Y.X.X`, represents the datacenter. The third octet, `X.X.Y.X`, represents the rack. The final octet represents the host, `X.X.X.Y`. Cassandra uses this information to determine which hosts are 'closest'. It is assumed that 'closer' nodes will have more bandwidth and less latency between them. Cassandra uses this information to send **Digest Reads** to the closest nodes and route requests efficiently.

There's more...

While it is ideal if the network conforms to what is required for `RackInferringSnitch`, it is not always practical or possible. It is also rigid in that if a single machine does not adhere to the convention, the snitch will fail to work properly.

See also...

The next recipe, *Manually specifying Rack and Datacenter configuration with property file snitch* to see how to use a configuration file to set the topology information.

Scripting a multiple datacenter installation

Testing out some multiple datacenter capabilities of Cassandra can sometimes require a large number of instances. This recipe installs and creates all the configuration files required to run a multiple datacenter simulation of Cassandra locally.

Getting ready

This recipe is an enhanced version of the recipe *Scripting a multiple instance installation* in *Chapter 1, Getting Started*.

It creates many instances of Cassandra, and each instance uses a minimum of 256 MB RAM. A Cassandra release in `tar.gz` format needs to be in the same directory as the script.

How to do it...

1. Open `<hpcbuild>scripts/multiple_instances_dc.sh` and add this content:

```
#!/bin/sh
#wget http://www.bizdirusa.com/mirrors/apache//cassandra/0.7.0/
apache-cassandra-0.7.0-beta1-bin.tar.gz
HIGH_PERF_CAS=${HOME}/hpcas
CASSANDRA_TAR=apache-cassandra-0.7.5-bin.tar.gz
TAR_EXTRACTS_TO=apache-cassandra-0.7.5
mkdir ${HIGH_PERF_CAS}
mkdir ${HIGH_PERF_CAS}/commit/
mkdir ${HIGH_PERF_CAS}/data/
mkdir ${HIGH_PERF_CAS}/saved_caches/
cp ${CASSANDRA_TAR} ${HIGH_PERF_CAS}
pushd ${HIGH_PERF_CAS}
```

This script will take a list of arguments such as 'dc1-3 dc2-3'. The string before the first dash is the name of the datacenter, and the string after the dash is the number of instances in that datacenter.dcnum=0

```
while [ $# -gt 0 ]; do
  arg=$1
  shift
  dcname=`echo $arg | cut -f1 -d '-'`
  nodecount=`echo $arg | cut -f2 -d '-'`
  #rf=`echo $arg | cut -f2 -d '-'`
  for (( i=1; i<=nodecount; i++ )) ; do
    tar -xf ${CASSANDRA_TAR}
    mv ${TAR_EXTRACTS_TO} ${TAR_EXTRACTS_TO}-${dcnum}-${i}
    sed -i '1 i MAX_HEAP_SIZE="256M"' ${TAR_EXTRACTS_TO}-${dcnum}-
${i}/conf/cassandra-env.sh
```

2. Use the datacenter number as the value of the second octet, and the node number in the fourth octet:

```
    sed -i '1 i HEAP_NEWSIZE="100M"' ${TAR_EXTRACTS_TO}-${dcnum}-
${i}/conf/cassandra-env.sh
    sed -i "/listen_address\|rpc_address/s/localhost/127.${dcnum}.
0.${i}/g" ${TAR_EXTRACTS_TO}-${dcnum}-${i}/conf/cassandra.yaml
    sed -i "s|/var/lib/cassandra/data|${HIGH_PERF_CAS}/
data/${dcnum}-${i}|g" ${TAR_EXTRACTS_TO}-${dcnum}-${i}/conf/
cassandra.yaml
    sed -i "s|/var/lib/cassandra/commitlog|${HIGH_PERF_CAS}/
commit/${dcnum}-${i}|g" ${TAR_EXTRACTS_TO}-${dcnum}-${i}/conf/
cassandra.yaml
```

```
    sed -i "s|/var/lib/cassandra/saved_caches|${HIGH_PERF_CAS}/
saved_caches/${dcnum}-${i}|g" ${TAR_EXTRACTS_TO}-${dcnum}-${i}/
conf/cassandra.yaml
    sed -i "s|8080|8${dcnum}0${i}|g" ${TAR_EXTRACTS_TO}-${dcnum}-
${i}/conf/cassandra-env.sh
```

3. Change the snitch from `SimpleSnitch` to `RackInferringSnitch`. This will use the listen address of the Cassandra machine to locate it in the datacenter and rack:

```
    sed -i "s|org.apache.cassandra.locator.SimpleSnitch|org.
apache.cassandra.locator.RackInferringSnitch|g" ${TAR_EXTRACTS_
TO}-${dcnum}-${i}/conf/cassandra.yaml
  done
  dcnum=`expr $dcnum + 1`
done
popd
```

4. Run this script passing arguments to create two datacenters with each having three nodes:

```
$ sh  scripts/multiple_instances_dc.sh  dc1-3 dc2-3
```

5. Start up each node in the cluster. Then, connect to a node with the cassandra-cli. Create a keyspace. Ensure the `placement_strategy` is the `NetworkTopologyStrategy` and supply it `strategy_options` to configure how many replicas to place in each datacenter:

```
[default@unknown] create keyspace ks33  placement_strategy = 'org.
apache.cassandra.locator.
NetworkTopologyStrategy' and strategy_options=[{0:2,1:2}];
```

How it works...

This script takes command-line arguments and uses those to set up multiple Cassandra instances using specific IP addresses. The IP addresses are chosen to work with the `RackInferringSnitch`. After starting the cluster, a keyspace using `NetworkTopologyStrategy` with a replication factor of 6 is created. The `strategy_options` specify three replicas in datacenter 0 and three in datacenter 1.

Determining natural endpoints, datacenter, and rack for a given key

When troubleshooting, it is valuable to know which rack and datacenter your snitch believes a node belongs to. Also, knowing which machines would store a specific key is important when troubleshooting specific failures or determining how your strategy is spreading data across the cluster. This recipe shows how to use JConsole to find this information.

How to do it...

Inside JConsole, select the **Mbeans** tab, expand the **org.apache.cassandra.db** tree, expand the **EndPointSnitch** Mbean, then select **Operations**. In the right pane, find the button labeled **getRack**. Enter the IP address of a node to find rack information in the text box next to the button. Enter `127.0.1.0`, then click the **getRack** button.

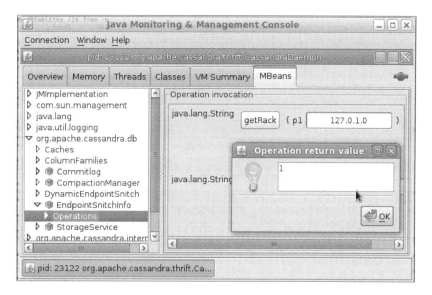

In the operations list, another method **getDatacenter** is defined. Supply the IP address of a node in the text box next to the button and then click **OK**.

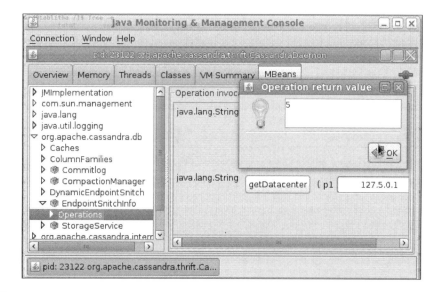

How it works...

This operation is used internally to intelligently route requests. Calling this operation is a way to check that the `PropertyFileSnitch` or `RackInferringSnitch` is working correctly.

See also...

Manually specifying Rack and Datacenter configuration with a property file snitch in this chapter.

Manually specifying Rack and Datacenter configuration with a property file snitch

The job of the **Snitch** is to determine which nodes are in the same **Rack** or **Datacenter**. This information is vital for multiple datacenter Cassandra deployments. The property file snitch allows the administrator to define a property file that Cassandra uses to determine what datacenter and rack nodes are a part of. This recipe shows how to configure the property file snitch.

Getting ready

Review the diagram in the *Choosing IP Addresses to work with RackInferringSnitch* recipe. We will be using the same theoretical network for this recipe.

How to do it...

1. Open `<cassandra_home>conf/cassandra-topology.properties` in your text editor. Create an entry for each host:

   ```
   10.1.2.5=ny:rack2
   10.1.2.6=ny:rack2
   10.1.3.7=ny:rack3
   10.2.5.9=tx:rack5
   10.2.3.4=tx:rack3
   10.2.3.9=tx:rack3
   ```

2. Edit `<cassandra_home>/conf/cassandra.yaml` in your text editor:

   ```
   endpoint_snitch: org.apache.cassandra.locator.PropertyFileSnitch
   ```

3. Replicate this file to all hosts in your cluster and restart the Cassandra process.

How it works...

The `cassandra-topology.properties` file is a simple Java properties file. Each line is an entry in the form of `<ip>=<data center>:<rack>`. The property file snitch reads this information on startup and uses it to route requests. This optimization attempts to handle digest reads to a host on the same switch or datacenter.

There's more...

See the previous recipe, *Determining natural endpoints, datacenter, and rack for a given key* to see how to test if you have performed this setup correctly.

Troubleshooting dynamic snitch using JConsole

The **Dynamic Snitch** is a special snitch that wraps another snitch such as the `PropertyFileSnitch`. Internally, Cassandra measures latency of read traffic on each host and attempts to avoid sending requests to nodes that are performing slowly. This recipe shows how to use JConsole to find and display the scores that the snitch has recorded.

Getting ready

The recipe in Chapter 1, *Connecting to Cassandra with JConsole* shows you how to connect.

How to do it...

In the left pane, expand the view for **org.apache.cassandra.db** and expand the **DynamicEndpointSnitch** item below it. An Mbean with a randomly chosen number will be below, which you need to expand again. Click on the **attributes** and the **Scores** information will appear in the right panel.

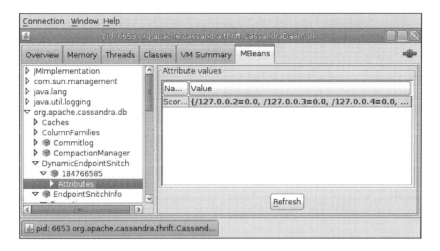

How it works...

When Cassandra nodes are under CPU or IO load due to a heavy number of requests, compaction, or an external factor such as a degraded RAID volume, that node should have a higher score. With dynamic snitch enabled nodes coordinating read operations will send fewer requests to slow servers. This should help balance requests across the server farm.

Quorum operations in multi-datacenter environments

Most applications use Cassandra for its capability to perform low-latency read and write operations. When a cluster is all located in a single physical location, the network latency is low and bandwidth does not (typically) have a cost. However, when a cluster is spread across different geographical locations, latency and bandwidth costs are factors that need to be considered. Cassandra offers two consistency levels: LOCAL_QUORUM and EACH_QUROUM. This recipe shows how to use these consistency levels.

Getting ready

The consistency levels LOCAL_QUORUM and EACH_QUORUM only work when using a datacenter-aware strategy such as the NetworkTopologyStrategy. See the recipe *Scripting a multiple datacenter installation* for information on setting up that environment.

READ.LOCAL_QUORUM returns the record with the most recent timestamp once a majority of replicas within the local datacenter have replied.

READ.EACH_QUORUM returns the record with the most recent timestamp once a majority of replicas within each datacenter have replied.

WRITE.LOCAL_QUORUM ensures that the write has been written to <ReplicationFactor> / 2 + 1 nodes within the local datacenter (requires network topology strategy).

WRITE.EACH_QUORUM ensures that the write has been written to <ReplicationFactor> / 2 + 1 nodes in each datacenter (requires network topology strategy).

How it works...

Each datacenter-aware level offers tradeoffs versus non-datacenter-aware levels. For example, reading at QUORUM in a multi-datacenter configuration would have to wait for a quorum of nodes across several datacenters to respond before returning a result to the client. Since requests across a **WAN** link could have high latency (40ms and higher), this might not be acceptable for an application that returns results to the clients quickly. Those clients can use LOCAL_QUORUM for a stronger read then ONE while not causing excess delay. The same can be said for write operations at LOCAL_QUORUM, although it is important to point out that writes are generally faster than reads.

It is also important to note how these modes react in the face of network failures. EACH_QUORUM will only succeed if each datacenter is reachable and QUORUM can be established in each. LOCAL_QUORUM can continue serving requests even with the complete failure of a datacenter.

Using traceroute to troubleshoot latency between network devices

Internet communication over long distances has inherent latency due to the speed of light; however, some areas of the world have more robust network links and better peering. A common tool used to check for network latency is **traceroute**.

How to do it...

1. Use `traceroute` to test the path to an Internet-based host.

   ```
   $ traceroute -n www.google.com

   traceroute to www.google.com (74.125.226.113), 30 hops max, 60
   byte packets

    1   192.168.1.1   2.473 ms   6.997 ms   7.603 ms
    2   10.240.181.29   14.890 ms   15.394 ms   15.590 ms
    3   67.83.224.34   15.970 ms   16.573 ms   16.947 ms
    4   67.83.224.9   22.606 ms   22.969 ms   23.324 ms
    5   64.15.8.1   23.841 ms   24.710 ms   24.283 ms
    6   64.15.0.41   30.699 ms   29.384 ms   24.861 ms
    7   * * *
    8   72.14.238.232   15.931 ms   16.388 ms   16.810 ms
    9   216.239.48.24   19.833 ms   16.504 ms   16.732 ms
   10   74.125.226.113   19.616 ms   19.158 ms   19.021 ms
   ```

How it works...

Traceroute tracks the route packets taken from an IP network on their way to a given host. It utilizes the IP protocol's **time to live (TTL)** field and attempts to elicit an ICMP `TIME_EXCEEDED` response from each gateway along the path to the host.

By analyzing the response time of each device, hops that are taking a long time can be identified as the source of problems. Depending on where the slowness occurs, you can take appropriate action. That may be contacting your network administrator or your ISP.

Ensuring bandwidth between switches in multiple rack environments

For clusters with a few nodes, it is generally advisable to place these nodes on a single switch for simplicity. Multiple rack deployments are suggested when the number of nodes is more than the ports on a typical switch or for redundancy. Cassandra does a high amount of intra-cluster communication. Thus, when nodes are divided across switches, ensure that the links between switches DO not become choke points. This recipe describes how to monitor network interface traffic.

How to do it...

Monitor the traffic on all interfaces, especially on the uplink interfaces between switches using a NMS such as mrtg or cacti. Know the maximum capacity of your network gear and plan for growth.

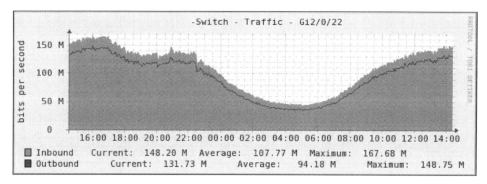

There's more...

If the uplinks between switches are network contention points, there are several solutions. One option is to spread your nodes out over more switches. Another option is to upgrade the uplink between your switches, for example if your switches supports 10 GB uplinks, these would give more bandwidth than the standard 1 GB uplinks. Enterprise-level switches often support **Link Aggregation Groups** (**LAG**), which bundle multiple interfaces together in an active/active fashion to make a single logical interface that is as fast as the sum of the links aggregated.

Increasing rpc_timeout for dealing with latency across datacenters

Cassandra servers in a cluster have a maximum timeout that they will use when communicating with each other. This is different than the socket timeout used for Thrift clients talking to Cassandra. Operations will have more latency with nodes communicating across large distances.This recipe shows how to adjust this timeout.

How to do it...

1. Open `<cassandra_home>/conf/cassandra.yaml` in a text editor. Increase the timeout value:

    ```
    rpc_timeout_in_ms: 20000
    ```

2. Restart Cassandra for this change to take effect:

How it works...

When clusters are spread out over large geographical distances, intermittent outages have a greater chance of making requests exceed the timeout value. Remember, if a client is using a consistency level such as ONE, they may receive a result quickly, but the cluster may still be working to write that data to replicas in other datacenters. Raising the timeout gives the cluster more time to complete the process in the background.

Changing consistency level from the CLI to test various consistency levels with multiple datacenter deployments

By default, the command-line interface reads and writes data at consistency level ONE. When using Cassandra with multiple node and multiple datacenter environments, being able to execute operations at other consistency levels is essential to testing and troubleshooting problems. This recipe shows to change the consistency level while using the CLI.

Getting ready

This recipe assumes a multiple data setup such as the one created in the recipe *Scripting a multiple datacenter installation*.

How to do it...

1. Use the `consistencylevel` statement to change the level the CLI will execute operations at:

    ```
    [default@unknown] connect 127.0.0.1/9160;
    Connected to: "Test Cluster" on 127.0.0.1/9160

    [default@unknown] create keyspace ks33 with  placement_strategy =
    'org.apache.cassandra.locator.
    NetworkTopologyStrategy' and strategy_
    options=[{0:3,1:3}];
    [default@unknown] use ks33;
    Authenticated to keyspace: ks33
    [default@ks33] create column family cf33;
    ```

    Down all the nodes that are in one of the datacenters.

    ```
    $ <cassandra_home>/bin/nodetool -h 127.0.0.1 -p 9001 ring
    ```

Address	Status State	Load	Owns	Token

```
127.1.0.3        Down    Normal   42.62 KB        42.18%
127.0.0.1        Up      Normal   42.62 KB        6.74%
127.0.0.2        Up      Normal   42.62 KB        11.78%
127.0.0.3        Up      Normal   42.62 KB        22.79%
127.1.0.2        Down    Normal   42.62 KB        4.62%
127.1.0.1        Down    Normal   42.62 KB        11.90%
```

2. Insert a row at the default consistency level of ONE:

```
[default@ks33] set cf33['a']['1']=1;
Value inserted.
```

3. Change the consistency level to EACH_QUORUM:

```
[default@ks33] consistencylevel as EACH_QUORUM;
Consistency level is set to 'EACH_QUORUM'.
[default@ks33] set cf33['a']['1']=1;
null
[default@ks33] get cf33['a']['1'];
null
```

4. Change the consistency level to LOCAL_QUORUM:

```
[default@ks33] consistencylevel as LOCAL_QUORUM;
Consistency level is set to 'LOCAL_QUORUM'.
[default@ks33] set cf33['a']['1']=1;
Value inserted.
[default@ks33] get cf33['a']['1'];
=> (column=31, value=31, timestamp=1304897159103000)
```

How it works...

The `consistencylevel` statement in the command-line interface changes the level operations run at. The default level of ONE will succeed as long as a single natural endpoint for the data acknowledges the operation. For LOCAL_QUORUM, a quorum of nodes in the local datacenters must acknowledge the operation for it to succeed. With EACH_QUROUM, a quorum of nodes in all datacenters much acknowledge the operation for it to succeed. If the CLI displays **null** after a `set` or `get`, the operation failed.

Using the consistency levels TWO and THREE

In multiple datacenter scenarios, replication factors higher than three are common. In some of these cases, users want durability of writing to multiple nodes, but do not want to use ONE or QUORUM. The Thrift code generation file, `<cassandra_home>/interface/cassandra.thrift`, has inline comments that describe the different consistency levels available.

* Write consistency levels make the following guarantees before reporting success to the client:
...

*   TWO   Ensure that the write has been written to at least 2 nodes' commit log and memory table

*   THREE   Ensure that the write has been written to at least 3 nodes' commit log and memory table
...

* Read consistency levels make the following guarantees before returning successful results to the client:
...

*   TWO   Returns the record with the most recent timestamp once two replicas have replied.

*   THREE   Returns the record with the most recent timestamp once three replicas have replied.

Getting ready

This recipe requires a multiple datacenter installation as described in the recipe *Scripting a multiple datacenter installation*.

How to do it...

1. Create a two-datacenter cluster with two nodes in each datacenter:

   ```
   $ sh multiple_instances_dc.sh dc1-3 dc2-3
   ```

2. Create a keyspace with a replication factor of 4 and two replicas in each datacenter:

   ```
   [default@unknown] create keyspace ks4 with placement_strategy =
   'org.apache.cassandra.locator.
   NetworkTopologyStrategy' and strategy_
   options=[{0:2,1:2}];

   [default@unknown] use ks4;
   [default@ks4] create column family cf4;
   ```

3. Down multiple nodes in the cluster inside the same datacenter:

   ```
   $ <cassandra_home>/bin/nodetool -h 127.0.0.1 -p 9001 ring
   ```

Address	Status	State	Load	Owns	Token
127.0.0.3	Down	Normal	42.61 KB	39.37%	
127.1.0.1	Up	Normal	42.61 KB	2.43%	
127.0.0.2	Down	Normal	42.61 KB	10.85%	
127.1.0.2	Up	Normal	42.61 KB	17.50%	
127.0.0.1	Up	Normal	42.61 KB	5.40%	
127.1.0.3	Up	Normal	42.61 KB	24.44%	

4. Set the consistency level to TWO and then insert and read a row:

```
[default@ks4] connect 127.0.0.1/9160;
[default@unknown] consistencylevel as two;
Consistency level is set to 'TWO'.


[default@unknown] use ks4;
[default@ks4] set cf4['a']['b']='1';
Value inserted.
[default@ks4] get cf4['a'];
=> (column=62, value=31, timestamp=1304911553817000)
Returned 1 results.
```

How it works...

Replication factors such as TWO and THREE can be helpful. An example of this is a two-datacenter deployment with a replication factor of four. QUORUM would require three natural endpoints, and since each datacenter has two replicas, this would mean that the operation depends on the system in a remote datacenter. If the remote datacenter is down—EACH_QUORUM would fail, and if a local replica was down—LOCAL_QUORUM would fail. Consistency level TWO would allow the first two acknowledgments, local or remote, to successfully complete the operation.

Calculating Ideal Initial Tokens for use with Network Topology Strategy and Random Partitioner

NetworkTopologyStrategy works in conjunction with an EndpointSnitch to determine a relative proximity of each of your Cassandra nodes and distribute replica data in an explicit user specified manner. The replica insertion behavior of NetworkTopologyStrategy requires that the "standard" ring concept of even token distribution between all nodes that span multiple datacenters is not used, but instead create mirrored logical rings between datacenters.

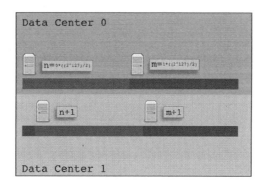

Getting ready

For `NetworkTopologyStrategy` to work, you must have a correctly configured Endpoint
Snitch. For absolute control, use `PropertyFileSnitch` to specify which Cassandra nodes
are in which datacenter and rack.

How to do it...

For this example, assume two datacenters each with two nodes. Calculate the tokens for the
nodes in a datacenter as if they were the entire ring.

1. The formula to calculate the ideal Initial Tokens is:

   ```
   Initial_Token = Zero_Indexed_Node_Number * ((2^127) / Number_Of_
   Nodes)
   ```

2. For the first node in the first datacenter (NODC0):

   ```
   initial token = 0 * ((2^127) / 2)
   initial token = 0
   ```

3. For the second node in the first datacenter (N1DC0):

   ```
   initial token = 1 * ((2^127) / 2)
   initial token = 85070591730234615865843651857942052864
   ```

   Now, for the second datacenter, do the exact same process, but no two nodes can
   have the same token, so offset the tokens by adding 1 to the token value.

4. For the first node in the second datacenter (NODC1):

   ```
   initial token = 1
   ```

5. For the second node in the second datacenter (N1DC1):

   ```
   initial token = 85070591730234615865843651857942052865
   ```

How it works...

Continuing with our two-datacenter example, a replica for token 3 is set to go from DC0 to
DC1. Cassandra determines which node will get the write in the remote datacenter the same
way it would do for primary insertion. Cassandra will write to the node whose Initial Token is
closest without being larger than the data's token. When using Network Topology strategy,
Cassandra only has nodes in the remote datacenter to choose from when placing the replica,
not the entire ring. Thus, the replica will write to DC1N0.

There's more...

`NetworkToplogySnitch` is versatile as it can be used with more than two datacenters and even when datacenters have differing numbers of nodes. However, it must be set up properly.

More than two datacenters

If there are more than two datacenters, follow the same steps but keep incrementing the offset so that no nodes have the same Initial Token. For example, add 2 in the third datacenter.

Datacenters with differing numbers of nodes

`NetworkTopologyStrategy` also works with multiple datacenters that each have different numbers of nodes. Follow the recipe of computing the tokens for that datacenter independently, and then check to make sure there are no token collisions on any other node in any datacenter. If the numbers collide, increment the token on one of those nodes.

Endpoint Snitch

Furthermore, using a different, or improperly configured Endpoint Snitch, will not guarantee you even replication.

See also...

In this chapter, the recipe *Specifying Rack and Datacenter configuration with a property file snitch*.

For a reference on how Cassandra uses tokens to select nodes to write to, see the recipe in *Chapter 1, Getting Started, Calculating Ideal Initial Tokens for use with Random Partitioner*.

9
Coding and Internals

In this chapter, you will learn the following recipes:

- ▶ Installing common development tools
- ▶ Building Cassandra from source
- ▶ Creating your own type by sub classing abstract type
- ▶ Using the validation to check data on insertion
- ▶ Communicating with the Cassandra developers and users through IRC and e-mail
- ▶ Generating a diff using subversion's diff feature
- ▶ Applying a diff using the patch command
- ▶ Customizing the sstable2json export utility
- ▶ Using strings and od to quickly search through data files
- ▶ Configure index interval ratio for lower memory usage
- ▶ Increasing phi_convict_threshold for less reliable networks
- ▶ Using the Cassandra maven plugin

Introduction

Cassandra has a simple and powerful API and data model. There are some components that are designed for user extensibility such as custom types and practitioners. Working with these components requires writing code that builds against the Cassandra code. Also, like many open source projects, users often become developers by searching for bugs or adding new features.

Installing common development tools

Several common tools are used to develop Java applications. These tools help fetch, build, and test code.

How to do it...

Use `yum` to install the following components:

```
$ yum install maven
$ yum install ant
$ yum install subversion
$ yum install git
$ yum install junit
```

How it works...

They can be downloaded and installed individually, but installing with the `yum` tool is faster.

Building Cassandra from source

The Cassandra code base is active and typically has multiple branches. It is a good practice to run official releases, but at times it may be necessary to use a feature or a bug fix that has not yet been released. Building and running Cassandra from source allows for a greater level of control of the environment. Having the source code, it is also possible to trace down and understand the context or warning or error messages you may encounter. This recipe shows how to **checkout** Cassandra code from **Subversion** (**SVN**) and build it.

How to do it...

1. Visit `http://svn.apache.org/repos/asf/cassandra/branches` with a web browser. Multiple sub folders will be listed:

    ```
    /cassandra-0.5/
    /cassandra-0.6/
    ```

    Each folder represents a branch. To check out the 0.6 branch:

    ```
    $ svn co http://svn.apache.org/repos/asf/cassandra/branches/
    cassandra-0.6/
    ```

2. Trunk is where most new development happens. To check out trunk:

```
$ svn co http://svn.apache.org/repos/asf/cassandra/trunk/
```

3. To build the release tar, move into the folder created and run:

```
$ ant release
```

This creates a release tar in `build/apache-cassandra-0.6.5-bin.tar.gz`, a release jar, and an unzipped version in `build/dist`.

How it works...

Subversion (SVN) is a revision control system commonly used to manage software projects. Subversion repositories are commonly accessed via the HTTP protocol. This allows for simple browsing. This recipe is using the command-line client to checkout code from the repository.

See also...

In this chapter, the recipe *Generating a diff using subversion's diff feature*

Creating your own type by sub classing abstract type

Cassandra stores columns as byte arrays and does not enforce any restrictions on them by default. This design principal allows users to quickly serialize and store data, but there are some drawbacks to this approach. For the high-level user using the CLI, raw byte arrays display as hex strings. Those working on the backend may be used to a storage system providing data integrity checks such as length or type of data. This recipe shows how to write a custom **type** in Cassandra by extending `AbstractType`.

How to do it...

1. Create `<hpc_build>/java/hpcas/c09/USFootballPlayerType.java` in a text editor:

```
package hpcas.c09;

import org.apache.cassandra.db.marshal.*;
import hpcas.c03.*;
import java.nio.ByteBuffer;
import org.apache.cassandra.thrift.*;
import org.apache.cassandra.utils.ByteBufferUtil;
```

```
class PlayerBean {
  String position, name;
  int rushingyards, receivingyards;

  public PlayerBean(){}
```

2. Create a method that writes this instance to a `ByteBuffer`:

```
public ByteBuffer writeToBuffer() {
  return ByteBufferUtil.bytes(position + "|" + name +"|"
      + rushingyards + "|" + receivingyards);
}
```

3. Create a method that returns an instance of `PlayerBean` from a ByteBuffer:

```
public static PlayerBean readFromBuffer(ByteBuffer bb){
  String s = ByteBufferUtil.string(bb);
  String [] parts = s.split("\\|");
  PlayerBean pb = new PlayerBean();
  pb.position= parts[0];
  pb.name=parts[1];
  pb.rushingyards=Integer.parseInt(parts[2]);
  pb.receivingyards=Integer.parseInt(parts[3]);
  return pb;
}

public String toString(){
  return name +" "+position+" "+rushingyards+" "+receivingyards;
}
}
```

4. Create a class that extends `AbstractType`:

```
public class USFootballPlayerType extends AbstractType{
```

5. Statically initialize an instance of the class:

```
public static final USFootballPlayerType instance =

      new USFootballPlayerType();

USFootballPlayerType(){}
```

6. Override the `getString` method, which controls the display in the command-line interface:

```
public String getString(ByteBuffer bb) {
  PlayerBean pb = PlayerBean.readFromBuffer(bb);
  return pb.toString();
}
```

7. Also, define a compare method, which is used to sort entries:

```
public int compare(ByteBuffer o1, ByteBuffer o2) {
    return ByteBufferUtil.compareUnsigned(o1, o2);
}

public void validate(ByteBuffer bb) throws MarshalException {
}
```

8. Create a main method that creates a new keyspace and a column family. Set the `validation_class` of the new column family to the type were created `hpcas.c09.USFootballPlayerType`:

```
public static void main(String[] args) throws Exception {
    FramedConnWrapper fcw = new FramedConnWrapper(Util.
envOrProp("host"),
            Integer.parseInt(Util.envOrProp("port")));
    fcw.open();
    Cassandra.Client client = fcw.getClient();
    client.set_keyspace("football");
    try {
        KsDef ksD = new KsDef();
        ksD.setname("football");
        CfDef cfD = new CfDef();
        cfD.setDefault_validation_class("hpcas.c09.
USFootballPlayerType");
        cfD.setName("teams");
        client.system_add_keyspace(ksD);
        cfD.setKeyspace("football");
        client.system_add_column_family(cfD);
    } catch (Exception e) {
        System.out.println(e.getMessage());
    }
```

9. Create an entry and insert it:

```
    PlayerBean pb = new PlayerBean();
    pb.name = "Ahmad Bradshaw";
    pb.position = "RB";
    pb.receivingyards = 413;
    pb.rushingyards = 1235;
    ColumnParent cp = new ColumnParent();
    cp.setColumn_family("teams");
    Column c = new Column();
    c.setName(ByteBufferUtil.bytes(pb.name));
    c.setValue(pb.writeToBuffer());
    client.insert(ByteBufferUtil.bytes("Giants"), cp, c,
ConsistencyLevel.ONE);
    fcw.close();
    }
}
```

10. Build the project and copy the resulting JAR to the `<cassandra_home>/lib` directory on all nodes. Then, restart Cassandra:

    ```
    $ host=127.0.0.1 port=9160 ant -DclassToRun=hpcas.c09.
    USFootballPlayerType run
    ```

11. List the column family from the command-line interface:

    ```
    [default@unknown] use football;
    Authenticated to keyspace: football
    [default@football] assume teams comparator as ascii;
    Assumption for column family 'teams' added successfully.
    [default@football] list teams;
    RowKey: Giants
    => (column=Ahmad Bradshaw, value=Ahmad Bradshaw RB 1235 413,
    timestamp=0)
    ```

How it works...

By creating types, users can control how columns are sorted by writing custom implementations of the `compare` method. This type uses a byte-level comparison. Display is controlled by providing a custom implementation of `getString`. This type removes the pipe characters used as delimiters for a display that is easier to read.

See also...

The next recipe, *Using the validation to check data on insertion*.

Using the validation to check data on insertion

Column Families can optionally support validation. A default validation class can be specified for a column family. The validation class can be overridden for columns of specific names. This recipe shows how to create a sub class of `AbstractType` and use this as a validation class.

Getting ready

This recipe is an enhancement on the previous recipe, *Creating your own type by sub classing abstract type*.

How to do it...

1. Edit `src/hpcas/c09/USFootballPlayerType.java` in a text editor. Add the highlighted code to detect invalid data:

```
public class USFootballPlayerType extends AbstractType{
...
    public void validate(ByteBuffer bb) throws MarshalException {
        PlayerBean pb = PlayerBean.readFromBuffer(bb);
        if (!( pb.position.equalsIgnoreCase("QB")
                || pb.position.equalsIgnoreCase("RB") )){
          throw new MarshalException("bad position");
        }
    }
}
```

2. Inside the `main` method, set the position to `LB`. This value will cause a validation failure:

```
public static void main(String[] args) throws Exception {
    ...
    PlayerBean pb = new PlayerBean();
    pb.name = "Ahmad Bradshaw";
    //pb.position = "RB";
    pb.position = "LB";
```

3. Build the project and copy the `hpcas.jar` to the lib directory of Cassandra. Restart the instance if it is already running:

```
$ cd <hpc_home> ; cd ant
$ cp dist/lib/hpcas.jar /home/edward/hpcas/apache-
cassandra-0.7.3-1/lib/
```

4. Build and run the application:

```
$ host=127.0.0.1 port=9160  ant -DclassToRun=hpcas.c09.
USFootballPlayerType run
[java] InvalidRequestException(why:[football] [teams]
[41686d61642042726164736861777] = [4c427c41686d6164204272616473861
777c313233357c343133] failed validation (bad position))
```

How it works...

If a validation class is enabled, during an insert the data being inserted is passed to the `validate` method. If the data is valid, the method should return. If the data is invalid, the method should throw a `MarshalException` and supply information as to why the validation failed. The ability to validate data on insertion helps incorrect data from being inserted. This technique can be used to enforce restrictions on the length or content of data.

Communicating with the Cassandra developers and users through IRC and e-mail

Cassandra has a vibrant community of users and developers. E-mail and IRC allows people across the world to collaborate. Amazingly, most of the project coordination is done over these mediums. This makes Cassandra more than just code with an open source license; anyone can become involved and become part of the project. This recipe shows how to connect with the community.

How to do it...

Connect via Internet Relay Chat: `irc://chat.us.freenode.net:6667`, and join any of the channels you may be interested in.

Channel	Description
#cassandra	General talk about Cassandra or other related topics
#cassandra-dev	Discussion related to the Cassandra code base
#cassandra-ops	Channel for discussing performance or installation characteristics

Other Channels of interest: #solandra, #thrift, #hive.

There are several mailing lists; send an e-mail to the specified addresses and a reply e-mail will be sent to you with further instructions on joining the list.

List Name	E-mail	Description
Users	user-subscribe @cassandra.apache.org	General questions and announcements
Developer	dev-subscribe @cassandra.apache.org	Discussions on development of the Cassandra code base
Commits	commits-subscribe@cassandra. apache.org	Auto-generated e-mails on commits to the source code
Clients development	client-dev-subscribe@cassandra. apache.org	High-level clients such as Thrift, Hector, or clients for other languages

How it works...

Always attempt to search for the answer first before asking a question on a mailing list or IRC. Many questions have been asked and answered before. Remember, most people on the lists are enthusiasts and are volunteering their time to help.

For those interested in developing or fixing features in Cassandra, it is common to join the `dev` mailing list and chat room. Typically, the key committers have insights into the problem and the code base and help code get committed faster.

Generating a diff using subversion's diff feature

Subversion is a popular revision control system. Any changes made to the source code after checkout will be tracked. Subversion can produces diff files. A `diff` is a file that stores the changes made. `diffs` are exchanged between developers so that they can share code without having entire copies of the project. This recipe shows how to use subversion to create diff files.

How to do it...

1. Use `svn stat` to determine if any files have changed since the code was checked out:

```
$ svn stat
?           src/java/org/apache/cassandra/cli/CliUserHelp.java
?           src/java/org/apache/cassandra/cli/CliCompleter.java
?           src/java/org/apache/cassandra/cli/CliClient.java
?           src/java/org/apache/cassandra/cli/Cli.g
```

2. Use the subversion add feature, `svn add` , to add these files to the project:

```
$ svn add  src/java/org/apache/cassandra/cli/*.java
```

3. Generate a `diff`, which captures the changes you have made to the source files:

```
$ svn diff > /tmp/cassandra-XXX-1.patch.txt
```

How it works...

Subversion with diff capabilities provide a way to track changes and share code with others.

There's more...

Diff files are human readable. Lines that start with a minus sign (-) indicate a line has been removed. Lines that start with a plus sign (+) indicate a line has been added. Lines above the change are also stored in the file. This can help resolve issues when the patch offsets do not match exactly due to other changes since the `diff` had been generated.

```
$ svn  diff | head -11
Index: src/java/org/apache/cassandra/cli/CliUserHelp.java
```

```
=====================================================================
--- src/java/org/apache/cassandra/cli/CliUserHelp.java    (revision
1082028)
+++ src/java/org/apache/cassandra/cli/CliUserHelp.java    (working
copy)
@@ -325,7 +325,11 @@
                state.out.println("example:");
                state.out.println("assume Users comparator as
lexicaluuid;");
                break;
 -
+          case CliParser.NODE_CONSISTENCY_LEVEL:
+                state.out.println("consistencylevel as <level>");
```

See also...

The next recipe, *Applying a diff using the patch command* shows how to apply a `diff` to your copy of the code.

Applying a diff using the patch command

A `diff` file represents the comparison of a file before and after a change. Unreleased source code updates or **patches** typically come in the form of `diff` files. This recipe shows how to use the `patch` command with a `diff` file to apply changes to a branch of Cassandra source code.

Before you begin...

Ensure the software being patched is the exact same revision of the software the patch was based on. Patches may apply incorrectly if it is not applied to the correct source. The output of the previous recipe, *Generating a diff using subversion's diff feature* can be applied with this recipe. If the patch did not apply correctly, `svn revert` will restore the contents of files back to the repository state.

How to do it...

1. Navigate to the Cassandra source directory. Ensure the source code is clean, run `svn stat`, and ensure it produces no output:

   ```
   $ cd <cassandra_source_home>
   $ svn stat
   ```

2. Run the `patch` command and use the shell's input redirection to feed it the contents of the patch file:

```
$ patch -p0 < /tmp/cassandra-2354-3.patch.txt
patching file src/java/org/apache/cassandra/cli/CliUserHelp.java
patching file src/java/org/apache/cassandra/cli/CliCompleter.java
patching file src/java/org/apache/cassandra/cli/CliClient.java
patching file src/java/org/apache/cassandra/cli/Cli.g
```

> **Problems patching**
>
> If any messages are displayed such as 'skipping hunk', this means that the `diff` file is not applying cleanly. It was probably generated from a different source.

How it works...

The `patch` command takes the content of a `diff` file and applies those changes to the local code. `diff` and `patch` files allow users to share and review code changes. All the updates to the Cassandra code base are always done by generating `diff` files.

Using strings and od to quickly search through data files

A user may wish to review Cassandra data files directly. This is a fast alternative to searching through data with range scanning using the API or exporting the data to JSON format. Because the Cassandra data files are written in a binary format, using standard text editing tools can be difficult. Two command-line tools that are helpful in this process are the command-line octal dump utility, od, and the strings utility, which displays human readable strings inside binary files. This recipe show how these tools can be used.

How to do it...

1. Run `strings` against a file in your data directory that matches the pattern '*Data*':

```
$strings /home/edward/hpcas/data/1/football/teams-f-1-Data.db
Giants
Ahmad Bradshaw
RB|Ahmad Bradshaw|1235|413
```

2. Run the od command with the -a switch:

```
[edward@tablitha hpcbuild]$ od -a /home/edward/hpcas/data/1/
football/teams-f-1-Data.db
0000000 nul ack   G   i   a   n   t   s nul nul nul nul nul nul
nul
0000020 nul nul nul dle nul nul nul etx nul nul nul soh nul nul
nul   0
0000040 nul  bs nul nul nul nul nul nul nul nul nul nul nul
nul nul
0000060 nul nul nul nul nul nul nul soh nul  so   A   h   m   a
d  sp
0000100   B   r   a   d   s   h   a   w nul nul nul nul nul nul
nul nul
0000120 nul nul nul nul sub   R   B   |   A   h   m   a   d  sp
B   r
0000140   a   d   s   h   a   w   |   1   2   3   5   |   4   1
3
0000157
```

Command-line tools such as od and strings are a fast way to extract data when troubleshooting, while tools such as SSTable2JSON have the startup overhead involved in sampling the index files. Od and strings can be combined with other command-line tools such as pipelines or grep. Command-line utilities to hex or octal dump still have shortcomings in their ability to decode data as they require a lower-level understanding of data files. The format of these files is also subject to change.

Customizing the sstable2json export utility

The sstable2json utility is designed to produce output that can be used with its counterpart program json2sstable. However, this is not very friendly for end users. This recipe shows how to customize the sstable2json program to output data in a user-defined format.

How to do it...

 This recipe is only applicable when your data is ASCII or UTF-8.

1. Run `sstable2json` against an **SSTable** file. The data is output as hex strings:

```
$ <cassandra_home>/bin/sstable2json
$ <cassandra_home>/data/1/football/teams-f-1-Data.db


{

"4769616e7473": [["41686d616420427261473686177", "52427c41686d616
420427261473686177c313233357c343133", 0, false]]


}
```

2. Copy the `SSTableExport.java` file from the Cassandra source code to the project source home:

```
$ <cassandra_src>/cassandra-0.7/src/java/org/apache/cassandra/
tools/SSTableExport.java <hpc_home>/src/java/hpcas/c09/
```

3. Change the package name to `hpcas.c09`. Search the file for calls to the `bytesToHex` method and replace them with the `ByteBufferUtil.string` method:

```
package hpcas.c09;
...
    private static void serializeColumn(IColumn column,
PrintStream out)
    {
      try{
        out.print("[");
        out.print(quote(ByteBufferUtil.string(column.name())));
        out.print(", ");
        out.print(quote(ByteBufferUtil.string(column.value())));
        ...
      } catch (CharacterCodingException ex) { }

    private static void serializeRow(SSTableIdentityIterator row,
      DecoratedKey key, PrintStream out)
    {
        ColumnFamily columnFamily = row.getColumnFamily();
        boolean isSuperCF = columnFamily.isSuper();

        //out.print(asKey(bytesToHex(key.key)));
        try{
          out.print(asKey(ByteBufferUtil.string(key.key)));
        } catch (CharacterCodingException ex) { }
```

4. Copy the `sstable2json` file. Edit it to invoke the class this recipe creates:

```
$ cp <cassandra_home>/bin/sstable2json <cassandra_home>/bin/
sstable2nicejson

$JAVA -cp $CLASSPATH  -Dstorage-config=$CASSANDRA_CONF \

        -Dlog4j.configuration=log4j-tools.properties \

    hpcas.c09.SSTableExport "$@"
```

5. Invoke the `sstable2nicejson` script. The output of the application should now be strings:

```
$ <cassandra_home>/bin/sstable2nicejson <cassandra_home>/data/1/
football/teams-f-1-Data.db

{

"Giants": [["Ahmad Bradshaw", "RB|Ahmad Bradshaw|1235|413", 0,
false]]

}
```

How it works...

The default export program outputs data as Hex encoded strings. This recipe uses the helper functions in the `ByteBufferUtil` class to convert byte data into strings. This assumption is not a good valid if the data stored is binary data.

There's more...

This application could be easily customized to produce XML, an SQL file to be bulk loaded, or a batch of inserts to replicate the data to another Cassandra cluster.

Configure index interval ratio for lower memory usage

The `index_interval` controls the sampling of row keys for each SSTable. The default value of 128 means one out of every 128 keys are held in memory. Index sampling happens during node startup and that data stays in memory until the SSTable is removed. The memory used by `index_interval` is independent of the **key cache**.

How to do it...

1. Edit `<cassandra_home>/casandra.yaml` and increase `index_interval` from 128 to 256:

   ```
   index_interval: 256
   ```

2. Restart Cassandra for this change to take effect.

How it works...

Raising the `index_interval` uses less memory, but makes the index less effective. A common use of this feature is systems that store a large amount of data but do not have much RAM memory. This knob is also useful because different use cases have different key size, key count, and key-to-row ratio. Raising the ratio can also help a node start up faster.

Increasing phi_convict_threshold for less reliable networks

The failure detector monitors **gossip** traffic, and if a node has not participated in the process for an interval, it marks the node as dead. This recipe shows how to increase the `phi_convict_threshold` for unstable environments.

How to do it...

1. Edit `<cassandra_home>/conf/cassandra.yaml` and change the `phi_conviction_threshold`:

   ```
   phi_convict_threshold: 10
   ```

   Cassandra must be restarted for this change to take effect.

How it works...

The higher the `phi_conviction_threshold` is set, the less chance of getting a false positive about a failure. However, it also takes longer to detect a failure. This setting should be changed when networks are unstable or with virtual machines that sometimes have resources stolen by other instances on the same hardware.

There's more...

The value of `phi_conviction_threshold` is not a number of seconds. The default value of eight is about nine seconds, while 10 is about 14 seconds.

Using the Cassandra maven plugin

With maven, it is simple to create a software project that has Cassandra support built in. The Cassandra maven plugin fetches all the dependencies and provides **goals** for starting and stopping Cassandra. This is an easy way to create self-contained projects that work with Cassandra. This recipe shows how to use the Cassandra maven plugin.

Getting ready

The recipe in this chapter, *Installing common development tools* is a pre-requisite.

How to do it...

1. Run the maven command with the archetype:generate argument:

    ```
    $ mvn archetype:generate
    110: remote -> maven-archetype-webapp
    Choose a number: 107: 110
    Choose version:
    1: 1.0
    Choose a number: 1: 1
    Define value for property 'groupId': : hpcas.ch09
    Define value for property 'artifactId': : webapp
    Define value for property 'version': 1.0-SNAPSHOT:
    Define value for property 'package': hpcas.ch09:
    Confirm properties configuration:
    groupId: hpcas.ch09
    artifactId: webapp
    version: 1.0-SNAPSHOT
    package: hpcas.ch09
    Y: y
    [INFO] -------------------------------------------------------------
    -------------

    [INFO] BUILD SUCCESSFUL

    [INFO] -------------------------------------------------------------
    -------------
    ```

2. Modify webapp/pom.xml with a text editor:

    ```
    <project xmlns="http://maven.apache.org/POM/4.0.0"
    xmlns:xsi="http://www.w3.org/2001/XMLSchema-instance"
       xsi:schemaLocation="http://maven.apache.org/POM/4.0.0 http://
    maven.apache.org/maven-v4_0_0.xsd">
    ```

```
<modelVersion>4.0.0</modelVersion>
<groupId>org.apache.wiki.cassandra.mavenplugin</groupId>
<artifactId>webapp</artifactId>
<packaging>war</packaging>
<version>1.0-SNAPSHOT</version>
<name>webapp Maven Webapp</name>
<url>http://maven.apache.org</url>
<dependencies>
  <dependency>
    <groupId>me.prettyprint</groupId>
    <artifactId>hector-core</artifactId>
    <version>0.7.0-25</version>
  </dependency>
</dependencies>
<build>
  <finalName>webapp</finalName>
  <plugins>
    <plugin>
      <artifactId>maven-compiler-plugin</artifactId>
      <version>2.3.2</version>
      <configuration>
        <source>1.6</source>
        <target>1.6</target>
      </configuration>
    </plugin>
  </plugins>
</build>
</project>
```

3. Create the following directories:

    ```
    $ mkdir -p webapp/src/cassandra/cli
    ```

    ```
    $ mkdir -p webapp/src/main/resources
    $ mkdir -p webapp/src/main/webapp/WEB-INF
    ```

    The Cassandra maven plugin will automatically execute the content in `webapp/src/cassandra/cli/load.script`.

    ```
    create keyspace WebappKeyspace with replication_factor=1;
    use WebappKeyspace;
    create column family Example with column_type='Standard' and
    comparator='UTF8Type';
    ```

4. Execute maven specifying the `cassandra:start` goal:

```
$ mvn cassandra:start -Dcassandra.jmxPort=7199
[INFO] Cassandra cluster "Test Cluster" started.
[INFO] Running /home/edward/arch/webapp/src/cassandra/cli/load.
script...
[INFO] Connected to: "Test Cluster" on 127.0.0.1/9160
[INFO] 30a5bc5b-8028-11e0-9b86-e700f669bcfc
[INFO] Waiting for schema agreement...
[INFO] ... schemas agree across the cluster
[INFO] Finished /home/edward/arch/webapp/src/cassandra/cli/load.
script.

[INFO] Cassandra started in 5.3s
```

How it works...

Maven projects are controlled by pom files. A pom file contains information on the project, including dependencies and plugin configuration information. Maven repositories across the Internet store project JARs and information on their dependencies. The Cassandra plugin for maven provides goals to start and stop Cassandra without having to explicitly bring Cassandra-related libraries into the project. This makes it easy to prototype and distribute an application using Cassandra.

There's more...

More information on the Cassandra maven plugin can be found at http://mojo.codehaus.org/cassandra-maven-plugin/

10

Libraries and Applications

In this chapter, you will learn

- ▶ Building the contrib stress tool for benchmarking
- ▶ Inserting and reading data with the stress tool
- ▶ Running the Yahoo! Cloud Serving Benchmark
- ▶ Hector, a high-level client for Cassandra
- ▶ Doing batch mutations with Hector
- ▶ Cassandra with Java Persistence Architecture (JPA)
- ▶ Setting up Solandra for full text indexing with a Cassandra backend
- ▶ Setting up Zookeeper to support Cages for transactional locking
- ▶ Using Cages to implement an atomic read and set
- ▶ Using Groovandra as a CLI alternative
- ▶ Searchable log storage with Logsandra

Introduction

Cassandra's popularity has led to several pieces of software that have developed around it. Some of these are libraries and utilities that make working with Cassandra easier. Other software applications have been built completely around Cassandra to take advantage of its scalability. This chapter describes some of these utilities.

Building the contrib stress tool for benchmarking

Stress is an easy-to-use command-line tool for stress testing and benchmarking Cassandra. It can be used to generate a large quantity of requests in short periods of time, and it can also be used to generate a large amount of data to test performance with. This recipe shows how to build it from the Cassandra source.

Getting ready

Before running this recipe, complete the *Building Cassandra from source* recipe discussed in *Chapter 9, Coding and Internals.*

How to do it...

From the source directory, run `ant`. Then, change to the `contrib/stress` directory and run `ant` again.

```
$ cd <cassandra_src>
$ ant jar
$ cd contrib/stress
$ ant jar
...
BUILD SUCCESSFUL
Total time: 0 seconds
```

How it works...

The build process compiles code into the `stress.jar` file.

See also...

The next recipe, *Inserting and reading data with the stress tool.*

Inserting and reading data with the stress tool

The stress tool is a multithreaded load tester specifically for Cassandra. It is a command-line program with a variety of knobs that control its operation. This recipe shows how to run the stress tool.

Before you begin...

See the previous recipe, *Building the contrib stress tool for benchmarking* before doing this recipe.

How to do it...

Run the `<cassandra_src>/bin/stress` command to execute 10,000 insert operations.

```
$ bin/stress -d 127.0.0.1,127.0.0.2,127.0.0.3 -n 10000 --operation INSERT
Keyspace already exists.
total,interval_op_rate,interval_key_rate,avg_latency,elapsed_time
10000,1000,1000,0.0201764,3
```

How it works...

The stress tool is an easy way to do load testing against a cluster. It can insert or read data and report on the performance of those operations. This is also useful in staging environments where significant volumes of disk data are needed to test at scale. Generating data is also useful to practice administration techniques such as joining new nodes to a cluster.

There's more...

It is best to run the load testing tool on a different node than on the system being tested and remove anything else that causes other unnecessary contention.

See also...

The next recipe, *Running the Yahoo! Cloud Serving Benchmark* for a more sophisticated load testing system.

Running the Yahoo! Cloud Serving Benchmark

The Yahoo! Cloud Serving Benchmark (YCSB) provides benchmarking for the bases of comparison between NoSQL systems. It works by generating random workloads with varying portions of insert, get, delete, and other operations. It then uses multiple threads for executing these operations. This recipe shows how to build and run the YCSB.

Information on the YCSB can be found here:

```
http://research.yahoo.com/Web_Information_Management/YCSB
```

```
https://github.com/brianfrankcooper/YCSB/wiki/
```

```
https://github.com/joaquincasares/YCSB
```

How to do it...

1. Use the git tool to obtain the source code.

   ```
   $ git clone git://github.com/brianfrankcooper/YCSB.git
   ```

2. Build the code using the ant.

   ```
   $ cd YCSB/
   ```

   ```
   $ ant
   ```

3. Copy the JAR files from your <cassandra_hom>/lib directory to the YCSB classpath.

   ```
   $ cp $HOME/apache-cassandra-0.7.0-rc3-1/lib/*.jar db/
   cassandra-0.7/lib/
   ```

   ```
   $ ant dbcompile-cassandra-0.7
   ```

4. Use the Cassandra CLI to create the required keyspace and column family.

   ```
   [default@unknown] create keyspace usertable with replication_
   factor=3;
   ```

   ```
   [default@unknown] use usertable;
   ```

   ```
   [default@unknown] create column family data;
   ```

5. Create a small shell script run.sh to launch the test with different parameters.

   ```
   CP=build/ycsb.jar
   for i in db/cassandra-0.7/lib/*.jar ; do
     CP=$CP:${i}
   done

   java -cp $CP com.yahoo.ycsb.Client  -t -db com.yahoo.ycsb.
   db.CassandraClient7 -P workloads/workloadb \
   -p recordcount=10 \
   -p hosts=127.0.0.1,127.0.0.2 \
   -p operationcount=10 \
   -s
   ```

6. Run the script ant pipe the output to more command to control pagination:

   ```
   $ sh run.sh | more
   ```

   ```
   YCSB Client 0.1
   ```

```
Command line: -t -db com.yahoo.ycsb.db.CassandraClient7 -P
workloads/workloadb -p recordcount=10 -p hosts=127.0.0.1,127.0.0.2

 -p operationcount=10 -s
Loading workload...

Starting test.

data

 0 sec: 0 operations;

 0 sec: 10 operations; 64.52 current ops/sec; [UPDATE
AverageLatency(ms)=30] [READ AverageLatency(ms)=3]

[OVERALL], RunTime(ms), 152.0

[OVERALL], Throughput(ops/sec), 65.78947368421052

[UPDATE], Operations, 1

[UPDATE], AverageLatency(ms), 30.0

[UPDATE], MinLatency(ms), 30

[UPDATE], MaxLatency(ms), 30

[UPDATE], 95thPercentileLatency(ms), 30

[UPDATE], 99thPercentileLatency(ms), 30

[UPDATE], Return=0, 1
```

How it works...

YCSB has many configuration knobs. An important configuration option is -P, which chooses the workload. The workload describes the portion of read, write, and update percentage. The -p option overrides options from the workload file. YCSB is designed to test performance as the number of nodes grows and shrinks, or scales out.

There's more...

Cassandra has historically been one of the strongest performers in the YCSB.

Hector, a high-level client for Cassandra

It is suggested that when available, clients should use a higher level API. Hector is one of the most actively developed higher level clients. It works as a facade over the Thrift API, and in many cases condenses what is a large section of Thrift code into a shorter version using Hector's helper methods and design patterns. This recipe shows how to use Hector to communicate with Cassandra.

How to do it...

Download the Hector JAR and place it in your applications classpath.

```
$wget https://github.com/downloads/rantav/hector/hector-core-0.7.0-26.tgz
$cp hector-core* <hpc_build>/lib
```

Open <hpc_build>src/hpcas/c10/HectorExample.java in a text editor.

```
public class HectorExample {
```

Hector uses serializers. The role of a Serializer is to take the encoding burden away from the user. Internally, the `StringSerializer` will do something similar to `"string".getBytes("UTF-8")`.

```
private static StringSerializer stringSerializer =
StringSerializer.get();
public static void main(String[] args) throws Exception {
```

Hector has its own client-side load balancing. The host list for `Hfactory.getOrCreateCluster` can be one or more host:port pairs separated by commas.

```
Cluster cluster = Hfactory.getOrCreateCluster
    ("TestCluster", Util.envOrProp("targetsHost"));
Keyspace keyspaceOperator = HFactory.createKeyspace(Util.
envOrProp("ks33", cluster);
```

The `HFactory` object has several factory methods. `HFactory.createStringColumn` is a one-liner for creating columns. This is an alternative to working with the `Column` in a JavaBean-like style.

```
Mutator<String> mutator = Hfactory.createMutator
        (keyspaceOperator, StringSerializer.get());
mutator.insert("bbrown", "cf33", HFactory.
createStringColumn("first", "Bob"));
```

One way to read data is by using a `ColumnQuery` object. `ColumnQuery` uses a builder pattern where set operations return an instance to the `ColumnQuery` object instead of void.

```
ColumnQuery<String, String, String> columnQuery =
        HFactory.createStringColumnQuery(keyspaceOperator);
columnQuery.setColumnFamily("cf33").setKey("bbrown").
setName("first");
QueryResult<HColumn<String, String>> result = columnQuery.execute();

System.out.println("Resulting column from cassandra: " + result.
get());

cluster.getConnectionManager().shutdown();
    }
}
```

How it works...

Hector provides a few key things. Firstly, remember that the bindings generated by Thrift are cross-platform and designed for compatibility. Higher level clients such as Hector bring more abstraction and take more advantage of language features such as Java's generics. For example, the `HFactory` class provides methods that reduce four lines of Thrift code to a single line factory method call. Hector also provides client-side load balancing because detecting and automatically failing-over between servers is important to achieve good uptime.

There's more...

The next recipe, *Doing batch mutates with Hector* shows how Hector's API design makes operations such as batch mutate easier.

Doing batch mutations with Hector

In an earlier chapter, we showed how batch mutations are much more efficient than doing individual inserts. However, the long complex method signature of the `batch_mutate` method is difficult to read and assembling that structure may clutter code. This recipe shows how to use the Hector API for the batch mutate operation.

How to do it...

1. Create a text file `<hpc_build>src/hpcas/c10/HectorBatchMutate.java`.

```
public class HectorBatchMutate {
  final StringSerializer serializer = StringSerializer.get();
  public static void main(String[] args) throws Exception {
    Cluster cluster = HFactory.getOrCreateCluster("test", Util.
envOrProp("target"));
    Keyspace keyspace = HFactory.createKeyspace(Util.
envOrProp("ks"), cluster);
```

2. Create a mutator as you would for a single insert and make multiple calls to the `addInsertion` method.

```
Mutator m = Hfactory.createMutator(keyspace,serializer);
m.addInsertion("keyforbatchload", Util.envOrProp("ks"),
HFactory.createStringColumn("age", "30"));
m.addInsertion("keyforbatchload", Util.envOrProp("ks"),
  HFactory.createStringColumn("weight", "190"));
```

The writes are not sent to Cassandra until the execute method is called.

```
    m.execute();
  }
}
```

How it works...

Hector's mutator concept is more straightforward than the elaborate nested object needed to execute a batch mutation through Thrift. Writing less lines of code to carry out a task is better in numerous ways as there is less code to review and less chance to make a mistake.

Cassandra with Java Persistence Architecture (JPA)

Data in memory being used by an application is typically in a different format than it's on-disk representation. Serialization and deserialization take data from an in-memory form and persist it to a back-end data store. This work can be done by hand.The Java Persistence Architecture (JPA) allows you to annotate a Java object and use JPA to handle the serialization and de serialization automatically. This recipe show how to use JPA annotation to persist data to Cassandra.

Before you begin...

This recipe requires the mvm command provided by the maven2 package.

How to do it...

1. Use subversion to download the kundera source code and maven to build it.

    ```
    $ svn checkout http://kundera.googlecode.com/svn/trunk/ kundera-read-only
    $ cd kundera-read-only
    $ mvn install
    ```

2. Create a text file <hpc_build>/src/hpcas/c10/Athlete.java.

    ```
    package hpcas.c10;
    ```

3. Apply the Entity annotation. Then, use the columnFamily annotation and supply the column family name.

    ```
    @Entity
    @Index (index=false)
    @ColumnFamily("Athlete")
    public class Athlete {
    ```

4. Use the `@id` annotation to signify the row key.

```
@Id
String username;
```

5. Any field with the `@Column` annotation will be persisted. Optionally, you can supply a string for the column name.

```
@Column(name = "email")
String emailAddress;
@Column
String country;
public Athlete() {
}
… //bean patterns
}
```

6. Kundera can configure itself from a Java properties file or from a Map defined in your code. Create a file `<hpc_build>src/hpcas/c10/AthleteDemo.java`.

```
public class AthleteDemo {
  public static void main (String [] args) throws Exception {
    Map map = new HashMap();
    map.put("kundera.nodes", "localhost");
    map.put("kundera.port", "9160");
    map.put("kundera.keyspace", "athlete");
    map.put("sessionless", "false");
    map.put("kundera.client", "com.impetus.kundera.client.
PelopsClient");
```

7. `EntityManager` instances are created from a factory pattern.

```
    EntityManagerFactory factory = new EntityManagerFactoryImpl("t
est", map);
    EntityManager manager = factory.createEntityManager();
```

8. Use the `find()` method to look up by key. All annotated fields of the object are automatically populated with data from Cassandra.

```
    try {
        Athlete athlete = manager.find(Athlete.class, "bsmith");
        System.out.println(author.emailAddress);
    } catch (PersistenceException pe) {
        pe.printStackTrace();
    }
  }
}
```

How it works...

JPA provides methods such as find and remove. JPA takes the burden off the developer of writing mostly repetitive serialization code. While this does remove some of the burden, it also takes away some level of control. Since JPA can provide access to many types of data stores such as relational databases, it also makes it easy to switch between backend storage without having to make large code changes.

There's more...

Hector also offers a JPA solution in a subproject called hector-object-mapper.

Setting up Solandra for full text indexing with a Cassandra backend

Solandra is a combination of Lucene, Cassandra, and Solr. Lucene is a reverse index system designed for full text search. Solr is a popular frontend that provides a web service for Lucene as well as caching warming and other advanced capabilities. Solandra integrates with both tools by storing Lucene's data inside Cassandra, allowing for a high level of scalability.

How to do it...

1. Use `git` to obtain a copy of the Solandra source code and use `ant` to build it.

   ```
   $ git clone https://github.com/tjake/Solandra.git
   $ ant
   ```

2. Prepare a temporary directory that Solandra will use to store data. Then, run these steps to start Solandra, download, and load sample data.

   ```
   $ mkdir /tmp/cassandra-data
   $ cd solandra-app; ./start-solandra.sh -b
   $ cd ../reuters-demo/
   $ ./1-download-data.sh
   $ ./2-import-data.sh
   ```

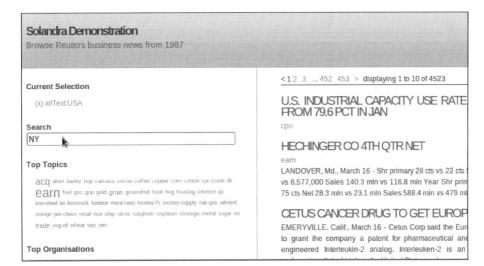

3. Open `./website/index.html` in your web browser. Place text in the search box to search for occurrences of it inside the documents loaded into Solandra.

How it works...

Solandra takes the data that Solr would normally store on local disk and instead stores it inside Cassandra. It does this by providing custom implementations of Lucene's `IndexReader` and `IndexWriter` and also runs Solr and Cassandra inside the same JVM. Solandra stores this data using `OrderPreservingPartitioner` because Lucene supports searching for ranges of terms (that is, albert to apple). Solandra provides a natural way to scale Solr. Applications can read data as soon it is written.

Setting up Zookeeper to support Cages for transactional locking

Cages API is used for distributed read and write locks. The Cages API is built around Apache Zookeeper. This recipe shows how to set up a single instance of Zookeeper to support Cages.

 Apache ZooKeeper is an effort to develop and maintain an open source server that enables highly reliable distributed coordination.

How to do it...

1. Download a binary Apache Zookeeper release and extract it.

   ```
   $ http://apache.cyberuse.com//hadoop/zookeeper/zookeeper-3.3.2/
   zookeeper-3.3.2.tar.gz

   $ tar -xf zookeeper-3.3.2.tar.gz

   cd zookeeper *
   ```

2. Create a configuration file from the sample. Make sure to set the `dataDir`.

   ```
   $ cp conf/zoo_sample.cfg conf/zoo.cfg
   tickTime=2000
   initLimit=10
   syncLimit=5
   dataDir=/tmp/zk
   clientPort=2181
   ```

3. Create the `dataDir` directory you referenced in the preceding configuration.

   ```
   $ mkdir /tmp/zk
   ```

4. Start the `zookeeper` instance.

   ```
   $ bin/zkServer.sh start

   JMX enabled by default

   Using config: /home/edward/cassandra-dev/zookeeper-3.3.2/bin/../
   conf/zoo.cfg

   Starting zookeeper ...

   ...

   STARTED
   ```

5. Confirm Zookeeper is running by checking for a process listening on the defined client port 2181.

   ```
   $ netstat -an | grep 2181
   tcp        0        0 :::2181                        :::*
   LISTEN
   ```

How it works...

Apache Zookeeper provides applications with distributed synchronization. It is typically installed on one to seven nodes so it is highly available and capable of managing a large number of locks and watches. Cassandra and Zookeeper are an interesting pairing: Cassandra providing high availability and high performance with Zookeeper providing synchronization.

See also...

The next recipe, *Using Cages to implement an atomic read and set* uses the `zookeeper` instance setup in this recipe.

Using Cages to implement an atomic read and set

In *Chapter 5, Consistency, Availability, and Partition Tolerance with Cassandra*, the recipe *Consistency is not locking or a transaction* shows what can happen when multiple applications read and update the same piece of data without synchronization. In the previous recipe, we set up Apache Zookeeper, a system for distributed synchronization. The Cages library provides a simple API to synchronize access to rows. This recipe shows how to use Cages.

Getting ready

Review the recipe *Demonstrating how consistency is not a lock or a transaction* discussed in *Chapter 5, Consistency, Availability, and Partition Tolerance with Cassandra*. To do this recipe, you must complete the previous recipe, *Setting up Zookeeper to support Cages for transactional locking*.

How to do it...

1. Use subversion to checkout a copy of the Cages source code and binary JAR.

    ```
    $ svn checkout http://cages.googlecode.com/svn/trunk/ cages-read-only
    ```

2. Copy the `cages` and `zookeeper` JARs to the library directory of the build root.

    ```
    $ cp cages-read-only/Cages/build/cages.jar <hpc_build>/lib/
    $ cp zookeeper-3.3.2/zookeeper-3.3.2.jar <hpc_build>/lib
    ```

3. Using the code from the *Chapter 5* recipe, *Demonstrating how consistency is not a lock or a transaction*, `<hpc_build>/src/java/hpcas/c05/ShowConcurrency.java` by adding imports for cages and zookeeper packages and classes.

    ```
    import org.apache.cassandra.thrift.*;
    import org.wyki.zookeeper.cages.ZkSessionManager;
    import org.wyki.zookeeper.cages.ZkWriteLock;
    ```

4. Next, add a reference to the `ZkSessionManager`, the object used to connect to Zookeeper.

```
public class ShowConcurrency implements Runnable {
    ZkSessionManager session;
    String host;
```

5. Initialize the session instance in the constructor.

```
public ShowConcurrency(String host, int port, int inserts) {
    this.host = host;
    this.port = port;
    this.inserts = inserts;
    try {
        session = new ZkSessionManager("localhost");
        session.initializeInstance("localhost");
    } catch (Exception ex) {
        System.out.println("could not connect to zookeeper "+ex);
        System.exit(1);
    }
}
```

6. Zookeeper has a hierarchical data model. The keyspace represents the top directory and the column family represents the second level. The third level is the row key to be locked. After instantiating the lock object, use the `acquire()` method, perform the operations inside the critical section, and when done working with the lock, call `release()`.

```
for (int i = 0; i < inserts; i++) {
    ZkWriteLock lock = new ZkWriteLock("/ks33/cf33/count_col") ;
    try {
        lock.acquire();
        int x = getValue(client);
        X++;
        setValue(client, x);
    } finally {
        lock.release();
    }
}
```

7. Run `hpcas.c05.ShowConcurrency` using four threads doing 30 inserts each.

```
$ host=127.0.0.1 port=9160 inserts=30 threads=4 ant
-DclassToRun=hpcas.c04.ShowConcurrency run
```

. . .

```
[java] wrote 119
[java] read 119
[java] wrote 120
[java] read 120
[java] The final value is 120
```

How it works...

Cages and Zookeeper provide a way for external processes to synchronize. When each thread is initialized, it opens a Zookeeper session. The critical section of the code reads, increments, and finally updates a column. Surround the critical section of the code with a Zookeeper Write Lock that prevents all other threads from updating this value while the current thread operates on it.

There's more...

Synchronization incurs extra overhead; it should only be used when necessary. Zookeeper does scale out to several nodes, but it does not scale out indefinitely. This is because writes to Zookeeper have to be synchronized across all nodes.

Using Groovandra as a CLI alternative

Groovy is an agile and dynamic language for the Java Virtual Machine. Groovandra is a library designed to work with Groovy for rapid exploration of data in Cassandra. It can be used for tasks the Cassandra CLI cannot do and that coding and deploying a Java application may not make much sense. Code can be written line by line or in Groovy scripts that do not need to be compiled and packaged before running.

How to do it...

1. Download a release of Groovy and extract it.

   ```
   $ wget http://dist.groovy.codehaus.org/distributions/groovy-
   binary-1.8.0.zip
   ```

   ```
   $ unzip groovy-binary-1.8.0.zip
   ```

2. Create a startup script that adds the JAR files in the `cassandra/lib` and the `groovandra.jar` to the classpath and then starts Groovy.

   ```
   $ vi groovy-1.8.0/bin/groovycassandraCASSANDRA_HOME=/home/edward/
   hpcas/apache-cassandra-0.7.3-1/lib
   GROOVANDRA_JAR=/home/edward/encrypt/trunk/dist/groovandra.jar
   CLASSPATH=${GROOVANDRA_JAR}:$CLASSPATH
   ```

```
for i in ${CASSANDRA_HOME}/*.jar ; do
  CLASSPATH=${CLASSPATH}:$i
done
export CLASSPATH
/home/edward/groovy/groovy-1.8.0/bin/groovysh
```

```
$ chmod a+x groovy-1.8.0/bin/groovycassandra
```

3. Start the Groovy shell.

```
$ sh <groovy_home>/bin/groovycassandra

bean=new com.jointhegrid.groovandra.GroovandraBean()

===> com.jointhegrid.groovandra.GroovandraBean@6a69ed4a

groovy:000> bean.doConnect("localhost",9160);

===> com.jointhegrid.groovandra.GroovandraBean@6a69ed4a

groovy:000> bean.withKeyspace("mail").showKeyspace()

===> KsDef(name:mail, strategy_class:org.apache.cassandra.locator.
SimpleStrategy, replication_factor:1, ...
```

How it works...

Groovandra is a simple way to interact with Cassandra without having to go through the steps of compiling, deploying, and running Java applications. Groovy allows users to approach the application line by line. This allows ad hoc programming and debugging and is helpful for accessing the features of Cassandra that are not accessible from the CLI such as setting up a call to the `multiget_slice` method, which requires numerous parameters to be set.

Searchable log storage with Logsandra

Logsandra is a project based around log storage in Cassandra. Logsandra is a project that provides a set of tools to parse logs, store them in Cassandra in a searchable fashion, and search for or graph the occurrence of keywords in logs. Logsandra includes two processes. The first parses logs and stores them in Cassandra. The second runs a web server that allows you to search for occurrences of keywords in logs or graph their frequency.

Getting ready

Logsandra needs a running instance of Cassandra to connect to and store data. This recipe also requires Python and the Python installer `pip`.

```
$ yum install python python-pip
```

How to do it...

1. Obtain a copy of the Logsandra source code using `git` and install Logsandra's dependencies using `pip`.

```
$ git clone git://github.com/thobbs/logsandra.git
$ cd logsandra
```

2. Elevate to root to install the requirements and then drop back to a standard user.

```
$ su
# cat requirements.txt | xargs pip-python install
# python setup.py install
# exit
```

3. Next, set up Logsandra's keyspace and load sample data.

```
$ python scripts/create_keyspace.py
$ python scripts/load_sample_data.py


Loading sample data for the following keywords: foo, bar, baz
```

4. Start the web server.

```
$ ./logsandra-httpd.py start
```

5. Open `http://localhost:5000/` and search for 'foo', which was added by `load_sample_data.py`.

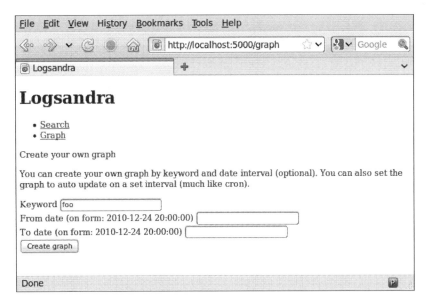

Logsandra presents a graph with occurrences of this keyword over time.

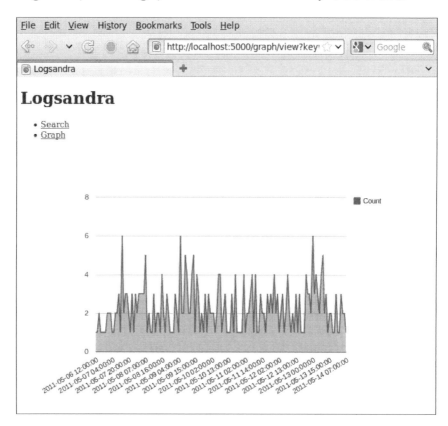

How it works...

Logsandra creates and uses a keyspace name `logsandra` with a column family inside it named `keyword`. It primarily retrieves events by looking up all logs containing a keyword from a range of time. To make this efficient, the event timeline is denormalized to produce one timeline per keyword. For each keyword that appears in a log, a separate copy of the log event will be appended to the corresponding timeline. Each timeline gets its own row, and within the row, each column holds one log event. The columns are sorted chronologically, using unique IDs (UUIDs) for column names to avoid clashes. Although this denormalization strategy uses more space on disk, a lookup query by Logsandra will only read a single contiguous portion of one row in Cassandra, which is very efficient.

```
[default@logsandra] show keyspaces;
Keyspace: logsandra:

    . . .
```

```
Column Families:
  ColumnFamily: keyword
    Columns sorted by: org.apache.cassandra.db.marshal.TimeUUIDType
```

Logsandra shows a versatile way to store and access log data in Cassandra. It is also important to note that Logsandra is written in Python, which demonstrates adoption for Cassandra outside the Java world.

There's more...

Inside the `logsandra/conf` directory, the `logsandra.yaml` file can be used to control which host and port the Logsandra web interface binds to, host and port information to connect to the Cassandra cluster, and directives that instruct it as to which folders to watch for log events.

11

Hadoop and Cassandra

In this chapter, you will learn the following recipes:

▶ A pseudo-distributed Hadoop setup

▶ A Map-only program that reads from Cassandra using ColumnFamilyInputFormat

▶ A Map-only program that writes to Cassandra using the ColumnFamilyOutputFormat

▶ A MapReduce program that uses grouping with Cassandra input and output

▶ Setting up Hive with Cassandra Storage Handler support

▶ Defining a Hive table over a Cassandra Column Family

▶ Joining two Cassandra Column Families using Hive

▶ Grouping and counting column values with Hive

▶ Co-locating Hadoop Task Trackers on Cassandra nodes

▶ Setting up a "Shadow" data center for running only MapReduce jobs

▶ Setting up DataStax Brisk the combined stack of Cassandra, Hadoop, and Hive

Introduction

The Apache Hadoop project develops open source software for reliable, scalable, and distributed computing. Hadoop includes two sub-projects.

▶ **HDFS**: A distributed file system that provides high throughput access to application data

▶ **MapReduce**: A software framework for distributed processing of large data sets on compute clusters

Hadoop is commonly used to store and process huge data sets. Cassandra integrates with Hadoop by implementing **Input Format** and **Output Format** interfaces. This allows MapReduce programs in Hadoop to read from and write to Cassandra. The pairing of Hadoop and Cassandra complement each other because Cassandra excels at low latency reading and writing and Hadoop provides a system to perform data mining and advanced searching.

A pseudo-distributed Hadoop setup

A production Hadoop cluster can span from a single node to thousands of computers. Each cluster has one of each of these components:

- ▶ **NameNode**: Component that stores the file system metadata
- ▶ **Secondary NameNode**: Checkpoints the NameNode
- ▶ **JobTracker**: Component in charge of Job Scheduling

These components are installed on multiple machines:

- ▶ **TaskTracker**: Component that runs individual tasks of a job
- ▶ **DataNode**: Component that stores data to disk

The communication between the components is depicted in the following image:

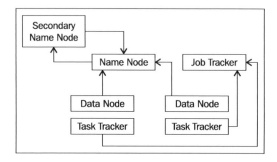

For Hadoop to be effective at grid computing, it needs to be installed on multiple machines, but the stack can be set up on a single node in a pseudo-distributed cluster. This recipe shows how to set up a pseudo-distributed cluster.

How to do it...

1. Determine the hostname of your system. Then, download and extract a Hadoop release:

```
$ hostname
tablitha.jtg.pvt
$ cd ~
```

```
$ wget  http://apache.mirrors.pair.com//hadoop/core/hadoop-0.20.2/
hadoop-0.20.2.tar.gz
$ tar -xf hadoop-0.20.2.tar.gz
$ cd hadoop-0.20.2
```

2. Edit `<hadoop_home>/conf/core-site.xml`. Use your hostname (`tablitha.jtg.pvt` in this example) in the value of `fs.default.name`:

```
<configuration>
  <property>
    <name>fs.default.name</name>
    <value>hdfs://tablitha.jtg.pvt:9000</value>
  </property>
</configuration>
```

3. Edit `<hadoop_home>/conf/mapred-site.xml`. Use your hostname (`tablitha.jtg.pvt` in this example) in the value of `mapred.job.tracker`:

```
<configuration>
  <property>
      <name>mapred.job.tracker</name>
      <value>tablitha.jtg.pvt:9001</value>
  </property>
</configuration>
```

4. Edit `<hadoop_home>/conf/hdfs-site.xml`. Since this test cluster has a single node, the replication should be set to one:

```
<configuration>
  <property>
   <name>dfs.replication</name>
   <value>1</value>
  </property>
</configuration>
```

5. Edit `<hadoop_home>/conf/hadoop-env.sh` to set the `JAVA_HOME` variable:

```
JAVA_HOME=/usr/java/latest
```

6. Format the NameNode (only do this once per install):

```
$ bin/hadoop namenode -format
11/03/09 19:09:01 INFO namenode.NameNode: STARTUP_MSG:
11/03/09 19:09:01 INFO common.Storage: Storage directory
/tmp/hadoop-edward/dfs/name has been successfully formatted.
/************************************************************
SHUTDOWN_MSG: Shutting down NameNode at tablitha.jtg.
pvt/192.168.1.100
************************************************************/
```

7. Start all the Hadoop components:

```
$ bin/hadoop-daemon.sh start namenode
$ bin/hadoop-daemon.sh start jobtracker
$ bin/hadoop-daemon.sh start datanode
$ bin/hadoop-daemon.sh start tasktracker
$ bin/hadoop-daemon.sh start secondarynamenode
```

8. Verify the NameNode and DataNode(s) are communicating by looking at the NameNode web interface and confirming one **Live Node**:

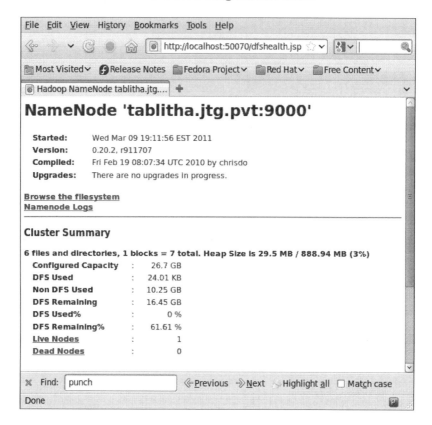

9. Verify that the JobTracker and TaskTrackers are communicating by looking at the JobTracker web interface and confirming one node listed in the **Nodes** column:

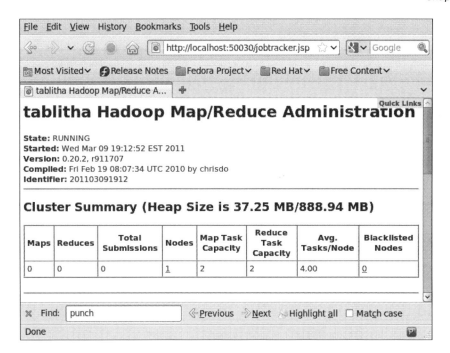

10. Use the `hadoop` command-line tool to test the file system:

```
$ hadoop dfs -ls /
$ hadoop dfs -mkdir /test_dir
$ echo "some info to test" > /tmp/myfile
$ hadoop dfs -copyFromLocal /tmp/myfile /test_dir
$ hadoop dfs -cat /test_dir/myfile
some info to test
```

How it works...

Each Hadoop component uses information in `core-site.xml` and either `mapred-site.xml` or `hdfs-site.xml` to bootstrap itself. For example, a DataNode uses the value of `fs.default.name` to locate and communicate with the NameNode.

There's more...

Hadoop is a large complex project. There are hundreds of configuration knobs for Hadoop and many features.

A Map-only program that reads from Cassandra using the ColumnFamilyInputFormat

The `ColumnFamilyInputFormat` allows data stored in Cassandra to be used as input for Hadoop jobs. Hadoop can then be used to perform many different types of algorithms on the data. This recipe shows how to use a map-only job to locate any key with a specific column and convert the value of the column to uppercase.

Big Data Ahead!

The `ColumnFamilyInputFormat` scans through all the data on all nodes!

How to do it...

1. Create a file `<hpc_build>/src/java/hpcas/c11/MapOnly.java`:

```java
package hpcas.c11;
import hpcas.c03.Util;
import java.nio.ByteBuffer;
import java.util.*;
import org.apache.cassandra.hadoop.ColumnFamilyInputFormat;
import org.apache.cassandra.hadoop.ConfigHelper;
import org.apache.cassandra.thrift.SlicePredicate;
import org.apache.hadoop.conf.Configuration;
import org.apache.hadoop.conf.Configured;
import org.apache.hadoop.fs.Path;
import org.apache.hadoop.io.Text;
import org.apache.hadoop.mapreduce.Job;
import org.apache.hadoop.mapreduce.lib.output.FileOutputFormat;
import org.apache.hadoop.util.Tool;
import org.apache.hadoop.util.ToolRunner;
```

Entry point programs for Hadoop typically extend **Configured** and implement **Tool**. This allows Hadoop to auto-configure settings and inherit features:

```java
public class MapOnly extends Configured implements Tool {
    public static final String CONF_COLUMN_NAME = "columnname";
    public static void main(String[] args) throws Exception {
        System.exit(ToolRunner.run(new Configuration(), new
MapOnly(), args));
    }
    public int run(String[] args) throws Exception {
```

```
    //Column names will be specified by the user.
    getConf().set(CONF_COLUMN_NAME, Util.envOrProp("columnname"));
    //Instantiate a job instance. 'Uppercase' will be the name of
the job.
Job job = new Job(getConf(), "Uppercase");
    job.setNumReduceTasks(0);
    job.setJarByClass(MapOnly.class);
```

A **Mapper** processes key-value pairs from the `InputFormat`. The mapper produces intermediate key-value pairs that are `Text` type. The `UpperCaseMapper` will be described in more detail in the following code:

```
    job.setMapperClass(UpperCaseMapper.class);
    job.setMapOutputKeyClass(Text.class);
    job.setMapOutputValueClass(Text.class);
    //The output directory inside HDFS will be chosen by user
input.
    FileOutputFormat.setOutputPath(job, new Path(Util.
envOrProp("output")));
```

The `ColumnFamilyInputFormat` requires information to connect to a Cassandra cluster initially. After connection, the split information is calculated. Splitting is the process by which MapReduce divides the input to be processed in parallel by multiple mappers.

```
    job.setInputFormatClass(ColumnFamilyInputFormat.class);
    ConfigHelper.setRpcPort(job.getConfiguration(), "9160");
    ConfigHelper.setInitialAddress(job.getConfiguration(),
"localhost");
    ConfigHelper.setPartitioner(job.getConfiguration(),
            "org.apache.cassandra.dht.RandomPartitioner");
    ConfigHelper.setInputColumnFamily(job.getConfiguration(),
```

Users will provide the **keyspace** and **column family** information as well as the column they are interested in.

```
            Util.envOrProp("KS"), Util.envOrProp("CF"));
    SlicePredicate predicate = new SlicePredicate().setColumn_
names(
            Arrays.asList(ByteBuffer.wrap(Util.
envOrProp("column").getBytes())));
    ConfigHelper.setInputSlicePredicate(job.getConfiguration(),
predicate);

    job.waitForCompletion(true);
    return 0;
  }
}
```

2. Create a file `<hpc_build>/src/java/hpcas/c11/MapOnly.java`:

```
package hpcas.c11;

import java.io.IOException;
import java.nio.ByteBuffer;
import java.util.SortedMap;
import org.apache.cassandra.db.IColumn;
import org.apache.cassandra.utils.ByteBufferUtil;
import org.apache.hadoop.io.Text;
import org.apache.hadoop.mapreduce.Mapper;
import org.apache.hadoop.mapreduce.Mapper.Context;
```

The signature of a Mapper allows the framework to know what Java types are input and output from the `map` method.

```
public class UpperCaseMapper extends
        Mapper<ByteBuffer, SortedMap<ByteBuffer, IColumn>, Text,
Text> {
        /*
    During a Map Reduce Job, the map method will be called many
times. Save
    object instantiation and cleanup by declaring class level
objects. */
    private Text akey = new Text();
    private Text value = new Text();
    private ByteBuffer sourceColumn;
```

The setup method is called once when the Mapper is initialized. Fetch the wanted column information here rather than in the map method since this data will not change for the entire run of the program.

```
    @Override
    protected void setup(org.apache.hadoop.mapreduce.Mapper.
Context context)
            throws IOException, InterruptedException {
        sourceColumn = ByteBuffer.wrap(context.getConfiguration()
            .get(MapOnly.CONF_COLUMN_NAME).getBytes());
    }
```

Data from the `InputFormat` is sent to the map method. Both the key and the value are treated as Strings and a conversion to uppercase is applied. The calculated values are then written to the context. Since no reducer has been defined, data is written directly to HDFS.

```
    public void map(ByteBuffer key, SortedMap<ByteBuffer,
IColumn> columns,
            Context context) throws IOException,
InterruptedException {
        IColumn column = columns.get(sourceColumn);
        if (column == null)
          return;
        value.set(ByteBufferUtil.string(column.value()).
toUpperCase() );
        akey.set(ByteBufferUtil.string(key).toUpperCase());
        context.write(akey, value);
    }
  }
```

3. Run the application supplying the name of a keyspace, column family, and column to process (this is a single command):

```
$ ant dist
$ columnname=favorite_movie column=favorite_movie \
KS=ks33 CF=cf33 output=/map_output \
<hadoop_home>/bin/hadoop  jar \
<hpc_home>/dist/lib/hpcas.jar \
hpcas.c11.MapOnly \
```

4. Use the `-libjars` switch and specify a comma-separated list of JAR files that are distributed with the job:

```
-libjars \
<cassandra_home>/lib/apache-cassandra-0.7.3.jar, <cassandra_home>/
lib/libthrift-0.5.jar,
<cassandra_home>/lib/guava-r05.jar,
<cassandra_home>/lib/commons-lang-2.4.jar

11/03/12 12:50:20 INFO mapred.JobClient: Running job:
job_201103091912_0034
...
11/03/12 12:50:41 INFO mapred.JobClient:     Map input records=3
11/03/12 12:50:41 INFO mapred.JobClient:     Spilled Records=0
11/03/12 12:50:41 INFO mapred.JobClient:     Map output records=3
```

5. Confirm the results by using the `<hadoop_home>/bin/hadoop dfs -cat`, which streams files on HDFS to the local console:

```
$ <hadoop_home>/bin/hadoop dfs -cat /map_output/*
STACEY DRDOLITTLE
ED      MEMENTO
BOB     MEMENTO
```

How it works...

Each time the `ColumnFamilyInputFormat` is run, the entire column family is used as input. This means that processing large column families can take a long time and be very intensive. The `ColumnFamilyInputFormat` first connects to Cassandra to plan the job. The result of this planning is a list of **splits**. Each split is processed by a **TaskTracker**. The larger the cluster, the more splits that can be processed in parallel.

See also...

The next recipe, *A Map-only program that writes to Cassandra using the CassandraOutputFormat* to write data from Hadoop directly to Cassandra.

A Map-only program that writes to Cassandra using the CassandraOutputFormat

The default `OutputFormat` writes objects to human-readable text files. Cassandra also implements a Hadoop `OutputFormat` allowing the results of MapReduce jobs to be written data directly to Cassandra. This recipe shows how to read data from Cassandra, update it, and then write it back using MapReduce.

Getting ready

This recipe will make modifications to the program in the previous recipe, *A Map-only program that reads from Cassandra using CassandraInputFormat*.

How to do it...

1. Add the highlighted lines to the following: `<hpc_build>/src/java/hpcas/c11/MapOnly.java`

```
ConfigHelper.setInputSlicePredicate(job.getConfiguration(),
predicate);
```

```
job.setMapOutputKeyClass(ByteBuffer.class);
job.setMapOutputValueClass(List.class);
job.setOutputFormatClass(ColumnFamilyOutputFormat.class);
ConfigHelper.setOutputColumnFamily(job.getConfiguration(),
        Util.envOrProp("KS"), Util.envOrProp("CF"));

job.waitForCompletion(true);
```

The output format accepts a **ByteBuffer** and a list of **Mutation** objects. Comment the existing `context.write()` call and replace it.

```
//context.write(akey, value);
context.write(key, Collections.singletonList(getMutation(source
Column, value)));
}
```

2. Construct a new mutation using the column name and the new value in uppercase:

```
private static Mutation getMutation(ByteBuffer word, Text value)
{
    Column c = new Column();
    c.name = word;
    c.value = ByteBuffer.wrap(value.getBytes());
    c.timestamp = System.currentTimeMillis() * 1000;

    Mutation m = new Mutation();
    m.column_or_supercolumn = new ColumnOrSuperColumn();
    m.column_or_supercolumn.column = c;
    return m;
}
```

3. Rebuild the `hpc_build` project and run the code again:

```
$ cd <hpc_build>
$ ant
```

The `OutputFormat` uses Avro and more JARs are required to run the job. Add the following files to the `-libjar` list and run the program again.

- ❑ avro-1.4.0-fixes.jar
- ❑ jackson-core-asl-1.4.0.jar
- ❑ jackson-mapper-asl-1.4.0.jar

4. Confirm that the values of the column are in uppercase:

```
[default@ks33] list cf33;
Using default limit of 100
-------------------
RowKey: stacey
```

```
=> (column=favorite_movie, value=DRDOLITTLE,
RowKey: ed
=> (column=favorite_movie, value=MEMENTO,
RowKey: bob
=> (column=favorite_movie, value=MEMENTO,
3 Rows Returned.
```

How it works...

The `OutputFormat` receives data from `MapReduce` and writes the data to Cassandra. Having support for both `InputFormat` and `OutputFormat` allows users to mix and match how they approach problems. This job reads from Cassandra, processes using Hadoop, and then writes the data back to Cassandra. However, users can read data from Hadoop and write to Cassandra or vice-versa.

Using MapReduce to do grouping and counting with Cassandra input and output

Many types of grid computing systems can divide a problem into smaller sub-problems and distribute this across many nodes. Hadoop's distributed computing model uses `MapReduce`. `MapReduce` has a map phase, a shuffle sort that uses a `Partitioner` to guarantee that identical keys go to the same reducer, and finally a reduce phase. This recipe shows a `word_count` application in the Cassandra contrib. Grouping and counting is a problem ideal for `MapReduce` to solve.

 More information on `MapReduce` can be found on http://en.wikipedia.org/wiki/MapReduce.

Getting ready

The complete code for this example is found here: http://svn.apache.org/repos/asf/cassandra/branches/cassandra-0.7/contrib/word_count/.

How to do it...

The mapper takes a column and breaks it into tokens (individual words) using `StringTokenizer`, a class that splits strings on common tokens such as spaces and columns.

```
public static class TokenizerMapper extends
    Mapper<ByteBuffer, SortedMap<ByteBuffer, IColumn>, Text,
IntWritable>
```

```
        {
            private final static IntWritable one = new IntWritable(1);
            private Text word = new Text();
            private ByteBuffer sourceColumn;
            . . . .
            public void map(ByteBuffer key, SortedMap<ByteBuffer, IColumn>
    columns,
                Context context) throws IOException, InterruptedException
            {
                IColumn column = columns.get(sourceColumn);
                if (column == null)
                    return;
                String value = ByteBufferUtil.string(column.value());
                StringTokenizer itr = new StringTokenizer(value);
                while (itr.hasMoreTokens())
                {
                    word.set(itr.nextToken());
                    context.write(word, one);
                }
            }
        }
```

Equal keys are guaranteed to be processed by the same reducer. This reducer counts how many times a given key occurs.

```
        public static class ReducerToFilesystem extends
            Reducer<Text, IntWritable, Text, IntWritable>
        {
            public void reduce(Text key, Iterable<IntWritable> values,
                Context context)        throws IOException,
    InterruptedException
            {
                int sum = 0;
                for (IntWritable val : values)
                    sum += val.get();
                context.write(key, new IntWritable(sum));
            }
        }
```

How it works...

MapReduce can efficiently parallelize many common algorithms. Grouping and counting is one such application. This application counts the number of times words appear in text. However, much of this code can be used to count hits to a website, or build a reverse index storing the positions of words in a body of text.

Setting up Hive with Cassandra Storage Handler support

Hive is a data warehouse infrastructure built on top of Hadoop that provides tools to enable easy data summarization, ad hoc querying, and analysis of large data sets stored in Hadoop files. It provides a mechanism to put structure on this data and provides a simple query language called Hive QL, which is based on SQL and which enables users familiar with SQL to query this data.

Hive has an API for Storage Handlers that allows data in other systems outside of HDFS to be used as input or output. This recipe shows how to set up Hive with the Cassandra Storage Handler.

Getting ready

You will need to have a working Hadoop deployment. Refer to the recipe *A pseudo-distributed Hadoop setup* in this chapter for more information. The Cassandra Storage Handler has not yet been integrated into a Hive release. You can either build hive from source: `http://wiki.apache.org/hadoop/Hive/GettingStarted#Building_Hive_from_Source` and apply the latest patch: `https://issues.apache.org/jira/browse/HIVE-1434` or you can follow the recipe *Setting up DataStax Brisk the combined stack of Cassandra, Hadoop, and Hive* to get a binary version hive with Storage Handler support.

How to do it...

1. Download and extract Hive release from `http://hive.apache.org`:

```
$ cd ~
$ wget <tar.gz for latest release>
$ tar -xf hive-0.8.0.tar.gz
$ cd hive-0.8.0
```

2. Copy all the JAR files from your Cassandra distribution to `auxlib`. Remove libraries that are not needed and may conflict with Hive versions:

```
$ mkdir auxlib
$ cp <cassandra_home>/lib/*.jar auxlib/
$ rm auxlib/antlr*
$ rm auxlib/commons-cli*
```

3. Export the environmental variable `HADOOP_HOME` to the directory of your Hadoop installation:

```
$ export HADOOP_HOME=~/hadoop-0.20.2
```

4. Start Hive:

```
$ bin/hive
hive>
```

How it works...

Hive is built on top of Hadoop. The HADOOP_HOME environment variable needs to be exported so Hive can use it to find required libraries as well as site-specific Hadoop settings such as the hostname and port of the NameNode and JobTracker.

The Cassandra Storage handler requires many libraries from Cassandra to be on the classpath since it uses classes such as the ColumnFamilyInputFormat provided by Cassandra.

See also...

▶ In this chapter, the recipe *Defining a Hive table over a Cassandra Column Family* shows you the next step in the Hive Cassandra integration

▶ In this chapter, the recipe *Joining two Cassandra Column Families using with Hive*

▶ In this chapter, the recipe *Grouping and counting column values with Hive* shows how to use the Storage handler for Analytic queries

Defining a Hive table over a Cassandra Column Family

Hive is designed on the concept that rows in the same table have a fixed number of columns, while a Cassandra row has multiple key value pairs associated with it. You can think of the process of overlaying Hive on Cassandra as turning a map into a fixed array based only on certain key value pairs in the map.

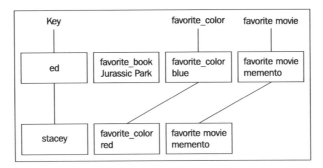

For this recipe, columns such as favorite_book will not be accessible. Additionally, if a row does not have a required column such as favorite_movie, a null value will be returned.

Getting ready

The recipe *Setting up Hive with Cassandra Storage Handler support* for information on installing and configuring Hive.

How to do it...

Tables that use the Cassandra Storage Handler must be **external**. External tables are not physically removed when they are dropped from Hive:

```
hive> CREATE EXTERNAL TABLE IF NOT EXISTS
```

1. Name the table `cf33` and specify two columns `key` of type string and `favorite_movie` of type string:

```
> cf33 (key string, favorite_movie string)
```

The special `STORED BY` clause instructs Hive to use the external storage handler:

```
>  STORED BY 'org.apache.hadoop.hive.cassandra.
CassandraStorageHandler'
```

The `cassandra.columns.mapping` maps the Hive columns to Cassandra columns. The format is `column_family:column_name` and the `special:key`, which means to use the row key:

```
> WITH SERDEPROPERTIES
> ("cassandra.columns.mapping" = ":key,cf33:favorite_movie" ,
```

2. Specify the column family name:

```
> "cassandra.cf.name" = "cf33" ,
```

3. Specify the initial contact host and the RPC port:

```
> "cassandra.host" = "127.0.0.1" , "cassandra.port" = "9160",
```

4. Specify the partitioner being used:

```
"cassandra.partitioner" = "org.apache.cassandra.dht.
RandomPartitioner" )
```

5. In the table properties, specify the keyspace name:

```
TBLPROPERTIES ("cassandra.ks.name" = "ks33");
```

6. After the table is set up, run a simple query that should select all rows and then order the results by the key:

```
hive> SELECT * FROM cf33 ORDER BY key;
Total MapReduce jobs = 1
Launching Job 1 out of 1
...
```

```
bob     memento
ed              memento
stacey drdolittle
Time taken: 37.196 seconds
```

How it works...

The parameters specified when the table is created are stored as the definition of the Hive table. Many of these parameters such as `cassandra.ks.name`, `cassandra.cf.name`, `cassandra.host`, `cassandra.port`, and `cassandra.partitioner` are passed internally to the `ColumnFamilyInput` format. Hive uses the `cassandra.columns.mapping` property to map the columns as they may have different names between the two systems.

Hive uses multiple mappers to fetch all the contents of the column family in parallel. The result of the map phase is then passed into a single reducer; the outputs of a reducer are naturally sorted.

See also...

- ▶ The next recipe, *Joining two Column Families with Hive.*
- ▶ The recipe *Grouping and Counting column values with Hive* in this chapter.

Joining two Column Families with Hive

Joining two data sets on a value is a common operation. This operation is typically done in SQL databases where data is in a normalized form. Data in Cassandra is typically stored in a de-normalized form; however, there are many cases where a user wishes to join columns from two-column families together on a key.

Getting ready

The recipe *Setting up Hive with Cassandra Storage Handler support* is a prerequisite.

How to do it...

1. Create entries in two column families that have the same row key:

```
$ <cassandra_home>/bin/cassandra-cli
[default@ks33] set cfcars['ed']['car']='viper' ;
[default@ks33] set cfcars['stacey']['car']='civic';
[default@ks33] set ed cf33['ed']['favorite_movie']='memento'
[default@ks33] set ed cf33['stacey']['favorite_
movie']='drdolittle'
```

2. Ensure a table is created for each column family:

```
$ <hive_home>/bin/hive
hive> show tables;
OK
cf33
cfcars
Time taken: 0.145 seconds
```

3. Issue a JOIN clause to combine both data sets on the row key:

```
hive> SELECT cf33.key, cf33.favorite_movie, cfcars.car FROM cf33
JOIN cfcars ON cf33.key = cfcars.key;
...
OK
key            favorite_movie      car
ed             memento             viper
stacey         drdoolittle         civic
Time taken: 41.238 seconds
```

How it works...

The Cassandra Storage Handler allows Hive to read data from Cassandra. After this data is read, it is no different than any other data from Hive. It can be joined with another Cassandra table as is done in this example, or it can be joined with a table of HDFS data. Equality joins are efficient in MapReduce as data produced from the map phase is naturally moved to a reducer based on the key.

Grouping and counting column values with Hive

Once a schema is defined inside Hive, many different ad hoc queries can be run against it. Based on the submitted query, Hive generates a plan that may be one or more MapReduce jobs. This recipe shows how to group and count on the values of a specified column using Hive.

How to do it...

1. Insert some entries ensuring that the 'favorite_movie' column is populated:

```
[default@ks33] set cf33['ed']['favorite_movie']='memento';
[default@ks33] set cf33['stacey']['favorite_movie']='drdolittle';
[default@ks33] set cf33['bob']['favorite_movie']='memento';
```

2. Create an HQL query that will count values of the `favorite_movie` column and then order the counts in ascending order:

```
hive> SELECT favorite_movie,count(1) as x FROM cf33 GROUP BY
favorite_movie ORDER BY x;
...
OK
drdolittle     1
memento        2
```

How it works...

Those familiar with Structured Query Language will notice that Hive has the **SELECT**, **GROUP BY**, and **ORDER BY** constructs.

Comparing this recipe with the recipe *A MapReduce program that uses grouping with Cassandra input and output* demonstrates the benefit of the code generation capability of Hive. Coding, compiling, testing, and deploying a MapReduce program can sometimes be replaced by a two-line Hive query!

See also...

In this chapter, the recipe *A MapReduce program that uses grouping with Cassandra input and output*.

Co-locating Hadoop Task Trackers on Cassandra nodes

When multiple applications are run on the same hardware, they affect the performance of each other by competing for the same resources. MapReduce jobs commonly run from several minutes to hours while processing gigabytes of data. Cassandra requests are low latency operations on small amounts of data.

One of the important concepts leveraged by Hadoop is that moving data is more intensive than moving processing. When a Hadoop **job** is divided into **tasks**, the scheduler attempts to run the task on a node where the data is. This is referred to as **data locality**.

This recipe shows how to achieve data locality when using Hadoop and Cassandra, as well as configuration suggestions so they run on the same hardware while isolating them from each other.

How to do it...

If your system has multiple disks, consider isolating the TaskTracker to its own disk(s).

1. Edit `<hadoop_home>/conf/mapred-site.xml`:

```
<property>
    <name>mapred.temp.dir</name>
    <value>/mnt/hadoop_disk/mapred/temp</value>
</property>
```

2. Set the values of `*.task.maximum` to low numbers:

```
<property>
    <name>mapred.tasktracker.reduce.tasks.maximum</name>
    <value>1</value>
</property>
<property>
    <name>mapred.tasktracker.map.tasks.maximum</name>
    <value>3</value>
</property>
```

3. Set the `-Xmx` size of forked processes:

```
<property>
    <name>mapred.child.java.opts</name>
    <value>-Xmx150m</value>
</property>
```

4. Restart the `TaskTracker` for the changes to take effect.

How it works...

MapReduce jobs are IO intensive. They work with large amounts of data, and during operations repeatedly spill data to disk. Having dedicated disks serve as the `mapred.temp.dir` is desirable as it isolates the disk traffic from Cassandra and Hadoop.

Both Cassandra and Hadoop will also compete for the CPU of the system. To control this from the Hadoop side, set `mapred.tasktracker.reduce.tasks.maximum` and `mapred.tasktracker.map.tasks.maximum` to low values. For example, if a system has eight CPU cores, you may only want to dedicate four of them to the `TaskTracker`, leaving the remaining four for Cassandra.

The `mapred.child.java.ops` property is used an argument when map and reduce tasks are forked. When setting the Xmx value in this property, multiply it by (`mapred.tasktracker.reduce.tasks.maximum` + `mapred.tasktracker.map.tasks.maximum`) to determine the maximum memory that can be used at a given time. Balance this out with the memory dedicated to Cassandra.

The next recipe, *Setting up a "Shadow" data center for running only MapReduce Jobs* shows how to use Cassandra's built-in replication to partition a cluster with nodes dedicated for ETL-type workloads and others dedicated for serving low-latency requests.

Setting up a "Shadow" data center for running only MapReduce jobs

MapReduce and other Extract Translate Load (ETL) processing can be intensive, which can interfere with the ability of Cassandra to serve other requests promptly. This recipe shows how to set up a second Cassandra data center for ETL, as depicted in the following image:

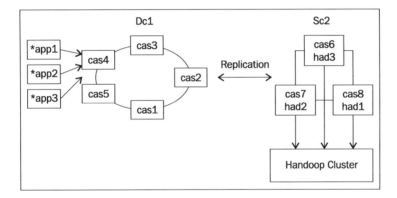

Review the chapter on *Multi datacenter deployments* for recipes on multi-data centers setups.

1. Create a keyspace that is replicated three times in DC1, but only once in DC2:

   ```
   [default@unknown] create keyspace ks33 with
   placement_strategy = 'org.apache.cassandra.locator.
   NetworkTopologyStrategy' and strategy_options=[{DC1:3,DC2:1}];
   ```

2. Open `<cassandra_home/conf/cassandra-topology.properties` in your text editor. Create an entry for each host. Put hosts 1-5 in DC1 and hosts 6-8 in DC2:

   ```
   10.1.2.1=DC1:rack1 #cas1
   10.1.2.2=DC1:rack1
   10.1.2.3=DC1:rack1
   ```

```
10.1.2.4=DC1:rack1
10.1.2.5=DC1:rack1
10.2.5.9=DC2:rack1 #cas6
10.2.3.4=DC2:rack1 #cas7
10.2.3.9=DC2:rack1 #cas8
```

3. Edit `<cassandra_home>/conf/cassandra.yaml` in your text editor:

   `endpoint_snitch: org.apache.cassandra.locator.PropertyFileSnitch`

How it works...

This design leverages the multi-data center capability of Cassandra. Application servers (app1-3) communicate exclusively with Cassandra servers in DC1 (cas1-5), while the Hadoop cluster communicates with DC2 (cas6-8). This division of resources allows ETL-type processes to run without having an impact on the nodes that serve requests to application servers.

There's more...

The hardware in the Shadow data center does not have to be the same class of hardware used for request serving. Also, the number of physical servers may be less. For example, the primary data center might have ten servers with fasts SCSI disks and large amounts of RAM to handle user requests. However, in your shadow data center, three servers with large SATA drives and less RAM may be sufficient for MapReduce or ETL workloads.

Setting up DataStax Brisk the combined stack of Cassandra, Hadoop, and Hive

Brisk contains versions of Cassandra, Hadoop, and Hive that are combined into a single package. This makes it fast and easy to deploy and manage these components as one entity.

How to do it...

1. Download and extract brisk:

```
$ mkdir brisk
$ cd brisk
$ wget --no-check-certificate https://github.com/downloads/
riptano/brisk/brisk-1.0~beta1-bin.tar.gz
$ tar -xf brisk-1.0~beta1-bin.tar.gz
```

2. Start brisk using the `-t` argument to start the Cassandra and Hadoop stack:

```
$ bin/brisk cassandra -t
  INFO 01:12:10,514 Started job history server at: localhost:50030
  INFO 01:12:10,514 Job History Server web address: localhost:50030
  INFO 01:12:10,519 Completed job store is inactive
  INFO 01:12:10,532 Starting ThriftJobTrackerPlugin
  INFO 01:12:10,549 Starting Thrift server
  INFO 01:12:10,553 Hadoop Job Tracker Started...
```

3. Execute `hadoop dfs` commands form inside the shell:

```
$ bin/brisk hadoop dfs -ls /
Found 1 items
drwxrwxrwx   - edward edward          0 2011-05-27 01:12 /tmp
```

4. Start Hive from the brisk shell:

```
$ bin/brisk hive
Hive history file=/tmp/edward/hive_job_log_
edward_201105270113_823009135.txt
hive>
```

How it works

Brisk removes the need to run separate NameNode, SecondaryNameNode, and DataNodes components by storing data directly in **Cassandra File System** (**CFS**), which works as a drop-drop-in replacement for HDFS. The Hive metadata, typically stored in a relational datastore, is also stored directly in Cassandra. Brisk is ideal for those wishing to use Cassandra and who do not wish to manage Hadoop components separately.

12
Collecting and Analyzing Performance Statistics

In this chapter, you will learn the following recipes:

- ▶ Finding bottlenecks with nodetool tpstats
- ▶ Using nodetool cfstats to retrieve column family statistics
- ▶ Monitoring CPU utilization
- ▶ Adding read/write graphs to find active column families
- ▶ Using Memtable graphs to profile when and why they flush
- ▶ Graphing SSTable count
- ▶ Monitoring disk utilization and having a performance baseline
- ▶ Profiling the effectiveness of caches with cache graphs
- ▶ Monitoring compaction by graphing its activity
- ▶ Using nodetool compaction stats to check the progress of compaction
- ▶ Graphing column family statistics to track average/max row sizes
- ▶ Using latency graphs to profile time to seek keys
- ▶ Tracking the physical disk size of each column family over time
- ▶ Using nodetool cfhistograms to see the distribution of query latencies
- ▶ Tracking open networking connections

Cassandra offers built-in support for performance counters that provide in-depth information into how the system is doing. Recording the information from these counters is an invaluable asset when troubleshooting and capacity planning. Cassandra provides access to this information through standard JMX MBeans (Java Management eXtension Managed Bean). MBeans make it possible for a variety of applications to collect, report, and alert on this information. This chapter looks in depth at techniques for both standard system monitoring and Cassandra-specific monitoring. It shows which information is important to capture and how to analyze this information.

Some of the recipes in this chapter use the Cacti network management system (`http://www.cacti.net`) and cassandra-cacti-m6 `http://www.jointhegrid.com/ cassandra/cassandra-cacti-m6.jsp` to collect and graph performance counters from Cassandra's JMX.

Finding bottlenecks with nodetool tpstats

The Cassandra server internals are designed with SEDA (Staged Event Driven Architecture). Rather than spawning a thread per request, the requests are transferred between queues of bounded size called **thread pools**. If thread pools are filled, requests get backlogged and clients will begin experiencing delays or exceptions. A good first step in diagnosing a performance problem is running **tpstats** (thread pool stats) and determining if any stage is backlogged.

How to do it...

Use `nodetool tpstats` to connect to the JMX port of the server you would like to gather statistics on.

```
$   <cassandra_home>/bin/nodetool -h 127.0.0.1 -p 8080 tpstats
```

Pool Name	Active	Pending	Completed
ReadStage	0	0	8
RequestResponseStage	0	0	210271
MutationStage	0	0	333208
ReadRepairStage	0	0	0
GossipStage	0	0	92134
AntiEntropyStage	0	0	0
MigrationStage	0	0	2
MemtablePostFlusher	0	0	5
StreamStage	0	0	0
FlushWriter	0	0	4
MiscStage	0	0	0

FlushSorter	0	0	0
InternalResponseStage	0	0	3
HintedHandoff	0	0	2

How it works...

Any stage that has a non-zero number in the **Active** or **Pending** column is backlogged. A healthy system shows near zero at most times in all stages for both the **Active** and **Pending** states.

There's more...

The **ReadStage** and **RequestResponseStage** search data and return the results to the client.

Some stages such as the **AntiEntropyStage** are entered by administrative actions such as running `nodetool repair`.

The **FlushStage** happens periodically when Memtables hit their thresholds and flush to disk. Sustained non-zero values for active and pending inside this stage are rare. Since flushing to disk is a serial operation, this would indicate an extremely overburdened disk subsystem.

MutationStage is the stage that handles write operations. Because the write stage is highly optimized, backlog in this stage would indicate either an extreme volume of write activity and that the disk with the commit log cannot sustain the write traffic.

Using nodetool cfstats to retrieve column family statistics

Each column family has a number of performance counters that provide in-depth diagnostics. The **cfstats** (column family statistics) option shows a high level summary of the column family information.

How to do it...

Use `nodetool cfstats` to retrieve the column family information.

```
$  <hpcas>/bin/nodetool -h 127.0.0.1 -p 8080 cfstats
Keyspace: Keyspace1
        Read Count: 0
        Read Latency: NaN ms.
        Write Count: 333208
        Write Latency: 0.020031103694989314 ms.
```

```
Pending Tasks: 0
        Column Family: Standard1
        SSTable count: 0
        Space used (live): 0
        Space used (total): 0
        Memtable Columns Count: 1666040
        Memtable Data Size: 84968040
        Memtable Switch Count: 0
        Read Count: 0
        Read Latency: NaN ms.
        Write Count: 333208
        Write Latency: 0.020 ms.
        Pending Tasks: 0
        Key cache capacity: 200000
        Key cache size: 0
        Key cache hit rate: NaN
        Row cache: disabled
        Compacted row minimum size: 0
        Compacted row maximum size: 0
        Compacted row mean size: 0
```

How it works...

Some values in the cfstats output represent values that are a current size such as **SSTable count**. Other fields such as **Write Count** represent counters that need to be sampled over time to determine a rate. Each column family has its own set of values. Averages of specific variables such as **Read Count** are used to summarize the activity of the keyspace.

See also...

Further information on many of these fields is described in other recipes across this chapter.

Monitoring CPU utilization

The CPU activity is one of the most important factors of performance. This recipe shows the CPU graph and describes how to interpret the following CPU graph:

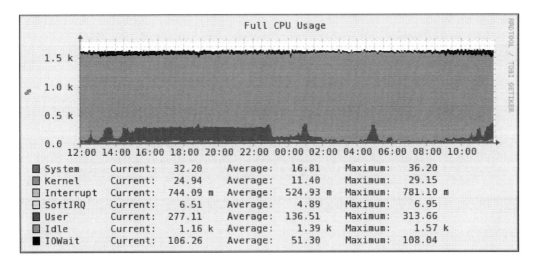

How to do it...

The following table lists descriptions of the major CPU states:

State	Description
user	Shows the percentage of CPU utilization that occurred while executing at the user level (application).
system	Shows the percentage of CPU utilization that occurred while executing at the system level (kernel).
idle	Shows the percentage of time that the CPU or CPUs were idle during which the system had an outstanding disk I/O request.
IOWait	Shows the percentage of time that the CPU or CPUs were idle and the system did not have an outstanding disk I/O request.

With this graph:

▶ Track each state and compare the results over time

▶ Ensure sufficient IDLE cycles for future growth

▶ Track IOWait to look out for disk and network bottlenecks

How it works...

Every workload is different. Sites that use Cassandra in a caching role have small data sets compared to RAM size. Under load, they will typically see the **User** and **System** states increase and become a bottleneck. For sites that use Cassandra to store significantly more data than RAM, **IOWait** will usually become the limiting factor.

The Java garbage collection process utilizes multiple threads to sweep through memory often and avoids pauses. Generally, if a system is spending time in **Idle** state there is spare capacity. However, the **IOWait** state, `wa` when using the `top` command, indicates the system is waiting on disk or network IO. Because the system is waiting on those resources, it can not fully utilize the CPU.

Make sure to collect IOWait and Idle information

Some NMS systems provide CPU graphs that do not record IOWait and other system states. High IOWait will prevent you from fully utilizing your CPU. Those only recording a few states such as **User**, **System**, and **Idle** could look at a graph showing 200 percent User, 700 percent Idle and wonder why Cassandra is not fully utilizing their processor. That reason could be that 300 percent of the CPU time is spent waiting for IO!

See also...

High `IOWait` usually means that your disk subsystem is overworked. Review the *Monitoring disk utilization and having a performance baseline* recipe to learn how to monitor hard disk activity.

Adding read/write graphs to find active column families

Each column family tracks the read and write requests to it. This recipe describes the CFStores Read/Write graph and the information it provides, which is depicted as follows:

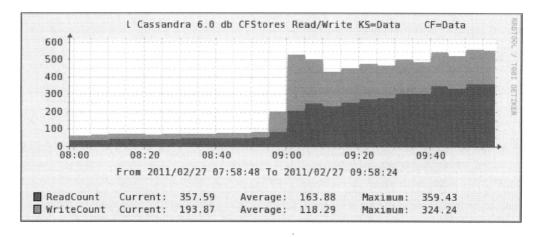

How to do it...

In this graph, the **ReadCount** is represented as an area in blue and the **WriteCount** is an area in green stacked above it. The more requests on a given column family, the more system resources are being used. Use this information to:

- ▶ Correlate with Disk and CPU usage graphs to determine approximately how many operations per second a system can support
- ▶ Track these values over time to monitor usage patterns

How it works...

Tracking, trending, and having a baseline for your read and write activity is critical. For example, a software release could accidentally triple read operations, and without knowing the normal rate, detecting the issue would be difficult. Knowing which column families are the most active is important when deciding where to allocate larger caches.

There's more...

The hinted handoff stores records that were destined to downed nodes. Currently, hinted handoff reads from the source system to find the data that needs to be replayed to the other nodes. This causes read traffic to temporarily increase on the nodes storing hints after a failed node comes back online.

Using Memtable graphs to profile when and why they flush

Memtables are in-memory sorted structures that data is written to. The Memtables flush when their time, size, or activity thresholds are triggered. This recipe describes how to interpret activity from the following Memtable graph:

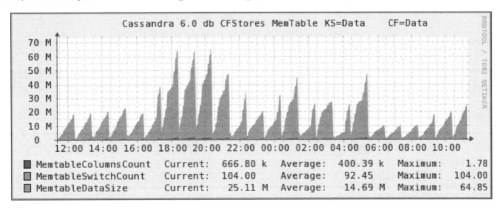

How it works...

In this graph, the orange area represents **MemtableDataSize**, which is the size of the Memtable including all keys and columns. The blue area, **MemtableColumnsCount**, is the number of columns in the Memtable. The size of the table grows until a flush to disk is triggered and the size and column count are reset to zero. Use this graph to:

▶ Ensure the saw tooth action of this graph is periodic

▶ Examine the cause of Memtable flushes

▶ Compare Memtable size with memory usage and ensure large Memtable settings are not causing memory contention

There's more...

If a column is written twice to a Memtable, it will be overridden. If Memtable settings are set higher, Memtables will flush less. This increases the chances that data will not be written to disk multiple times. Flushing often creates multiple SSTables, which may in turn trigger more compaction. If this disk is flushing and compacting often, it has less resources to spend responding to user's requests.

See also...

In *Chapter 4, Performance Tuning*, the recipe *Memtable tuning for write-heavy workloads*.

The recipe *Monitoring compaction by graphing its activity* in this chapter.

Graphing SSTable count

Cassandra's SSTables are written once and never modified. For an active column family with frequent writes and/or deletes, new SSTables are created often. The compaction manager has thresholds that are triggered and combine multiple SSTables into one. This recipe shows how to interpret the data from the SSTable graph, which is shown as follows:

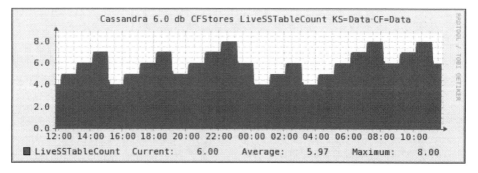

How to do it...

The blue area represents the **LiveSSTableCount**. Each **SSTable** also has an **Index** and **Bloom Filter** file. Each read may have to check for data in all the SSTables in a column family. Having more SSTables slows down the read path. SSTables that have to be part of a snapshot may still exist on disk, but are not counted by this graph. Use this graph to:

▶ Ensure that the SSTable count stays low (single digits)

▶ Compare the SSTable count with historical information

There's more...

The compaction thresholds try to ensure that the SSTable count stays low. It may grow temporarily during a large compaction, or possibly if compaction is disabled for a bulk load. However, if SSTable count begins to grow, it may be time to tune Memtable or compaction settings, or get more hardware.

Monitoring disk utilization and having a performance baseline

For deployments where the data on disk is larger than the amount of RAM on system, disk performance becomes a larger factor in performance. This recipe shows how to monitor the activity of a hard disk, as depicted in the following graph:

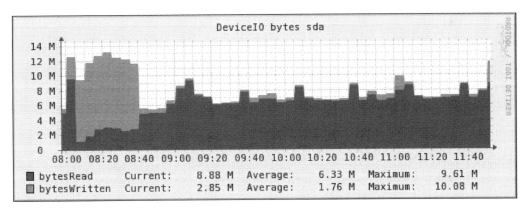

How to do it...

The area of the graph in blue is **bytesRead** that represents the bytes read from disk per second. The area stacked on top of **bytesRead** in green is **bytesWritten**, the bytes written to disk per second. Use this graph to:

- ▶ Keep track of disk utilization over time

- ▶ Ensure disk activity is not maxed out during peak times

- ▶ Correlate the activity of this graph with the Cache Activity graph to determine the I/O savings that different cache configurations provide

How it works...

Disks on platters are capable of reading and writing fast serially. However, seeking across disk is slower. The majority of use cases exhibit a random read pattern. Random reads cause the hard disk to spend more time seeking than reading and thus limit throughput.

There's more...

Solid State Drives (SSD) offer an interesting solution to random read challenge. A solid state drive has no moving parts and never has to seek access to any data location. This technology is new and more expensive than standard spinning disks.

See also...

See the recipes *Using a dedicated commit log disk*, *Choosing a high performing RAID Level*, and *File system optimization for hard disk performance* in *Chapter 4, Performance Tuning* for information on tuning physical disks.

How to do it...

Towards the bottom of the graph, the **Cache Hit Rate** represents the number of **Requests** divided by the number of **Cache Hits**. The higher the **Cache Hit Rate**, the more effective the cache. Use this graph to:

- ▶ Compare the cache hit ratio with yesterday or last week and ensure changing traffic patterns are not affecting the hit rate

- ▶ Correlate the activity of this graph with the Device I/O graph to determine how much I/O savings different cache configurations provide

- ▶ Ensure caches are not growing large when they are set as a percentage rather than a fixed size

How it works...

Caching can make a drastic difference in performance if the situation is right and the caches are employed correctly. Understanding the concept of **active set** is helpful. Active set can be considered as the portion of your data that is in use at a given time. As a hypothetical example, a node has 400 GB of data storing information on 100,000,000 users. At any given time, a small portion of those users may be active, such as five percent. If you employ correctly sized caches, a small amount of memory can effectively cache the five percent of active users, making the service responsive for them.

Cache tuning involves making caches large enough to achieve a high hit rate. The goal is to keep as much of the active set in memory as possible as this lowers disk activity.

The law of diminishing returns may apply to cache sizes. For example, a 50,000 item cache might achieve a 90 percent hit rate, while a 100,000 item cache may achieve a 92 percent hit rate. It may not make sense to double the memory in that case to achieve only a two percent higher rate.

See also...

In *Chapter 4, Performance Tuning* the recipes *Boosting read performance with the Key Cache* and *Boosting read performance with the Row Cache*

Monitoring compaction by graphing its activity

Compaction is a necessary process in the life cycle of the data in Cassandra's structured log format. Compaction removes old data and optimizes the data on disk. Rows marked for deletion with tombstones are candidates to be removed entirely. This recipe shows how to monitor compaction graphically.

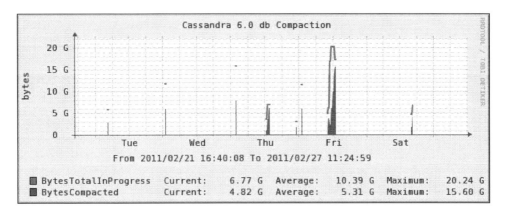

Network Management Systems typically monitor at five-minute intervals. Due to the way compaction counters are kept, it is possible that a graph sampling at five-minute intervals could miss a compaction event. However, generally these smaller compactions are not performance impacting.

How it works...

When a compaction starts, the red line in the graph records **BytesTotalInProgress**, which is the amount of data that needs to be compacted. The blue area renders **ByteCompacted**, which is the current progress. When the blue area meets with the red line, the compaction is done. An absence of graph elements indicate no compaction is happening at that time.

▶ Review this graph periodically and ensure your system is not compacting often

▶ Find slow periods to do long compaction operations such as repairs and joins

There's more...

Compaction should not be looked at as a negative. After all, compaction removes old data and optimizes the data on disk. However, if systems are in a compaction state often, user requests will have more latency. In most cases, it is desirable for compactions to finish as quickly as possible, and short quick spikes in the compaction graph show just that. A health system should be able to compact many gigabytes of data in a short time period. If a system is beginning to become overloaded, its compaction process could become long and drawn out.

Adjusting your Memtable settings so that they flush less should cause less compaction. It is also possible to manually run major compaction at specified times. This lowers the chance a larger compaction will automatically trigger during peak request load.

See also...

In *Chapter 4, Performance Tuning* the recipe *Setting compaction thresholds* shows how to change the criteria that cause compaction.

The next recipe, *Using nodetool compaction stats to check the progress of compaction* for a command-line alternative to this graph.

Using nodetool compaction stats to check the progress of compaction

Nodes can compact for several reasons. They can compact automatically when the compaction thresholds are reached. A **major compaction** is a compaction of all the SSTables for a column family that is triggered by the user. Joining and leaving nodes trigger **anti compactions**, as does **anti entropy repairs** . This recipe shows how to check and monitor compaction using `nodetool`.

How to do it...

The `nodetool compactionstats` command allows you to quickly see if a compaction is in progress.

```
$  <cassandra_home>/bin/nodetool -h 127.0.0.1 -p 8080 compactionstats
compaction type: Major
column family: standard1
bytes compacted: 49925478
bytes total in progress: 63555680
pending tasks: 1
```

How it works...

This command is a quick way to determine if a node is compacting and monitoring how close it is to finishing. Use this to determine if a compaction is the reason for performance degradation or to see how a node join is progressing.

Graphing column family statistics to track average/max row sizes

Rows can have between a single column and up to two billion columns inside them. During compaction, information is collected about the rows that were compacted. This recipe shows how to interpret this graph and the implications of row size in Cassandra, which is depicted as follows:

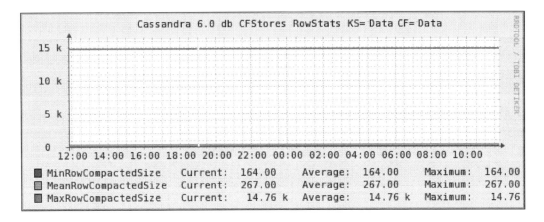

How to do it...

The red, green, and blue lines represent max, mean, and min row compacted size. These values are the raw byte size of rows. That is, a key and all its columns.

▶ Use **MaxRowCompactedSize** to ensure that rows are not growing larger than expected

▶ Use the **MeanRowCompactedSize** to help determine how much space a particular cache will use

Row cache and large rows

Using the row cache creates memory pressure when rows are very large. Remember that all the columns of a row must be cached when using the row cache.

Using latency graphs to profile time to seek keys

Latency is an important factor when serving data to clients. Cassandra tracks latency, which does not include the network latency; it counts time the request is received to the time it is found or inserted to disk. This recipe shows how to interpret the graph.

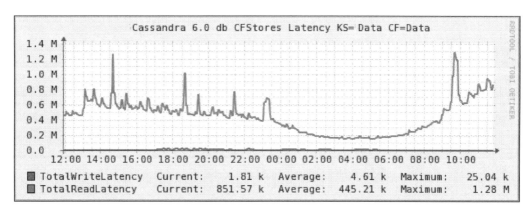

How to do it...

During read operations, Cassandra tracks information on the cumulative time spent searching for data and makes this available as **TotalReadLatencyMicros**. When this value is divided by the read count, the result is average read latency per request. This graph displays that calculated value. Use this information to:

▶ Ensure that latency stays within acceptable values

▶ Compare this latency with results from yesterday or last week

Because the write path of Cassandra involves writing to a sorted-in memory table and serially to a disk, write operations typically have very low latency and are constant. Constant low values are typically not useful to graph.

How it works...

Latency is a function of many things: data size, disk search speed, load from other requests, and caching. This means that smaller column families will search faster than larger ones. Disks capable of more Revolutions Per Minute, such as SCSI, will search faster than SATA disks. More simultaneous requests will cause more contention and more latency. Caching in the form of Cassandra's built-in key cache and row cache as well as VFS cache (system RAM) reduce latency by serving some or possibly all of the data from memory.

Tracking the physical disk size of each column family over time

It is common to graph your system's total disk usage. Each column family has its own statistics that record disk size. This recipe shows how to interpret data from the Column Family Store graph, as depicted in the following graph:

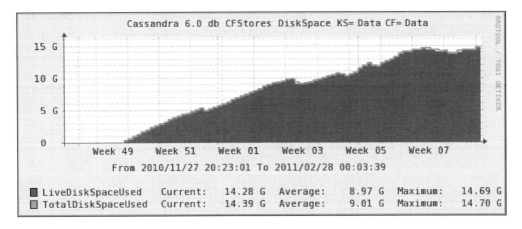

How to do it...

The blue area, **LiveDiskSpaceUsed**, represents storage being used by Data, Index, and Bloom Filter files. The green line, **TotalDiskSpaceUsed**, also tracks temporary files being created by compaction.

▶ Track the size of column families and project the growth rate

▶ Ensure that during compaction that **TotalDiskSpaceUsed** is not filling the disk

How it works...

Column Family size is also important to the performance of read and write operations. As a hypothetical example, on a given server it may be possible to serve 1,000 requests per second when the column family size is 10 GB, but only 750 requests per second when the column family size is 15 GB. Thus, it is important to be able to correlate column family size with other information such as latency and request rate.

Using nodetool cfhistograms to see the distribution of query latencies

Nodetool provides the `cfhistograms` command to display the latency information of requests. This is helpful for determining the performance of requests without having to record information in an external NMS.

How to do it...

Run `nodetool cfhistograms` command.

```
$<cassandra_home>/bin/nodetool -h 127.0.0.1 -p 8080 cfhistograms
testkeyspace testcf | awk '{print $1 $3 $5}'
```

Offset	Read Latency	Column Count
1	0	0
2	1	4
3	998	7
4	7729	4
5	22844	15
6	44439	10

How it works...

Histograms are useful for seeing the distribution of request times. This is helpful in cases where knowing the average request time is not enough. For example, a request hitting the row cache may have low latency where requests not cached may be considerably slower.

See also...

In this chapter, the recipe *Using latency graphs to profile time to seek keys* shows a way to visualize latency information such as the cfhistogram stats.

Tracking open networking connections

Cassandra is a client server application. Each client that connects uses resources. In the operating system, each open socket requires CPU and memory to manage it. Inside the virtual machine each thread uses resources as well. This recipe shows how to interpret what the following TCP connection graphs are showing. The first shows current established connections:

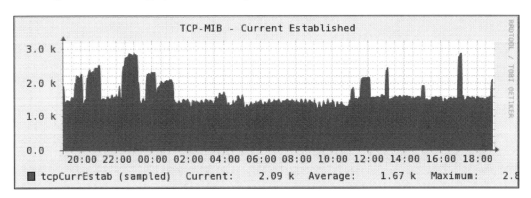

The second graph shows how many connections are listening:

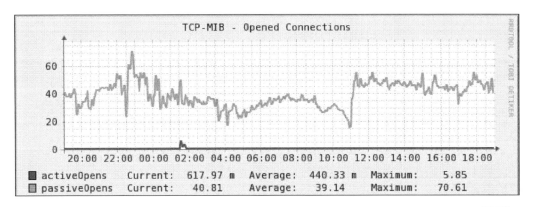

How to do it...

In the **Current Established** graph, the **tcpCurrEstab** area shows how many sockets are open across the system. Use this information to do the following:

- ▶ Ensure open connections are not exceeding operating system thresholds.
- ▶ Ensure that connections are not being left open by clients.
- ▶ In the **Opened connections** graph, the **passiveOpens** line shows the number of times TCP connections have made a direct transition to the SYN-RCVD state from the LISTEN state. Use the information to monitor how many listening sockets are open on the system.

How it works...

The Management Information Base for the Transmission Control Protocol (TCP) provides a spec that systems implementing TCP should implement. Numerous counters are available that can be used to get performance information and troubleshoot the TCP stack. This information is important to Cassandra because of the high request rate and amount of internode communication.

There's more...

The SNMP Management Information Base file, which describes the information that can be monitored: `https://www.ietf.org/rfc/rfc4022.txt`.

13

Monitoring Cassandra Servers

In this chapter, you will learn:

- ▶ Forwarding Log4j logs to a central server
- ▶ Using top to understand overall performance
- ▶ Using iostat to monitor current disk performance
- ▶ Using sar to review performance over time
- ▶ Using JMXTerm to access Cassandra JMX
- ▶ Monitoring for Garbage Collection Events
- ▶ Using tpstats to find bottlenecks
- ▶ Creating a Nagios Check Script for Cassandra
- ▶ Keep an eye out for large rows with compaction limits
- ▶ Reviewing network traffic with IPTraf
- ▶ Keep on the lookout for Dropped Messages
- ▶ Inspecting Column Families for dangerous conditions

Introduction

Getting Cassandra running at maximum efficiency involves understanding how it is utilizing the hardware and the operating system. It also requires understanding the inner workings of Cassandra to know when things are working non-optimally. This chapter focuses on applying conventional and Cassandra-specific monitoring techniques.

Forwarding Log4j logs to a central sever

The faster a problem can be diagnosed and corrected, the better. In environments with only a few systems, connection to the server over SSH and using command-line tools to examine logfiles is usually sufficient. Since a Cassandra cluster can range from one to a few hundred nodes, a better way to aggregate and review logs is needed. This recipe shows how to configure Cassandra's logging mechanism, Log4J, to send events to its local logfile as well as a remote syslog server.

Getting ready

Syslog is a simple text-based protocol designed to transfer log messages over UDP. Modern Linux distributions have a syslog server installed by default. Designate a system as a syslog server and prepare it to accept remote messages.

1. Edit `/etc/syslog.conf`:

   ```
   # Provides UDP syslog reception
   $ModLoad imudp.so
   $UDPServerRun 514
   ```

2. Restart the `rsyslog` service:

   ```
   # /etc/init.d/rsyslog restart
   Shutting down system logger:                                      [  OK  ]
   Starting system logger:                                           [  OK  ]
   ```

3. Check to make sure the UDP port 514 is listening.

   ```
   # netstat -nl | grep 514
   udp        0        0 0.0.0.0:514              0.0.0.0:*
   udp        0        0 :::514                   :::*
   ```

How to do it...

The Log4j messages in Cassandra do not always contain the hostname of the system generating the message. The `${HOSTNAME}` environment variable is available on Linux systems. Capture the hostname by adding the following line in `cassandra-env.sh` to use later:

```
JVM_OPTS="$JVM_OPTS -Dlogging.hostname=${HOSTNAME}"
```

1. Add an appender named `SYSLOG_LOCAL1` to the `log4j-server.properties` file:

   ```
   INFO,stdout,R,SYSLOG_LOCAL1
   ```

2. Configure the `SYSLOG_LOCAL1` appender to send messages to syslog:

```
log4j.appender.SYSLOG_LOCAL1=org.apache.log4j.net.SyslogAppender
log4j.appender.SYSLOG_LOCAL1.threshold=INFO
log4j.appender.SYSLOG_LOCAL1.syslogHost=sylogserver.domain.pvt
log4j.appender.SYSLOG_LOCAL1.facility=LOCAL1
log4j.appender.SYSLOG_LOCAL1.facilityPrinting=false
log4j.appender.SYSLOG_LOCAL1.layout=org.apache.log4j.PatternLayout
```

3. Use the `logging.hostname` variable defined in `cassandra-env.sh` to ensure each log includes the hostname of the system that generated:

```
log4j.appender.SYSLOG_LOCAL1.layout.conversionPattern=[%p]
${logging.hostname} %c:%L - %m%n
```

4. Restart Cassandra for these changes to take effect:

How it works...

Log4j is a versatile logging framework that is used by numerous projects. Log4j uses Java property files for configuration and has many options to control how logs are formatted and how large they can get before a new one is created. Log4j also has a number of built-in appenders such as the `SyslogAppender` used in this recipe. The `SyslogAppender` transmits messages using Syslog protocol to a remove logging host. By aggregating logs from multiple Cassandra servers to a single host, events from multiple servers can be correlated when troubleshooting.

There's more....

Syslog is a simple protocol for sending text-based log messages over UDP. UDP messages have less overhead compared to TCP; however, there are no transmission guarantees. This means that syslog messages could be lost. There are more advanced syslog servers that have more features such as syslog-ng. Another interesting tool is Splunk (`http://www.splunk.com/download`), which indexes logs and offers a web-based interface to search. It is seen in the following screenshot:

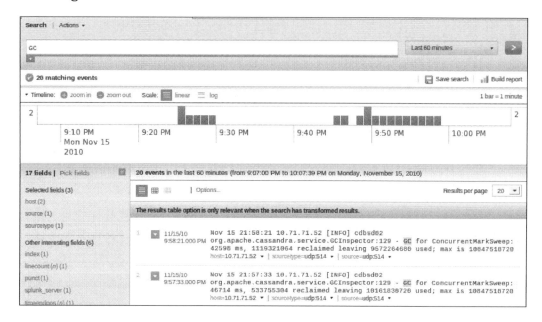

Using top to understand overall performance

`top` gathers a variety of performance information from across the system. It uses this information and updates the console display on an interval. This information combined with knowledge of Cassandra's inner workings is invaluable in understanding how to optimize your deployment. This recipe shows how to use `top` to determine how Cassandra is operating.

How to do it...

The section demonstrates `top` output on two separate server class machines with the same RAM, disk, and CPU running Cassandra. For the purpose of this example, the second system either has more data or is seeing more requests.

1. Run `top` from the command line. This was run against a server with moderate load:

```
$ top
top - 21:51:59 up 6 days,  8:30,  1 user,
```

Each OS calculates this differently. However, it is generally described as the number of active processes. Load averages below one indicate there is ample spare processing.

load average: 0.74, 0.92, 0.81

Tasks: 223 total,   1 running, 222 sleeping,   0 stopped,   0 zombie

Low user (us) and low wait (wa) indicate that the system is not CPU or disk-bound. This should mean that your node can handle more requests than it currently is handling.

Cpu(s): 1.2%us,   0.2%sy, 0.0%ni, 97.0%id, 1.5%wa, 0.0%hi, 0.1%si, 0.0%st

Mem: 16410904k total, 14979268k used,   1431636k free,
      29192k buffers

Swap: 0k total,   0k used,   0k free,

VFS caches files data in memory. Cache is not removed until other programs need memory or other items are added to the cache. Any disk information in cache can be read from memory instead of the hard disk.

9435876k cached

```
 PID USER        PR  NI  VIRT  RES   SHR
S %CPU %MEM    TIME+   COMMAND
20181 cassandr  20   0   244g 8.3g 3.7g S 29.6 52.8 804:55.01 java
```

2. Run top in thread mode. The following is the output against a server with heavy load:

   $top -H

   top - 22:10:31 up 6 days, 10:03,   1 user,

   The load averages are higher than one.

   load average: 7.64, 9.08, 9.85

   In the thread mode, top displays thread counts instead of process counts. Two threads are running in this output.

   Tasks: 472 total,   2 running, 470 sleeping,   0 stopped,   0 zombie

   While the user state (us) looks low, the wait is 12 percent. This means that the processor cannot be fully utilized.

   Cpu(s): 5.3%us,   1.0%sy, 0.5%ni, 80.6%id, 12.2%wa, 0.0%hi,
           0.3%si, 0.0%st
   Mem: 16411688k total, 16351132k used,   60556k free,
              2592k buffers
   Swap: 0k total,   0k used,   0k free,

3. The Cassandra process has consumed more memory. This has limited the cache memory available:

```
       7256672k cached
  PID USER      PR  NI  VIRT  RES  SHR S %CPU %MEM    TIME+
COMMAND
28569 cassandr  16   0  536g  11g 4.0g S 16.6 73.3  0:54.39 java
```

4. Processes in the D state are in an unimplementable sleep state. These are likely to be threads waiting for data from the disk. These contribute to the wait as seen previously:

```
29190 cassandr  20   4  536g  11g 4.0g D 12.9 73.3 126:52.95 java
28551 cassandr  16   0  536g  11g 4.0g D  9.2 73.3   0:52.12 java
10201 cassandr  16   0  536g  11g 4.0g S  7.4 73.3  38:46.43 java
```

How it works...

Top gathers information from numerous sources and displays it in a display that refreshes every few seconds. Top is one of the best ways to determine what resources are being used and by which processes.

There's more...

For terminals that are capable of displaying color and have other advanced features, the htop command can be used in combination with top.

Using iostat to monitor current disk performance

The iostat command uses counter information from the /proc file system to calculate system utilization. For those using Cassandra for data sets significantly larger them main memory, disk performance is a major factor in the read and write throughput of Cassandra. This recipe shows how to use the iostat command to examine disk performance.

Getting ready

Ensure the sysstat package is installed.

```
# rpm -qa sysstat
sysstat-7.0.2-3.el5_5.1
```

If the package is not installed, install it with yum (or similar package fetch tools).

```
# yum install sysstat
```

How to do it...

Run `iostat` at five-second intervals for three intervals; use `awk` to limit the columns displayed:

```
# iostat -xd 5 3 sda | awk '{print $6" "$7" "$10" "$12}'
rsec/s wsec/s await %util
34078.47 2582.45 4.46 76.44

rsec/s wsec/s await %util
20982.40 67.20 10.91 76.42

rsec/s wsec/s await %util
17952.00 588.80 10.57 66.06
```

How it works...

The first output from `iostat` is the sum of information since system startup. After that, the statistics are calculated by the interval specified (five seconds). The columns `rsec` and `wsec` show blocks read and written per second respectively. `Await` represents the average milliseconds a disk request takes. `%util` represents the portion of time the disk is working over the time it is idle.

As the disk utilization becomes closer to 100 percent servicing, read and write requests will begin to take longer. Short bursts of high disk activity are normal during compaction. However, systems with high utilization may not have enough disk IO. Solutions to high disk utilization may include dedicating more memory to caching. It also may be an indication that new nodes need to be added to the cluster, or that the current cluster nodes need a high performing disk subsystem.

See also...

The next recipe, *Using sar to review performance over time*

Using sar to review performance over time

Most sites have traffic patterns that vary throughout the day and week. The `system activity data collector, sadc,` collects and stores performance information over time. The `sar` command allows users to view this data. This recipe shows how to use `sar` to understand Cassandra system utilization over time.

Getting ready

The data collection may not be enabled by default. Creating a file `/etc/cron.d/sysstat` allows crontab to manage the collection of this data.

```
# Run system activity accounting tool every 10 minutes
*/10 * * * * root /usr/lib64/sa/sa1 -S DISK 1 1
# 0 * * * * root /usr/lib64/sa/sa1 -S DISK 600 6 &
# Generate a daily summary of process accounting at 23:53
53 23 * * * root /usr/lib64/sa/sa2 -A
```

How to do it...

Run the `sar` command. `%nice` and `%steal` columns have been omitted:

```
# sar -u | tail -5
02:00:01 AM        CPU     %user    %system    %iowait    %idle
02:00:01 PM        all      3.51      1.05       6.18      89.26
02:10:01 PM        all      4.29      0.98       6.00      88.74
02:20:01 PM        all      3.78      0.98       5.87      89.37
02:30:01 PM        all      3.97      1.07       6.40      88.56
Average:           all      3.71      0.95       4.12      91.13
```

How it works...

The `sar` utility shows processor utilization over time. The information provided by `sar` can be used in several ways. First, it can help determine if CPU or IOWait is high during times of the day. The best time to schedule intensive operations such as joining new nodes, scheduling major compaction, or running anti-entropy repair is during lulls so they have the lowest impact.

Using JMXTerm to access Cassandra JMX

JMX uses RMI for communication. Because of the design of RMI, it typically has issues working across Network Address Translation Devices, Tunnels, or VPNs. This recipe shows how to use JMXTerm to connect to a JMX application and retrieve statistics from it.

Getting ready

JMXTerm can be found at `http://www.cyclopsgroup.org/projects/jmxterm/`.

How to do it...

1. Start JMXTerm:

   ```
   # java -jar jmxterm-1.0-alpha-4-uber.jar
   Welcome to JMX terminal. Type "help" for available commands.
   ```

2. Open a connection to a Cassandra server on the JMX port:

   ```
   $>open 127.0.0.1:8080
   #Connection to 127.0.0.1:8080
     is opened
   ```

3. JMX objects are organized into **domains**. Use the `domains` command to list them:

   ```
   $>domains
   #following domains are available
   org.apache.cassandra.concurrent
   org.apache.cassandra.db
   ...
   ```

4. Choose the `org.apache.cassandra.db` domain:

   ```
   $>domain org.apache.cassandra.db
   #domain is set to org.apache.cassandra.db
   ```

5. List the beans/objects inside the domain:

   ```
   $>beans
   org.apache.cassandra.db:type=Commitlog
   org.apache.cassandra.db:type=CompactionManager
   ```

6. Select the `Commitlog` bean:

   ```
   $>bean org.apache.cassandra.db:type=Commitlog
   #bean is set to org.apache.cassandra.db:type=Commitlog
   ```

7. Get information on the bean with the `info` command:

   ```
   $>info
   #mbean = org.apache.cassandra.db:type=Commitlog
   #class name = org.apache.cassandra.db.commitlog.
   PeriodicCommitLogExecutorService
   # attributes
      %0    - ActiveCount (int, r)
      %1    - CompletedTasks (long, r)
      %2    - PendingTasks (long, r)
   #there's no operations
   #there's no notifications
   ```

8. Retrieve a value using the get operation:

```
$>get ActiveCount
#mbean = org.apache.cassandra.db:type=Commitlog:
ActiveCount = 1;
```

How it works...

Because JMXTerm can be run on a machine without a windowing subsystem, it can typically be run from the machine Cassandra is running on or another node on the same local network. It provides a way to access all the same JMX attributes and call JMX operations that can be accessed with JConsole.

See also...

In *Chapter 1, Getting Started* the recipe *Connecting to Cassandra with JConsole*.

Monitoring the garbage collection events

In Java programs do not explicitly *deallocate* or free objects from memory. Garbage collection is a background process that navigates the objects in memory to determine which are no longer reachable. Objects no longer reachable can then be removed. If the object creation rate exceeds the object delete rate, the JVM might have a pause, often called stop-the-world. These pauses cause Cassandra to stop responding to requests. This recipe shows how to watch logs for garbage collection events.

How to do it...

Use `grep` to look for the string "`GC inspection`" inside the Cassandra log.

```
$ grep "GC inspection" /var/log/cassandra/system.log

 INFO [GC inspection] 2010-11-15 18:06:44,137 GCInspector.java (line
129) GC for ConcurrentMarkSweep: 49428 ms, 1306542968 reclaimed leaving
7482369272 used; max is 9773776896
```

How it works...

Cassandra has options in the `conf/cassandra-env.sh` that cause Java to print garbage collection messages to the logfile. When the JVM garbage collector returns from a pause, it logs a message containing the information on how long the garbage collection took as well as how much memory was freed during the collection. If these events happen often, this indicates that the system may be overworked.

There's more...

A solution for avoiding pauses is assigning Cassandra more heap memory. However, garbage collections may be caused by inadequate Memtable, cache, or other settings.

Using tpstats to find bottlenecks

Cassandra is written using a SEDA architecture. This architecture is designed to control resource utilization in a high concurrency environment. This recipe shows how to use the tpstats command to diagnose performance bottlenecks in your cluster.

> You can learn more about SEDA from http://www.eecs.harvard.edu/~mdw/proj/seda/.

How to do it...

Use the nodetool tpstats command to supply the hostname and JMX port:

```
$ <cassandra_home>/bin/nodetool -h 127.0.0.1 -p 8080 tpstats
```

Pool Name	Active	Pending	Completed
FILEUTILS-DELETE-POOL	0	0	224
STREAM-STAGE	0	0	0
RESPONSE-STAGE	0	0	88445499
ROW-READ-STAGE	1	1	14665446
LB-OPERATIONS	0	0	0
MISCELLANEOUS-POOL	0	0	0
GMFD	0	0	814173
LB-TARGET	0	0	0
CONSISTENCY-MANAGER	0	0	1181879
ROW-MUTATION-STAGE	0	0	69218180
MESSAGE-STREAMING-POOL	0	0	0
LOAD-BALANCER-STAGE	0	0	0
FLUSH-SORTER-POOL	0	0	0
MEMTABLE-POST-FLUSHER	0	0	322
FLUSH-WRITER-POOL	0	0	322
AE-SERVICE-STAGE	0	0	0
HINTED-HANDOFF-POOL	0	0	161

How it works...

In a healthy cluster, the **Active** and **Pending** columns should be near zero at all times. If any column has a high number of pending operations, this generally indicates a bottleneck.

A high number of pending operations **ROW-READ-STAGE** could indicate the hard disk is over-utilized. Buildup in the **ROW-MUTATION-STAGE** would mean the write path is bottlenecked. Activity in the HINTED-HANDOFF-POOL stage shows other nodes in the cluster are under load and hints are being stored on other nodes. If multiple Memtables are being flushed to disk, **MEMTABLE-POST-FLUSHER** stage will be higher than zero.

See also...

- ▶ In this chapter, the recipe *Using iostat to monitor current disk performance*
- ▶ *Chapter 4, Performance Tuning* the recipe *Tuning concurrent readers and writers for throughput* if **READ-STAGE** or **MUTATION-STAGE** is high but disk is not over-utilized

Creating a Nagios Check Script for Cassandra

Nagios is the de facto standard **Network Monitoring System** (**NMS**). Nagios uses executable programs or scripts to probe the state of services and typically sends e-mails if the services are down. This recipe shows how to build an executable that can be used by Nagios to check Cassandra. Even if you are not using Nagios, you may be able to use this script with your system.

How to do it...

1. Create `<hpc_build>/src/java/hpcas/c13/NagiosCheck.java` with a text editor:

```
package hpcas.c13;
import hpcas.c03.FramedConnWrapper;
import hpcas.c03.Util;
import org.apache.cassandra.thrift.*;

public class NagiosCheck {
  public static void main(String[] args) {
    String host = Util.envOrProp("host");
    String sport = Util.envOrProp("port");
    String expected = Util.envOrProp("clusterName");
    if (host == null || sport == null || expected == null) {
```

```
        System.out.println("Cassandra Fail: specify host port
    clustername");
        System.exit(1);
    }
    int port = Integer.parseInt(sport);
    String gotName = null;
```

2. Connect to the cluster and for a test attempt to read its name:

```
    try {
        FramedConnWrapper fcw = new FramedConnWrapper(host, port);
        fcw.open();
        Cassandra.Client client = fcw.getClient();
        gotName = client.describe_cluster_name();
        fcw.close();
```

If the code takes the exception branch, the operation failed.

```
    } catch (Exception ex) {
        System.out.println("Cassandra FAILED: got exception: " +
    ex);
        System.exit(2);
    }
```

3. If the name retrieved from the server equals the user supplied name, print an **OK** message and then return 0:

```
    if (expected.equalsIgnoreCase(gotName)) {
        System.out.println("Cassandra OK: " + gotName);
        System.exit(0);
    }
```

4. If the name does not match the expected name, print an error condition:

```
    else {
        System.out.println("Cassandra FAILED: Expected:" + expected
    + " got:" + gotName);
        System.exit(2);
    }
  }
}
```

5. Test the script against a live node:

```
$ host=127.0.0.1 port=9160 clusterName="Test Cluster" ant
-DclassToRun=hpcas.c13.NagiosCheck run
```

```
    [java] Cassandra OK: Test Cluster
```

6. Test to see if the failure code works as expected by running the program with the wrong cluster name:

```
$ host=127.0.0.1 port=9160 clusterName="Test Clusterdfd" ant
-DclassToRun=hpcas.c13.NagiosCheck run

    [java] Cassandra FAILED: Expected:Test Clusterdfd got:Test
Cluster
    [java] Java Result: 2
```

7. Supply the wrong connection settings and ensure the test fails:

```
$ host=127.0.0.13 port=9160 clusterName="Test Clusterdfd" ant
-DclassToRun=hpcas.c13.NagiosCheck run

    [java] Cassandra FAILED: got exception: org.apache.thrift.
transport.TTransportException: java.net.ConnectException:
Connection refused
    [java] Java Result: 2
```

Keep an eye out for large rows with compaction limits

In some use cases, a row can have several columns. However, in other use cases such as time series data, a row can have thousands or millions of columns. This recipe shows how to check if the in_memory_compaction_limit_in_mb is being reached.

How to do it...

Use the grep command to search for the string Compacting large row inside the Cassandra logfile.

```
$ grep "Compacting large row" /var/log/cassandra/system.log
Compacting large row null (103343904 bytes) incrementally
```

How it works...

The default value for in_memory_compaction_limit_in_mb is 64. This value is set in conf/cassandra.yaml. For use cases that have fixed columns, the limit should never be exceeded. Setting this value can work as a sanity check to ensure that processes are not inadvertently writing to many columns to the same key. Keys with many columns can also be problematic when using the row cache because it requires the entire row to be stored in memory.

Reviewing network traffic with IPTraf

Issues that manifest on one system are sometimes caused by another. These type of issues include clients not closing connections, faulty network cards, and applications unintentionally degrading the service by over-utilizing it. This recipe gives a basic introduction to IPTraf. IPTraf is a ncurses-based application to view network statistics in real time.

Getting ready

IPTraf is a popular utility and likely packaged with your distribution. More information on IPTraf can be found at `http://iptraf.seul.org/`.

How to do it...

Set up a filter to monitor all traffic to the Cassandra Thrift port 9160 and the Cassandra store port 7000.

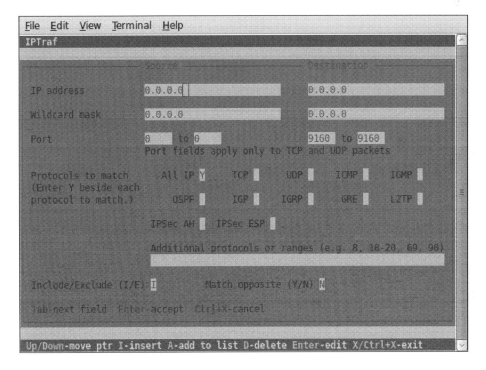

Apply these filters and begin monitoring network traffic. The result is an interactive display that shows network activity.

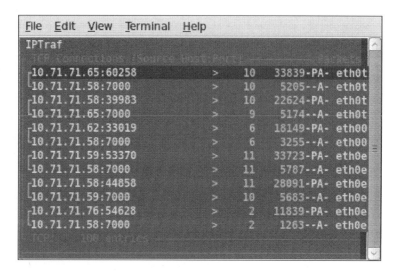

How it works...

IPTraf allows users to filter traffic and display the results in real time.

Keep on the lookout for dropped messages

Cassandra has a concept of back pressure. **Back pressure** is a technique used in staged SEDA architectures in which, if a stage is already full of requests, it will not accept requests from earlier stages. As a result of back pressure, Cassandra will drop already timed-out requests without processing, and log an error. This recipe shows how to search for this error.

How to do it...

Use `grep` to search for the string "DroppedMessageLogger" in the Cassandra logs:

```
$ grep "DroppedMessagesLogger" /var/log/cassandra/system.log
WARN [DroppedMessagesLogger] 2010-11-15 16:09:17,691 MessagingService.
java (line 501) Dropped 67 messages in the last 1000ms


WARN [DroppedMessagesLogger] 2010-11-15 16:09:18,693 MessagingService.
java (line 501) Dropped 90 messages in the last 1000ms
```

How it works...

Clients' requests throw `TimedOutException` when messages are dropped. Clients receiving this exception should try the failed operation again. If dropped messages appear frequently in logs, this indicates that the server is not able to keep up with the request load.

Inspecting column families for dangerous conditions

One optimization for doing bulk inserts is to set both the minimum and maximum compaction threshold to 0. This prevents multiple compaction operations on the same data. If compaction does not become re-enabled, this can end up being bad for performance as multiple `sstables` slow down the read path. This recipe shows how to check for these dangerous conditions.

How to do it...

1. Create `<hpc_build>/src/hpcas/c04/RingInspector.java` in a text editor:

```
package hpcas.c13;
import hpcas.c03.Util;
import java.util.*;
import java.util.Map.*;
import org.apache.cassandra.db.ColumnFamilyStoreMBean;
import org.apache.cassandra.tools.NodeProbe;

public class RingInspector {
   public static void main(String[] args) throws Exception {
      String host = Util.envOrProp("host");
      String sport = Util.envOrProp("port");
      int port = Integer.parseInt(sport);
```

2. Here, we connect using JMX rather than Thrift:

```
NodeProbe probe = new NodeProbe(host, port);
```

3. Next, we iterate across all of the column families:

```
Iterator<Map.Entry<String, ColumnFamilyStoreMBean>> cfamilies
=
         probe.getColumnFamilyStoreMBeanProxies();
while (cfamilies.hasNext()) {
   Entry<String, ColumnFamilyStoreMBean> entry = cfamilies.
next();
   ColumnFamilyStoreMBean cfsProxy = entry.getValue();
```

4. Check for conditions that could be harmful to performance such as too many `sstables`, large rows, or compaction being disabled:

```
if (cfsProxy.getLiveSSTableCount() > 20) {
    System.out.println(cfsProxy.getColumnFamilyName() +" "
            +cfsProxy.getLiveSSTableCount() + " sstables");
}
if (cfsProxy.getMaximumCompactionThreshold() == 0) {
    System.out.println("maxCompactionThreshold is off.");
}
if (cfsProxy.getMinimumCompactionThreshold() == 0) {
    System.out.println("minCompactionThreshold is off.");
}
if (cfsProxy.getMaxRowSize() >10000000){
    System.out.println("row larger than 10,000,000 bytes");
}
    }
  }
}
```

5. Run this program again with the JMX information:

```
$ host=127.0.0.1 port=8080 clusterName="Test Clusterdfd" ks=ks22
cf=cf22 ant -DclassToRun=hpcas.c13.RingInspector run
```

Successful runs produce no output.

How it works...

Nodetool uses **Remote Method Invocation** (**RMI**) to invoke methods on the server. This program calls methods from the `ColumnFamilyStoreMBean` object. With an instance of the `ColumnFamilyStoreMBean`, it is possible to obtain information about the column families on the server, including read latency, write latency, and Memtable information.

Index

Symbols

@BeforeClass 55
<cassandra_src>/bin/stress command 219
-p option 221

A

acquire() method 230
active column families
  searching, by read/write graphs addition 266,
    267
activity
  interpreting, with memtable graphs 268
addInsertion method 223
Ant 19
anti compactions 272
anti-compacts 161
Anti-Entropy Repair
  about 162, 167
  nodes, joining without auto-bootstrap 167
  Replication Factor, raising 167
  using 167
  working 167
anti entropy repairs 272
AntiEntropyStage 263
apache-ant build tool
  URL 15
Apache Cassandra Project 7
Apache Hadoop project
  about 237
  HDFS subproject 237
  MapReduce subproject 237
assume keyword
  about 39
  working 40
atomic read
  implementing, with Cages 229-231
auto_bootstrap 162

B

back pressure 294
bandwidth
  ensuring, between switches 191, 192
batch_mutate method 223
batch mutate operation
  performing, with Hector 223, 224
batch mutations
  about 69, 71
  working 71
benchmarking
  stress tool, building for 218
Bloom Filter file 269
Bloom Filters 170
Bonnie++ 83
bottlenecks
  searching, with nodetool tpstats 262, 263
build.xml file 16
ByteBuffer 247
ByteBufferUtil class 212

C

cache effectiveness
  profiling, with cache graphs 270, 271
cache graphs
  cache effectiveness, profiling with 270, 271
cache tuning 271
Cacti network management system
  URL 262
Cages
  atomic read, implementing with 229-231
  supporting, for Zookeeper set up 228

CAP theorem 102

Cassandra

about 8, 262

Anti-Entropy Repair, using 167

Application Programmer Interface 48

bandwidth, ensuring between switches 191, 192

batch mutations 69, 70

bottlenecks, searching with nodetool tpstats 262, 263

building, from source 200, 201

cache effectiveness, profiling with cache graphs 270, 271

CLI functions, using 41

column families, inspecting 295, 296

column family, creating 49-51

column family statistics, graphing 274

column family statistics, retrieving with nodetool cfstats 263, 264

columns of key, iterating 66, 67

Commit Log disk, using 80

Commit Log disk, working 81

common development tools, installing 200

community, connecting with 206, 207

compaction, monitoring 272

compaction thresholds, setting 94, 95

complex network scenarios, simulating using IPTables 181

Concurrent Readers and Writers, tuning 92, 94

connecting, CLI used 30

connecting, with Java and thrift 27, 28

consistency ANY, using 121, 122

consistency, demonstrating 122-125

consistency level ALL, using 120, 121

consistency level ONE, using 114-117

consistency levels TWO and THREE 194-196

consistency QUROUM levels, mixing 119, 120

consistency QUROUM, using 118, 119

CPU utilization, monitoring 265

custom type, creating by extending AbstractType 201-203

datacenter, determining 185

data directories, cleaning up 56, 57

data directory, coping to new hardware 164

data exporting, to JSON with sstable2json 175

data, reading with CLI 34, 35

data, reading with map-only-program 242-245

data, serializing into large columns 130, 131

data, writing with CLI 33, 34

data, writing with map-only-program 246, 247

diff, applying using patch command 208, 209

diff files, creating using subversion 207

disk utilization, monitoring 269, 270

distributed caching 145

downed node, removing 159

DroppedMessageLogger, searching 294

dynamic snitch, troubleshooting using jconsole 188

edge graph data, searching 147-150

edge graph data, storing 147-150

environment setup 15-19

excess data, removing 176

file system optimization 83

formula for strong consistency, working with 102-104

garbage collection events, monitoring 288

garbage collections, tuning to avoid JVM pauses 95, 96

gc_grace, lowering 169

Hector, communicating with 221-223

hinted handoff mechanism, disabling 106

Ideal Initial Tokens, calculating 20-22

Ideal Initial Tokens, calculating 196, 197

index interval ratio, configuring for lower usage 212, 213

Initial Tokens, selecting for using with Partitioners 22, 23

in_memory_compaction_limit_in_mb, checking 292

iostat command, using 284, 285

IP addresses, selecting 182, 183

IPTables, using for simulating complex network scenarios 181

Java Virtual Machine, selecting 79

Jconsole connection 24

Jconsole connection, over SOCKS proxy 26

Jconsole, using 185-187

JMXTerm, using 286-288

keyspace, creating 49-51

keyspace or column family, dropping 37, 38

large objects, storing 142-144

latency graphs, using 275

live node, removing 160, 161

Log4j logs, forwarding to central server 280, 281

low level client, generating using thrift 58

major compaction, forcing 177

major compaction, scheduling 170, 171

MapReduce, using 248, 249

Memory Mapped IO, enabling 89

memory, saving on 64-bit architectures with compressed pointers 92

Memtable, tuning 90, 91

multiget, using 51-53

multiple datacenter installation, scripting 183-185

multiple instance installation, scripting 13, 14

multiple instances, running on single machine 11-13

Nagios Check Script, creating 290, 291

natural endpoints, determining 185

network traffic, reviewing with IPTraf 293, 294

node join, achieving using external data copy methods 165, 166

node position, adjusting with nodetool move 157-159

nodes, joining with auto_bootstrap set to false 161

nodetool drain, using 168

Nodetool Move 157, 159

nodetool snapshot, using for backups 171, 172

od command, using 209, 210

open file limit, raising 97, 98

open networking connections, tracking 277, 278

operating system, selecting 78

performance baseline, monitoring 269, 270

performance, increasing by scaling up 98

performance tuning 78

phi_convict_threshold, increasing 213

physical disk size, tracking 275, 276

property file snitch, configuring 187

quorum operations, in multi data center environments 189, 190

rack for key, determining 185

RAID levels, selecting 81

read path, debugging 180, 181

read repair chance, adjusting 107, 108

Replication Factor 137

rows and columns, deleting from CLI 35, 36

rows, listing in column family 36, 37

rows, paginating in column family 36, 37

rpc timeout, increasing 192

running, in foreground 19

running, with specific debugging levels 19

sar command, using for reviewing performance over time 285, 286

schema agreement, confirming across cluster 109, 110

secondary data orderings or indexes, developing 150-153

secondary indexes, working with 74

seed nodes, defining for Gossip communication 156

single node installation 8-10

slice columns order, reversing 68

snapshot, restoring 174

snapshots, clearing with nodetool clearsnapshot 173

source data, storing in separate column family 145, 147

SSH key pair, generating 162, 163

sstable2json export utility, customizing 210-212

SSTable count, graphing 268, 269

stopping, from using swap 89

Storage Proxy API, using 59-61

strings, using 209, 210

Super Columns 134

Super Columns, using 134-136

Swap Memory, disabling 88

test data, reading and writing using CLI 10, 11

thrift bindings, generating 58

time series data, storing 131-134

timestamp value, supplying with write requests 105

top, using 282-284

tpstats command, using for finding bottlenecks 289

TTL, using for creating columns with self-deletion time 72-74

two data sets, joining with Hive 253, 254

unit tests, writing with server 53-55
URL 8
validation, using for checking data on
    insertion 204, 205
working, with JPA 224, 225

cassandra-cacti-m6
URL 262

Cassandra datacenter
setting up, for ETL 257, 258

Cassandra instances
connecting, using Jconsole 23-25
disk space, saving by using small column
    names 128, 129

Cassandra JMX
accessing, JMXTerm used 286-288

Cassandra maven plugin
about 214
using 214, 215
working 216

CassandraOutputFormat 246

Cassandra server
connecting to 48, 49

Cassandra Storage handler 251

Cassandra Storage Proxy
using 59-62

CentOS 79

cfhistograms command
about 276
using, for distribution of query latencies 276,
    277

cfstats
about 263
column family statistics, retrieving with 263,
    264
graphing, to track average row size 274
graphing, to track max row sizes 274
retrieving, nodetool cfstats used 263, 264

clean target 17

CLI
about 10, 11
assume keyword, using 39
column meta data, using 42, 43
consistency level, changing 43, 44
help statement 44, 45
keyspace, creating 30, 31
rows and columns, deleting 35, 36
Time To Live (TTL), providing 40

using, for connecting Cassandra 30
working, with Super Columns 38

CLI alternative
Groovandra, using as 232

CLI functions
using 41

CLI statements
loading, from file 45, 46

CMSInitiatingOccupancyFraction 96

CMSParallelRemarkEnabled 96

column families
inspecting 295, 296

column family
about 31, 84
creating 49-51
creating, with CLI 31, 32
rows, listing 36, 37
rows, paginating 36, 37

ColumnFamilyInputFormat
about 242
using 242-245

Column Family Meta Data 87

column family statistics. *See* **cfstats**

column meta data
using 42, 43

columns, of key
iterating 66-68

column values
grouping and counting, with Hive 254, 255

command-line interface. *See* **CLI**

Commit Log disk
using 80
working 81

common development tools
installing 200

community
connecting with 206, 207

compaction
about 90, 271
monitoring 272

compaction progress
verifying, with nodetool compaction stats 273

compaction thresholds
settings 94, 95

Comparator 131

complex network scenarios
simulating, IPTables used 181

Composite Key 132
ConcurrentMarkSweep 96
Concurrent Readers and Writers
  tuning 92, 94
consistency
  demonstrating 122-125
consistency ANY
  using 121, 122
  working 122
consistency level
  changing, from CLI 193, 194
consistency level ALL
  about 120, 138
  drawback 121
  using 120
consistency level , CLI
  changing 43, 44
consistency level ONE 193
  about 114
  using 114-117
  working 117, 118
Consistency Level Quorum 138
consistency levels TWO and THREE
  using 194-196
consistency QUROUM
  levels, mixing 119, 120
  using 118, 119
Consistent Hashing 20, 157
context.write() 247
continuous integration 53
Counter class 132, 133
CPU activity 264
CPU states
  idle 265
  IOWait 265
  system 265
  user 265
CPU utilization
  monitoring 265
custom type
  creating, by extending AbstractType 201-203
Cygwin 26

D

data
  exporting, to JSON with sstable2json 175

inserting, with stress tool 219
reading, with CLI 34, 35
reading, with stress tool 219
serializing, into large columns 130, 131
writing, with CLI 33, 34
dataDir directory 228
data directories
  cleaning up 56, 57
data directory
  coping, to new hardware 164
data locality 255
data resurrection 169
DataStax Brisk 259
  setting up 258
  working 259
DateFormat classes 132
decommission 160
describe_cluster_name() 28
describe keyspace command 32
describe_keyspace method 108, 139
describe_schema_versions() 110
diff
  about 207
  applying, patch command used 208, 209
  creating, subversion used 207
different hash algorithms
  using 142
disk performance testing 83
disk space
  saving, by using small column names 128, 129
disk utilization
  monitoring 269, 270
distributed caching 145
distribution, of query latencies
  viewing, with nodetool cfhistograms 276, 277
DroppedMessageLogger
  searching 294
dynamic proxy 26
dynamic snitch
  about 188
  troubleshooting, jconsole used 188

E

EACH_QUROUM 189
echo command 11

edge graph data
earching 147-150
storing 147-150
EmbeddedCassandraService
using 53
Endpoint Snitch 198
eventual consistency 117
excess data
removing, nodetool cleanup used 176
EXT4 file system
about 83
configuring 83
extra_info 147

F

file system optimization
about 83
working 84
find() method 225
FlushStage 263
Free-Form project 19
full text search
performing, with Solandra 226, 227

G

garbage collection events
monitoring 288
Garbage Collections
tuning, to avoid JVM pauses 95, 96
Garbage-First garbage collector (G1) 97
gc_grace
lowering 169
GCGracePeriod 169
GCGraceSeconds 169
getString method 202
git 226
Gossip 156
Groovandra
about 231
using, as CLI alternative 232
Groovy 231

H

Hadoop
about 237, 238

pseudo distributed cluster, setting up 238-241
hadoop command line tool 241
hadoop dfs command 259
Hadoop job 255
Hadoop Task Trackers
co-locating, on Cassandra nodes 255, 256
working 256
handleResults() method 64
Hardware RAID 82
Heap Memory 91
Heap Size 92
Hector
batch mutate operation, performing with 223, 224
communicating, with Cassandra 221-223
hector jar
downloading 222
help statement, CLI 44, 45
HFactory object 222
Hinted Handoff 159
hinted handoff mechanism
disabling 106
histograms 277
Hive
about 250
setting up, with Cassandra Storage Handler support 250
working 251
Hive QL 250
Hive table
defining, over Cassandra Column Family 251, 252
working 253
hpcas directory 12

I

Ideal Initial Tokens
calculating 196, 197
Index 269
index_interval 212
index interval ratio
configuring, for lower usage 212, 213
IndexReader 227
IndexWriter 227

Initial Tokens
  about 20, 157
  calculating 20-22
  selecting, for using with Partitioners 22, 23
in_memory_compaction_limit_in_mb
  checking 292
inode 84
iostat command
  using, for monitoring current disk performance 284, 285
IOWait state 266
IOZone 83
IP addresses
  selecting, to work with RackInferringSnitch 182, 183
IPTables
  about 181, 182
  working 182
IPTraf 293, 294

J

Java Management eXtension Managed Bean.
  See **JMX Mbeans**
Java Native Access (JNA) jar 89
Java Native Architecture
  about 78
  installing 89
Java Persistence Architecture. *See* **JPA**
Java SDK
  URL 15
Java SE JVM 79
Java Virtual Machine
  selecting 79
Jconsole
  about 23
  using 185
Jconsole connection
  over SOCKS proxy 26
JMX (Java Management Extensions) 12
JMX Mbeans 262
JMX port 9
JMXTerm
  using, for accessing Cassandra JMX 286, 288
JPA
  about 224
  Cassandra, working with 224, 225

JUnit jar
  URL 15
Just a Bunch Of Disks (JBOD) 82
JVM 95
JVM (Java Management Extensions) 23
JVM pauses 95

K

Key Cache
  about 84
  using, for boosting read performance 84-86
keyspace
  about 48
  creating 49-51
  creating, from CLI 30, 31
  describing 32
  working 31, 33
Keyspace 81
keyspace or column family
  dropping 37, 38
kundera source code 224

L

large objects
  storing 142-144
latency
  about 274
  troubleshooting, traceroute used 190
latency graphs
  using 275
Link Aggregation Groups (LAG) 192
Linux 78
live node
  nodetool decommission used 160, 161
LOCAL_QUORUM 189
Log4j
  about 280
  working 281
Log4j logs
  forwarding, to central server 280, 281
Logsandra
  about 232, 234
  working 234, 235
logsandra keyspace 234
logsandra.yaml file 235
Long Comparator 133

M

main() method 61
major compaction
about 272
forcing 177
scheduling 170
working 171
Makefile 16
map-only program
using 242-245
working 246
Mapper 243
MapReduce
about 248
using 248, 249
working 249
maven2 package 224
MaxCompactionThreshold 95
md5 checksum 140
md5hash() method 142
memory
saving, on 64-bit architectures with
compressed pointers 92
Memory Mapped IO
enabling 89
Memtable
about 80
criteria for flushing 90
threshold criteria 90
tuning 90, 91
memtable_flush_after_mins variable 90
memtable graphs
activity, interpreting with 268
benefits 268
memtable_operations_in_millions variable 90
memtables 267
memtable_throughput_in_mb variable 90
MinCompactionThreshold 95
multiget
about 51
using, to limit round trips and overhead 51-53
multiget_slice method 232
multiple datacenter installation
scripting 183-185
multiple instance installation
scripting 13, 14

scripting, with OOP 142
multiple instances
running, on single machine 11-13
MutationStage 263
mvm command 224

N

Nagios 290
Nagios Check Script
creating, for Cassandra 290, 291
Natural Endpoints 162
Network Management Systems (NMS) 131
Network Time Protocol (NTP)
about 99
enabling 99
working 100
NetworkTopologyStrategy 196
network traffic
reviewing, with IPTraf 293, 294
NMS systems 266
node join
achieving, using external data copy methods
165, 166
node position
adjusting, nodetool move used 157, 158
nodes
about 272
joining, with auto_bootstrap set to false 161
removing, nodetool removetoken used 159,
160
nodetool 276, 296
nodetool cfstats 85, 87
nodetool cleanup
using 176
nodetool clearsnapshot command 173
nodetool compact 177
nodetool compaction stats
compaction progress, verifying with 273
nodetool decommission
using 160
working 161
nodetool drain command
about 168
using 168
working 168
nodetool info 84

Nodetool Move
about 159
working 159
nodetool program 9
nodetool removetoken
using 159
nodetool repair 167, 263
nodetool ring
running 157
nodetool setcachecapacity command 87
nodetool snapshot
using, for backups 171, 172
NotFoundCount events 122
ntp server pools 99

O

od command
using 210
open file limit
raising 97, 98
OpenJDK 80
open networking connections
tracking 277, 278
OpenSSH 26
OpenSSL tools 162
operating system
selecting 78
Order Preserving Partitioner (OPP)
about 138, 139, 227
using 138-141
Ordinary Object Pointer (OOP) 92

P

ParNewGC 96
Partitioner 138
patch command 209
performance baseline
monitoring 269, 270
performance, Cassandra
increasing, by scaling up 98
performance tuning 76
phi_convict_threshold
about 213
increasing 213
working 213
physical disk size

tracking, of each column family over time
275, 276
pip 232
placement_strategy 31
property file snitch
configuring 187
pseudo distributed cluster, Hadoop
DataNode 238
JobTracker 238
NameNode 238
NSecondary NameNode 238
setting up 238
TaskTracker 238

Q

Quorum 111, 167
quorum operations
in multi data center environments 189, 190

R

Rack Aware Strategy 156
RackInferringSnitch 182
Rack Unaware Strategy 156
RAID-1 82
RAID-5 82
RAID-10 82
RAID level
selecting 81
Random Partitioner (RP) 138
range scans
using, for finding and removing old data 62-
65
read path
debugging 180, 181
read performance
boosting, with Key Cache 84-86
boosting, with Row Cache 86, 87
read repair chance
adjusting 107, 108
disabling 109
lowering 109
Read Repair process 162
ReadStage 263
read/write graphs
adding, for active column families search
266, 267

RedHat Enterprise Linux 79
Remote Method Invocation (RMI) 26, 296
Replication Factor
    about 10, 30, 81, 137, 160
    adjusting, to work with quorum 111-114
    using, for disk space saving 137
    using, for performance enhancements 137
RequestResponseStage 263
resurrection 169
Ring 156
Row Cache
    about 86
    using, for boosting read performance 86, 87
rpc timeout
    increasing 192
rsync command 164

S

sar command
    using, for reviewing performance over time
        285, 286
SATA 99
schema agreement
    confirming, across cluster 109, 110
SCSI 275
searchFrom method 152
secondary data orderings or indexes
    developing 150-153
secondary indexes
    working with 74
SEDA 92, 262
seed nodes
    defining, for Gossip communication 156
    IP address, using in seed list 156
    seed list, synchronizing 157
Seeds 156
setTimestamp method 105
setup() method 55
single node Cassandra installation 8, 9, 10
slice results order
    reversing 68, 69
snapshot
    clearing, with nodetool clearsnapshot 173
    restoring 174
socks proxy 26
software RAID 82

Solandra
    about 226
    full text search, performing with 226, 227
Solaris 78
Solid State Drives (SSD) 99, 270
Solr 227
source data
    storing, in separate column family 145, 147
split brain scenario 181
splits 246
SSH key pair
    generating 162, 163
sstable2json
    specific keys, excluding 175
    specific keys, extracting 175
    using 175
sstable2json export utility
    customizing 210-212
SSTable count
    about 264
    graphing 268, 269
SSTables 81
Staged Event Driven Architecture. *See* SEDA
StorageProxy 62
strategy_options 31
streams 161
stress.jar file 218
stress tool
    about 218
    building, for benchmarking 218
    data, inserting with 219
    data, reading with 219
    running 219
strings
    using 209
StringTokenizer class 248
striping 81
Subversion (SVN) 201
Super Columns
    about 38, 134
    CLI operations 38
    using 134, 135, 136
    working 137
Swap Memory
    about 88
    disabling 88
swapoff command 88

Swapping 88
Syslog 280, 281
System.getCurrentITimeMillis() 133
system_update_column_family method 108

T

TaskTracker 246
TCP 278
test data
  reading and writing, command-line interface
    used 10, 11
test environment
  setting up 15-19
thread pools 262
thread pool stats. *See* tpstats
thrift 58
thrift bindings
  generating, for other languages 58, 59
Thrift port 9
time series data
  storing 131-134
timestamp 99
timestamp value
  supplying, with write requests 105
Time To Live (TTL)
  about 40
  providing 40
  using, for creating columns with self-deletion
    time 72-74
Token Ring 162
tombstone 169, 170
top command
  about 282
  using, for understanding overall performance
    282-284
TProtocol 49
tpstats
  about 262
  bottlenecks, searching with 262, 263
  using, for finding bottlenecks 289
traceroute
  about 190
  using, for troubleshooting latency 190
  working 191

Transmission Control Protocol. *See* TCP
tunable consistency 118
two data sets
  joining, with Hive 253, 254

U

Ubuntu 79
unit tests
  writing, with embedded Cassandra server
    53-56
UpperCaseMapper 243
UseCMSInitiatingOccupancyOnly 96
user_info 147

V

validate method 205
validation
  using, for checking data on insertion 204,
    205
VFS Cache (Virtual File System Cache) 91

W

Windows 78

X

xxd command
  using, for decoding hex values 176

Y

Yahoo! Cloud Serving Benchmark. *See* YCSB
YAML™
  URL 9
YCSB
  running 220, 221
  URL, for info 220

Z

Zookeeper
  setting up, for supporting Cages 228

About Packt Publishing

Packt, pronounced 'packed', published its first book "*Mastering phpMyAdmin for Effective MySQL Management*" in April 2004 and subsequently continued to specialize in publishing highly focused books on specific technologies and solutions.

Our books and publications share the experiences of your fellow IT professionals in adapting and customizing today's systems, applications, and frameworks. Our solution based books give you the knowledge and power to customize the software and technologies you're using to get the job done. Packt books are more specific and less general than the IT books you have seen in the past. Our unique business model allows us to bring you more focused information, giving you more of what you need to know, and less of what you don't.

Packt is a modern, yet unique publishing company, which focuses on producing quality, cutting-edge books for communities of developers, administrators, and newbies alike. For more information, please visit our website: www.packtpub.com.

About Packt Open Source

In 2010, Packt launched two new brands, Packt Open Source and Packt Enterprise, in order to continue its focus on specialization. This book is part of the Packt Open Source brand, home to books published on software built around Open Source licences, and offering information to anybody from advanced developers to budding web designers. The Open Source brand also runs Packt's Open Source Royalty Scheme, by which Packt gives a royalty to each Open Source project about whose software a book is sold.

Writing for Packt

We welcome all inquiries from people who are interested in authoring. Book proposals should be sent to author@packtpub.com. If your book idea is still at an early stage and you would like to discuss it first before writing a formal book proposal, contact us; one of our commissioning editors will get in touch with you.

We're not just looking for published authors; if you have strong technical skills but no writing experience, our experienced editors can help you develop a writing career, or simply get some additional reward for your expertise.

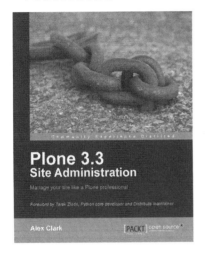

Plone 3.3 Site Administration

ISBN: 978-1-847197-04-7   Paperback: 240 pages

Alex Clark's book will get you managing and enhancing
your Plone website like a seasoned expert

1. Covers Plone basics from a site administrator's
   perspective

2. Learn how to use Buildout to develop, deploy, and
   maintain a modern Plone site

3. Enhance the functionality and appearance of your
   web site by using third-party add-ons

4. Features many useful Buildout recipes from the
   Python Package Index

MySQL for Python

ISBN: 978-1-849510-18-9   Paperback: 440 pages

Integrate the flexibility of Python and the power of MySQL
to boost the productivity of your Python applications

1. Implement the outstanding features of Python's
   MySQL library to their full potential

2. See how to make MySQL take the processing
   burden from your programs

3. Learn how to employ Python with MySQL to power
   your websites and desktop applications

4. Apply your knowledge of MySQL and Python
   to real-world problems instead of hypothetical
   scenarios

Please check **www.PacktPub.com** for information on our titles

Made in the USA
Lexington, KY
10 May 2013